HALF HIM HALF HER

Half Him Half Her

When do I get to be
ME

STEPHANIE VAUGHAN

COCKATOO
PUBLISHING

A catalogue record for this
book is available from the
National Library of Australia

NATIONAL
LIBRARY
OF AUSTRALIA

Publishing Details
Publisher: Cockatoo Publishing
Title: Half Him Half Her
First published 2021

Interior and cover layout: Pickawoowoo Publishing Group -
www.pickawoowoo.com

ISBN: 978-0-6488609-0-7   (paperback)
ISBN :978-0-6488609-1-4   (ebook)

Author Website: www.steps2stephanie.com

Contents

Introduction

I was born in March 1961, the youngest of three children, to a well-known Yorkshire farming family. I had two older brothers aged two and nearly four. Memories of my early childhood are sketchy. My father worked long hours, as the farm was predominantly a dairy farm and as he did the milking both morning and night, we saw little of him. Mum was a teacher, and to help make ends meet she went back to teaching not long after I was born. For the most part, I was looked after by a nanny.

From a very early age my brothers and I were expected to help on the farm as there were calves and hundreds of chickens to feed, and eggs to gather, clean and pack. I generally enjoyed this aspect of my life. On the outside I was a happy young boy being brought up in what I now know was a very privileged environment which taught right from wrong and in general gave a good start to understanding how life and the world worked.

From that same early age I had a strange feeling that some things didn't add up correctly but was unable to articulate why. One incident which stands out goes back to when I was probably eight or nine. My parents enjoyed Scottish dancing and we were also encouraged to participate. We were all decked out in kilts and sporrans to look the part and, without really knowing why, I very much enjoyed wearing the kilt. My particular tartan was red based and Mum didn't like the fact that when I spun around my white underpants were visible and so she bought me some girls red ones, as boys' pants were either white or grey at best. I enjoyed the whole outfit; to me it was just like wearing a skirt and matching girls' pants which somehow just felt right. The feeling of confusion remained with me and I think it was around then that I first questioned my gender. This continued as I progressed to senior school, and one day in the showers, after a rugby match on a typically muddy pitch, I realised I was not like the other boys in my class. Even taking into account the various shapes and sizes of my classmates, I was different. I had developed breasts, a condition which I learned some thirty years later is called gynecomastia, apparently not unusual in boys going through puberty, but not usually as severe. Sadly, this soon came to the attention of my classmates and the physical and mental bullying started there. My nickname became "tits" and life became a whole lot less pleasant. I used every possible excuse to skip school, especially when any form of sports was on the agenda and when I couldn't skip school with my parents' permission then I just didn't go. How I didn't get caught I don't know.

"Half him, half her" is a story of the three stages of my life. The first is about my teenage years, my early working years before moving into the motor trade, my first marriage and my eventual relocation to Western Australia. It also covers my second marriage to Jayne and the years which followed until the marriage came to an abrupt end in 2012. The second stage covers the years between Jayne and me parting and December 2015. It describes my ups and downs medically and my long battle with an endocrine system which seemed to have a completely different set of rules from anyone else's. It also covers the gradual unravelling of the truth which came to a head on December 21st, 2015 in a specialist's office in West Perth.

The third part of the book reveals the roller coaster ride which consumed the next two and a half years of my life after the revelations on that day in West Perth. I emerged from the specialist's office utterly shell-shocked; my life would never be the same again. Everything I had believed about my beginnings would be destroyed on that day and I look back on the months which followed in amazement; partly because I don't know how I survived them. I certainly wouldn't have done, if not for my best friend and soulmate, Denise. What she has done for me is more than any person should ever have had to do but she has stuck with me through thick and thin and is my hero. She has brought me back from the brink on many occasions, talked sense into me and guided me through the most challenging times. I often look back at two photos of Robin which I keep in my purse; one from 2006 and one from 2011 and I can't believe the difference between then and now. None of it would have happened without the amazing care that I have received from the medical profession both in Busselton and Perth. The two General Practitioners who have looked after me have been outstanding as has the gender specialist in Perth, my psychologist in Busselton, my endocrinologist and the psychiatrist who wrote the recommendation that I proceed to surgery after fast tracking me through the system. They have all played a vital role in my transition and I cannot thank them enough for bringing me a level of peace and happiness I could only have dreamed about before.

Chapter Summary - Part I

Living in Limbo
1961 - 2012

CHAPTERS
1. All is not as it should be
2. Learning to live with it and Stephanie
3. The family meeting
4. A change of direction
5. Maximum effort and the importance of PK
6. First shot at management
7. New beginnings
8. Ongoing confusion
9. The inevitable and Transformation
10. An unexpected twist
11. The attentions of a younger woman
12. Station road and MG Rover
13. An amazing trip and an unexpected bonus
14. Keeping the secret
15. A new life Down Under
16. Settling into life in Australia and first guests
17. The wedding and decision time
18. Test after test and a very bad day

Chapter 1

All is not as it should be

The journey home from school that wet and cold day was one of confusion and uncertainty. Confusion because I didn't know why I was different and uncertainty because I didn't know what to do about it. The bus ride took about forty-five minutes, much of it spent in a very empty double decker bus, so there was plenty of seats to choose from. I usually sat on the top deck at the front as I have never been a good passenger but to sit with an uninterrupted view of the road ahead seemed to help.

For whatever reason, I decided not to say anything at home for the time being. I had jobs to do on the farm when I arrived home, so quickly got changed and went about my usual routine of feeding calves and chickens. The calves were okay and I enjoyed tending to them, watching them grow and develop. Most of them were quite tame and I enjoyed stroking them. The chickens, on the other hand, I didn't like dealing with. I'm not a fan of birds in any way but it was a means to an end, as I received a small amount of money each week for the jobs I did. I have always believed this instilled in me, in the best possible way, an understanding of how money works, how the world works financially, and it gave me a sense of worth from an early age.

Having made the observation that I was different made me much more conscious of how I looked. Tight clothes were definitely off the agenda and I made a great effort to cover up my chest at all times. Unfortunately, this wasn't possible during numerous activities at school, like physical education and games lessons. Then there was the dreaded school swimming pool. Thankfully it was over-subscribed as it catered for lots of smaller schools as well, so we didn't have swimming lessons on a regular basis. But I knew that when we did, I would be in for some serious teasing and bullying. Consequently, I made every excuse not to go swimming even though I actually enjoyed being in the water. I invented every form of imaginary illness to excuse me from taking part; verruca, athlete's foot and ring worm to name a few and for the most part it worked. The downside to this was that I never really learned to swim, which I regret.

As time passed, the teasing and bullying got worse and eventually I had to confront my parents with the issue. Dad had been very helpful in writing "sick" notes for me; I often went to him when he was busy milking his beloved red poll cows so he had no time to question or argue as to why I needed to skip various lessons, but it had been growing more difficult to convince him even so. I chose my moment when there were just the three of us in the room and voiced my concerns. Dad was immediately instructed by Mum to take me to the doctors the following day. An appointment was made first thing; at least I would get to miss some school, but as the surgery was in the same town as the school I was still expected to go afterwards. The consultation was short; I was told to take off my shirt and the doctor had a press here, a squeeze there and then informed Dad that I needed to see a specialist. Nothing more was said; I put my clothes on again and we went back to the car. I pleaded with Dad to let me have the rest of the day off but he was having none of it, so I was duly taken to school.

The appointment with the specialist was a couple of weeks later, this time in Scarborough so in the opposite direction to school. Hopefully I would be taken home after this one and not to school. The appointment was at Scarborough hospital. I have never liked hospitals, they always seemed to have this strange smell which scared me to death. The specialist was a very formal, important looking man. He studied my referral and asked me to undress. Like the doctor, he felt here, touched me there and had a squeeze somewhere else, then announced that he was not the right person to see and wrote a referral to another specialist in Leeds. As hoped, I didn't get taken to school on this occasion. Dad actually asked me if I wanted to go, as if he didn't already know the answer. I was taken home and told to "do homework or something".

This was a very big milestone day for me. Mum was a teacher and was at work so I was in the house alone. Having been told many, many times while being teased at school that I should wear a bra I decided to see what it would feel like. I searched through Mum's underwear drawer until I found one that I thought might fit. After considerable fumbling I managed to get it on. I just stood there in front of Mum's dressing table mirror and stared at myself. The bra, a size 34b pink flowery thing, fitted perfectly and it was as though I was glued to the spot. I must have stood there looking at the vision in front of me for ages, just staring and wondering why was I like this; why did I have breasts and worst of all why did it feel right? Why did it feel like I was meant to be a girl?

The appointment in Leeds was arranged for an afternoon the following week and as much as I wasn't looking forward to it, I knew I would most likely get the day off school. The drive to Leeds had its own excitement as Dad was not a comfortable driver in any way, shape or form. He had zero mechanical sympathy and the car was made to take corners in top gear; not in a speeding way but just a lack of commitment on his part to changing gear. Once around the corner his foot was firmly grounded on the right pedal and if the poor car couldn't cope then a very rough jerky gear change followed and an insulting comment on how useless the car was. Nevertheless, we made it and managed to find the specialist's address, which was his private home. One of the reception rooms had been converted into his study and there were a handful of chairs in the hallway outside where we were instructed to wait. After a few minutes a lady and a girl, probably a little older than me, came out and we were called in. The specialist sat behind a huge old desk; he wore half rimmed glasses which he seemed to peer over at us as we walked in. He had a very brusque manner and I immediately got the impression it was not going to be a pleasant experience. There was an area separated off with a curtain and he told me to go behind it and undress fully. I stood there totally naked and waited for what seemed like an age before he finished a conversation with Dad which I unfortunately couldn't quite hear. Finally he pulled the curtain aside and came in, looked me up and down and then, in a completely different persona, quietly asked me to lie on the bed. His manner changed from being frustrated and impatient to that of a gentle, caring person. He felt my breasts, had a very brief look at the rest of my body including my genitals then asked me to get dressed as he left. There then followed an almost whispered conversation with Dad which I was unable to hear but when I emerged from behind the curtain Dad was standing at the door waiting for me and we left in silence.

The drive home was long and unpleasant in every way. Dad hardly spoke to me all the way home, appearing to be preoccupied with something and drove faster than usual. I decided it must have been because he would have to make up the time he had spent with me today and somehow resented that. I made the decision that when I got home I would put on my old clothes and try to be of help to him on the farm. It did cross my mind that it was strange that Mum didn't take me to the appointment as she was a good deal more confident as a driver, especially in unfamiliar places and it was a day when she didn't work. It would have allowed Dad to do the things he needed to do, so maybe he was frustrated about that also.

On arriving home I went upstairs to get changed into my old clothes in order to help Dad, but when I came downstairs I was met in the kitchen by both my parents and was told "so the reason you have breasts is that you are overweight and you need to lose some weight and then they will go away". I just stood there in disbelief. Yes, I was overweight, but there were two boys in my class who were either my size or bigger and neither had breasts like mine. I thought back to the man in Leeds and how kind he had seemed to me. Somehow it didn't ring true to me and I wondered why he hadn't told me it was because I was overweight?

So, that was how it was; basically having breasts was my own fault for eating too much of the wrong things and not getting enough exercise. I wondered what measures would be put in place to control my weight and how draconian they would be. I must admit I had, and still do have, a huge liking for anything chocolate and neither Mum nor Dad were particularly thin. It was a consequence of living on a dairy farm, drinking lots of full cream milk and having a constant supply of cakes and pastries in the cupboard as was the norm in those days on a farm in Yorkshire.

Chapter 2

Learning to live with it and Stephanie

My weight loss campaign didn't last long, and it was soon forgotten by my parents. I knew even then that there was more to it than losing weight. Even if I was stick-thin it wouldn't change what was going on in my head. I became more of a loner and spent a great deal of time in my room. My parents thought I was doing homework but much of the time was spent lying on my bed just trying to figure out what was happening to me. I usually went to bed early, often between eight and nine. It was my time to dream, and the more I thought about it the clearer it became. I wanted to be a girl! I believed that I should have been a girl from the start and couldn't figure out what had gone wrong. When it came time for me to go to sleep I would pray that by some miracle I would wake up the next day as a girl. This happened night after night until one night I had the thought that if I did wake as a girl then what would I call myself? Being able to choose your own name is cool and I started to think of what I would like to be known as. With that, the name Stephanie came into my mind and it stuck there, so much so that I have never even considered any other name.

I'm not sure where it came from, I didn't know anyone called Stephanie but I had obviously heard it somewhere and loved it. I have lived every day since then with Stephanie in my head occupying a section of my mind, never far from the front. I can't tell you how many hours I have spent over the last forty plus years thinking about her and dreaming of being her.

My life at school gradually got harder as hiding my breasts became more difficult and my nickname became "Tits". There was a glimmer of happiness though, in a friendship with a boy in my class called David. He lived in Driffield, the town where the school was located. He was very interested in farm life and I lived on a farm, so we had some sort of bond right from the start. After a while I was asked if I'd like to go to his house after school for tea. I asked Mum if this would be okay as one of my parents would have to bring me home afterwards as the farm was seven miles from the town. She agreed so I accepted the invitation and met his mum and dad for the first time. They were lovely; his mum made a fuss of me, fed me well and I formed an immediate bond with her which was to go on long after David and I had finished school. This was a perfect opportunity to get David to come to the farm. He very much wanted to be involved in farming in some way and this was the perfect place to start. Soon he was cycling from Driffield every Saturday to help on the farm and we had a great time together. We laughed a great deal and it was the perfect thing to get me through the week, looking forward to Saturday when David and I could spend the day on the farm. Then if the weather was bad, he would stay for tea and Dad would take him and his bike back to Driffield in the Land Rover. Mum and Dad really liked David as I think they thought he was everything I wasn't. He was ultra-polite, helpful and hard-working; I'm sure they thought much more of him than me at times and I was told on numerous occasions that I should be more like David.

At the age of twelve or thirteen, opportunities to be alone in the house were limited but I managed to fake illness on a regular basis on the days that Mum was at work so I would be left in the house with regular visits from Dad who was busy on the farm. This gave me opportunities to wear Mum's underwear and even some of her clothes at times. Her underwear drawer was crammed full of different things and over time I must have tried every single item on. Some fitted much better than others and I soon learned that the original bra I had tried on which was a 34b was too tight; it felt like it would cut me in half! Thankfully there was a great deal of choice as Mum's weight had gone up and down over the years and I soon found one which was much better, a 36b. It had blue and turquoise flowers on it. Walking across Mum and Dad's bedroom to the dressing table was a problem though. Their bedroom was above the kitchen which was the hub of the house as it is in any farmhouse. Sometimes I wouldn't know whether someone else was in the house so I had to tread very carefully indeed to avoid creaking floorboards. I devised a plan to avoid this, I worked out which items of underwear Mum used regularly by observing the washing line. The well-fitting bra was not one of them so instead of putting it back I kept it in my room, hidden under a big pile of clothes at the bottom of my wardrobe where she would never look. This bra I considered to be mine now, and I cherished it and wore it often. I think with anyone who crossdresses there is a buzz to be got from the risk factor; the risk of getting caught heightened my enjoyment and sooner or later I was pretty sure I would get caught. This happened one night after I had been in my room for some time and decided I would go to bed so went downstairs to say good night.

Mum was in the room alone, so I said goodnight to her. Dad was in his office and as I didn't want to disturb him I went to bed. Thinking I would now be alone until morning I put on the bra and went to bed dreaming. A few minutes later Dad opened the door to say good night so I quickly pulled up the covers, but he must have seen the straps. He came over and asked what I was wearing and pulled down the covers. He asked why I was wearing a bra. I have never been slow with comebacks but this one surprises me even now; I just said "because it fits". He nodded, covered me up, said goodnight and left the room. My mind was racing - what would happen next? Surely in the next sixty seconds Mum would walk in, put the light on and demand to know what was going on. The thing was, I was so busy thinking of what to say I never thought of taking off the bra. Nothing happened and Dad never discussed it ever again. He must not have told Mum for some reason and I was thankful that my secret was still safe.

At this point a little bit of luck came my way. Some years earlier we had some alterations done in the house. It was a very old farmhouse built in an L shape with what was referred to as a "Hind house" or "Foreman house" attached to the smaller end. This had not been lived in for some time so, to give us more space in the house, the bedroom nearest to our part was joined to what used to be my bedroom when I was very small and turned into a bedroom for my eldest brother. It had its own staircase from Dad's office, so it allowed a little more privacy as my brother was getting older. By this stage Nigel was eighteen and heading for college in Scarborough so I was offered the room. I'm not sure if my middle brother Greg was ever offered the room but as soon as the offer was made, I took it up. While the room was a little smaller than the one I was in, it had several advantages. Firstly, the door between it and the room I had when I was little had a lock on it. The little room had been turned into a dressing room for Mum so there was no one in it full time. This meant that I could make more noise with my music without getting shouted at and it provided me with a good deal of privacy for me to cross-dress more often. The stairs from Dad's office were pretty lethal; they were very steep and narrow, so no one came up them in a hurry which gave me time to cover myself up in the event of an unannounced visitor.

As I got older I went to school less and less. It caused many arguments between Mum and Dad but, as he regularly had no help on the farm, he relished the fact that I would be able to help him. But for Mum, my lack of education was a serious problem, particularly as she was a teacher herself. For me at that time it made my life much less stressful not having to be at school. I knew at that time I wanted to work on the farm and eventually take over when Dad retired so couldn't see the need to waste any more time at school. Mum also had a conflict of interest. As much as she thought I should go to school, having me home meant that Dad finished work at a more civilised hour as I did the work which would normally have been done by a labourer. It also helped on the financial side of things as, whilst I did get paid a little for my time working, it was nowhere near what an employee would have received.

Eventually I made it to sixteen, a milestone in anyone's life who lives on a fairly remote property but longs for some independence. Shortly after my birthday I bought myself a Suzuki 50cc moped. 50cc was as big as you were allowed to ride at sixteen at that time. It was not swift; it had a maximum speed of about 50mph, but it did the job - I was mobile! We were taught to drive tractors on the farm from about ten years old, although driving on public roads was forbidden until you passed a test at sixteen. This didn't deter me at all, and I regularly went for a joy ride around a seven-mile block on one of the tractors when no one was around. This gave me a fairly good knowledge of road rules et cetera so I took to the bike quickly. Another favourite pastime for me was driving the Land Rover around the same block and seeing how fast I could get it to go on some of the straights. I'm sure Dad knew I did it, as the thing had a huge thirst for petrol, so he would soon figure out that it had been driven.

Being mobile was such a big thing for me. I soon joined a group of similar aged local boys who all had bikes and I have to say that we were pretty much out of control at times. Well, as far out of control as you can get on a 50cc machine! It also allowed me to visit a very good friend who lived on a farm about six miles away. He was a year older than me, but we were friends due to our parents being friends. I used to go to his house every Friday night; his mum and dad liked me, and we used to go into the front room and listen to music. Both Phil and I had a similar taste in music but he introduced me to bands like Fleetwood Mac and 10cc of whom he was a great fan. It was due to Phil that I bought the album Rumours which I still rate as one of the classic albums of all time. Phil's mum was the mothering kind and obviously thought I looked undernourished so at around nine pm supper arrived. It was like heaven; there were sandwiches, cakes, chocolate, everything which I liked. I usually ate far more than I should have done but thoroughly enjoyed my time there.

I often thought of wearing my bra when I went out, especially when I went out riding on my own but the thought that I could be knocked off and hurt and the embarrassment which would follow meant that wearing it was confined to home and around the farm. I just felt so much closer to Stephanie wearing it. I had conversations with her, calling myself "she" all the time, longing for a time when I could experiment more with different clothes. But being in a family of males apart from Mum had its limitations and at that point I didn't have the confidence to go into a shop and buy girls clothes, so I had to make do for the time being.

Chapter 3

The family meeting

I left school at the earliest possible moment in May 1977. I was supposed to be on study leave for the upcoming exams to be held in June and early July but very little studying was ever done by me. My learning methodology has always been fairly simple. If it is something I am interested in, then I only need telling once and it is there in my memory for ever. If it is something I am not very interested in, then it goes one of two ways. The first is, if I understand what I have been taught then that is fine - into the memory it goes - but if I don't really understand it or feel it is useless information, then my view has always been that it gets discarded at the first opportunity. I worked on the farm almost every day from then, faking some revision time in the evenings after work and before bed. The reality was that I wanted to earn as much money as possible so that at the first opportunity I could upgrade my bike or, once I had obtained my car license, buy a car. So, there was no time to be wasted on revision during the day and the evenings were reserved for Stephanie time.

The exams came and went. I attended all that I should have done and in the case of physics ended up attending and completing two exams. Our group was of mixed ability and as I was borderline between 'O' level and the easier CSE level I was entered for both. Physics was one subject I enjoyed and I finished up with a grade B 'O' level and grade one CSE, so in effect I had two 'O' levels as grade one CSE counted as an 'O' level pass. Sadly, the good news finished there. I failed maths which was not surprising really. I remember the day of the exam well. I rode my motorbike to school and parked it in the staff carpark, as there was no real space for even small motorbikes in the normal area. When it came time for the exam to start, I turned over the paper and started to read the first question. It made no sense to me at all so I moved on to the second. That made no sense either and that was how it went. I got to the last question and, like all the others, it might as well have been written in a different language so I made sure my name was filled in correctly, looked around to see if there was anyone else doing the same then stood up, walked to the front, put my paper on the teacher's desk and went home. I did pass all the other exams except Accounts. So, given that I had done next to no revision, I actually felt I had done okay. My parents were less impressed, especially with the maths result but that was the end of school for me and I was free.

I worked on the farm for the next year and then, after a conversation with Dad it was decided that in order to gain some experience in how other farms worked it would be a good idea to work for someone else for a couple of years. I found an opening at a farm in the next village, working for a sizeable organisation with seven farms. It was great fun and I got to operate some huge machines, often with little tuition. I remember the first time I drove a harvester, the farm manager came to me and said "You can take the harvester today. You'll manage it won't you? Just press a few buttons, move a few levers and see what happens". I did and after a very short time I was comfortable with it and enjoyed the job. As there were multiple farms we were moved around a fair bit and got to do all sorts of jobs which I thought would be great experience for when I went back to the family farm after a couple of years. This was not to happen!

One night in early 1980 Dad came to me and said "we are having a family meeting on Tuesday so don't go to the pub as you usually do. It's at 7pm and your brothers will both be here so don't be late". I asked what it was about, but he would say nothing. I asked Greg what he thought it was about, but he was no wiser. In the end we decided that Mum must be sick and it was to give us the bad news together.

We all sat around the kitchen table in anticipation and Dad started to talk. He wasn't one for public speaking and seemed almost embarrassed. He thanked us for being there and just said, "Your mum and I are emigrating to Australia. You are all welcome to join us, but we are going anyway." There was a long silence and the three of us looked at each other for some time before Greg asked, "What's brought this on?". Dad then explained that the people who owned our farm wanted to sell it and the best way for my parents to come out of it with a good amount of money was to let them sell it with vacant possession. While Mum and Dad had been on holiday the previous year in Australia they had seen a perfect farm near Kojonup in Western Australia. The owner had since passed away and they were going to buy it. We were all shocked. I had a job, a girlfriend, a nice car and a life. Why would I want to uproot and go and live somewhere I had never seen? Not much else was said. Greg and I decided to continue the conversation at the pub, so the meeting ended.

Greg was in a similar position to me. He had a girlfriend who looked like being long term, a job and he was part way through a college course which he obviously didn't want to leave. We were both quite shocked as we sat behind our pints at the pub. I started to think of the Pros and Cons. The big thing for me was that my expected career path had ended earlier that evening. Mum and Dad had gone through a probable timescale and the long and the short of it was, by about August I would be homeless. I would be nineteen in a few weeks' time and was probably a bit naive when it came to things like finding somewhere to live. It had never even been on the horizon up to now, so it was all going to be a big learning curve.

As the time for leaving the farm came closer, I started to go through the memories that I had accumulated throughout my nineteen years. When I came in from work I would go for walks around the farm; one last look, as it were, and it was a sad time for me. My relationship with my girlfriend was complicated and I was not ready to move in with her so I went about finding somewhere to live by myself. I enlisted the help of a family friend who I had always been close to. He worked at the Auctioneers and Estate Agents business which had been started by my great grandfather and was quick to point me in the direction of buying rather than renting. I was far from convinced but the more he explained, the more logical it seemed so we left it that he would locate somewhere for me.

Sure enough, a couple of weeks later he called me and told me he had found the ideal house and asked me to meet him in Driffield the following morning. Whatever the house was like it was going to be a big shock from living on the farm. Whitehall farm was quite remote by English standards; a big rambling old farmhouse with no other houses around it; the sort of place where no one would hear you scream! Number 6 Cranwell street was everything the farm wasn't; one of a terrace of five houses; the one in the middle. It was no more than about thirteen feet wide, with a small front yard and a communal back yard with a small shed in it for each house. It had been modernised to some extent; a small extension incorporated the kitchen and bathroom. It had a very small cloakroom and one of the two upstairs bedrooms had been divided, making two unusable rooms instead of one decent sized one. There were some positive points though. Firstly, it fitted my budget which was very important; secondly it would be very cheap to run; and thirdly it was within walking distance to town. In the end I decided to put in an offer which was accepted and the challenge of getting a mortgage at nineteen began. My banking history with the Abbey National building society stood me in good stead and I was soon informed that the mortgage had been approved and a completion date set; I was just required to go in and sign the paperwork and wait for the date.

I had no furniture to speak of, but people were very kind and donated enough things for me to be comfortable to start with and I moved in at the end of November 1980, a very proud nineteen-year-old homeowner. I think during the next six months I matured more than I had in the previous nineteen years, learning to budget for things like the mortgage, electricity, gas and water bills, council rates etc. It was a huge challenge but one which, looking back, made me a much sharper and focused person, intent on making something from what was a huge shock to my system.

There was one very big advantage to living in my own little house. I was free to be Stephanie whenever I was at home and it felt amazing. I soon got into the habit of changing into my bra as soon as I got home and wearing it all night. It allowed me to explore my feelings at a deeper level but there was limited external information available to cross-dressers, so I limited myself to just wearing the bra and dreaming.

I was also learning to be thoughtful to neighbours. I had never experienced them before and either side of me were elderly ladies. Sadly, shortly after I moved in, the one to the left passed away and the house remained empty for some time. The lady on the right became a friend and I would often spend a few hours in an evening at her home. She didn't get around very well and I regularly went shopping for her. The other advantage was that she kept her house very warm. I could go around to see her, turn my gas fire right down and make use of her heat. Being a terraced house, you could feel the warmth of her house through my walls; they were a huge contrast to the other side which was now empty and cold.

1981 had one further milestone and one huge shock left in store for me. As I mentioned earlier, the relationship with my girlfriend was complicated and I had the impression it was not to be long-term, but I persevered. She was aware of my long-ing to wear women's underwear and had reservations about it. I very rarely wore it in her company and when questioned about it I didn't really know what to say. I knew in my own mind I would much rather be a girl, but such things were not discussed in the early eighties so it was just left as a bit of a fetish and she thought I would grow out of it. We needed to go to Bridlington for something and while we were there, we visited Marks and Spencer's. I wasn't much of a clothes shopper in those days, but she needed some underwear and I watched with interest as she picked out several bras to try on. I so wished I could do the same. She was much smaller than me across the back so only needed a size 34 which would not have fitted me; but I noticed on the rack of bras I particularly liked that the sizes went up to 38. How I longed to buy one. My opportunity came only a few days later as I was back in Bridlington for something else and decided to do it. I walked into the store and confidently walked up to the lingerie de-partment and picked out a size 38b which I thought would fit nicely and took it to the till. The lady at the till gave me a bit of a strange look and checked the size was what I needed and said if it doesn't fit when you get home you should get the lady to call in and get measured. I thanked her and said I would pass on her advice, paid the money and walked out so pleased with myself. I had bought my first bra.

The good news for 1981 ended there. In October I was laid off from my job, something almost unheard of in the farming industry, but as my employer had little in the way of livestock there would not be much for me to do during the winter. I was told that I would be welcome to return in Spring but somehow I needed to make it through to Spring financially. I finished at the end of the month and didn't really have much of an idea where to start. I had been doing a day release course since leaving school, at Driffield Further Education Centre and had enjoyed it and got on particularly well with the course tutor so thought I would pay him a visit to see if he had heard of any vacancies in the area. He hadn't, but said he would make some enquiries on my behalf. At that time I didn't have a phone at home but the lady next door was happy to take messages for me so I gave the tutor her number. A couple of days later he called and asked me to go in and see him. I went the next day thinking he had a hot tip for me, but his plan was of a different nature. He wanted me to go to Agricultural College. My first reaction was a straight "not interested" - after all I had a mortgage to pay; but the more he talked about it the more interesting an option it seemed. He also offered to help me obtain a grant which would help on the financial side if I went for it. There was one problem, the course was a specialist 20 week course in arable machinery and one of the conditions of entry was to have completed the NCA (National Certificate in Agriculture) which I hadn't. But he said the course tutor would like to meet me and would possibly overlook that if he thought I was a good candidate. An appointment was made and I arrived in good time hoping to get a word with my day release tutor first but as I walked in they were already talking. He looked me up and down and said to me "You must be quite something the way Tom has spoken about you. He is willing to put his name to a waiver of the NCA course requirement in your favour". I was very taken aback and it almost seemed a forgone conclusion that I would be enrolling there and then.

Chapter 4

A change of direction

My college course started on January 2nd, 1982. The first day was a "getting to know your way about" day and a day for meeting the tutors. I was very much in the minority as there was only me and one other student who hadn't done the NCA course (someone I had known for a few years as his cousin was one of my best friends). The only other student who didn't know his way around the place was a lad from Newcastle. He had done the NCA but up in the north east and came down to us as it was one of only three agricultural colleges in the country offering this course, the other two being in the south of England. There were twenty-two of us in total of whom I only knew four (all former Driffield Further Education Centre students), but we were a friendly group and all got along well.

I had always shied away from full time further education as I thought it would remind me too much of school but of course this was totally different. We were on first name terms with all the tutors, regardless of age, which gave for a very relaxed atmosphere and a much more adult feeling than I expected. I soon got to know all of them and enjoyed every minute of my time there. We had a great deal of fun but there was also a serious side to the learning. We were told on the first day – "You are all hand-picked students so we don't expect anyone to fail this course". The whole "being treated as an adult thing" was very evident in every aspect. There wasn't a great amount of homework but there was an expectation that it would be completed, and it was. I really took to one of the tutors who took us for welding. He was, I would say, in his early sixties, very old school and was famous for his phrase "gather round lads". He would then explain something such as an unexpected occurrence when someone had been welding in a particular way, or with a certain type of metal or rod. He would end with just an "as you were" and everyone just went back to what they had been doing. I think he liked me because I had done a fair amount of welding before and didn't need telling the basics. During his "gather round lads" interludes, he would often turn to me and ask why I thought something had happened, knowing that he would get a sensible answer and we soon built up a close relationship. He always called me Rob, a name I liked but which few people actually used. At the beginning of a lesson, after explaining what we were going to cover in the day's session, he would often turn to me and say "I have a little job for you Rob. You don't need to do today's exercise do you? You will have done it a hundred times before". He would then take me outside to a piece of machinery which someone had brought in which was in need of some welding work of some sort. He would explain what the problem was and just leave me to it. I enjoyed this very much as I have always liked welding, loved the precision of it and making it look perfect rather than just functional. I still admire good welding to this day. He also introduced me to the oxyacetylene cutter or "gas axe" as it is more frequently known. Now this was a piece of equipment I took to very quickly. The amount of destruction you could cause with it in a very short time was astonishing and I relished the opportunity to use it. Farmers would bring in old equipment which I would cut up into small pieces either for the NCA students to practice welding on or just so it would fit into the scrap bin. It was great fun indeed.

The main aim of this course was to firstly give you a real insight into how farm machinery worked and secondly how to repair it when it didn't. The idea was that if you were a farmer's son going back to work on the family farm you would be able to maintain your machinery yourself rather than getting the local dealer involved, which invariably turned out to be a very expensive exercise. If you were a farm labourer then the hope was that firstly, you would get a job more easily as you had a set of skills which most farm workers didn't have, and secondly be of more value to the owner and therefore be able to command a higher wage. It all added up for me as it was the machinery side of farming which appealed to me and it was becoming more mechanised every day. It was also a time of farmers cutting costs as margins were very much getting tighter.

Throughout the duration of the course I could feel myself gaining confidence, not just in what I was doing, but in myself as well and I started to think that maybe I should be looking more at working for a dealer rather than a farmer. As the twenty weeks were drawing to an end, thoughts of what to do next were high on my list of priorities. Going to college had made a serious dent in what little savings I had and if it hadn't been for some help from my aunt (my father's sister) and uncle things would have been very difficult. From the day my parents left the country they seemed to step in and take their place. The difference was that with them there was a caring and nurturing that I had not enjoyed with my parents. Virtually as soon as Mum and Dad left for Australia I was asked to join them for the weekly Sunday lunch, a habit which just became the norm and went on for many years. It worked well for all of us as I was able to help my uncle on his farm as he worked it on his own and there are lots of jobs which are a good deal easier with two people. Over the years a tremendous bond grew between us. I became known as their "adopted son" and I loved it. I enjoyed every minute with them and look back on this time with very happy memories. I looked after the farm when they went on holiday. It was a time I enjoyed very much as it was an idyllic place with a river running down the side of the property and looked like a picture postcard. I can't tell you how many times they have helped me in so many ways; they looked after me when I was sick, sorted me out when I needed legal help and were just always "there for me". I often wonder how I would have survived without them.

At the end of the course there was a lunch organised for us all where the tutor would be giving out the results and some awards for the high achievers. I would have been very satisfied to have just passed the course and was very happy to hear that all except one of us had passed. I sat next to the welding tutor with whom I had become good friends. We enjoyed our lunch and the tutor stood up. He firstly thanked us all for our commitment to the course. He remarked that it had been the most successful yet and they were considering making it a full year the following year. Then came the awards – three in total. Most of the students were pretty evenly matched, I thought, but as the first award was announced I was soon to learn that my day release tutor had done a great job. All the recipients had been students at the Driffield Further Education Centre. The first award was for the best practical student and it went to one of the lads I shared a car with to and from college. He had always been outstanding in the workshop part of the course. Second up was the best theory student. There was no surprise with this one as the recipient was the other lad I shared a car with - he was very articulate and his written work was also very good. Then it came time for the "best overall student" and I simply couldn't believe my ears when he read out my name. The welding tutor stood up and started to clap. I was so embarrassed as the whole room did the same. He shook hands with me and I went to the front to collect my award. The tutor congratulated me and I turned to the room and just said thank you to all the tutors and staff. I was overwhelmed.

On the last day of the course I was talking to one of the tutors and he asked what I was going to do next. I told him I needed to find a job and he mentioned that he knew someone looking for a tractor driver/mechanic. He gave me his name and phone number and said he would call him and let him know I would be phoning him in the next day or two. This I did and we arranged to meet at his house in Stamford Bridge which is about twenty miles from Driffield. When I arrived it was nothing like I had expected. I had anticipated a farm-like place but this was a stately home; it was huge! We talked for some time, discussing what he was looking for and what he was prepared to pay and a deal was done. He was a contractor so the work was spread over hundreds of miles and I spent a good deal of time traveling. I enjoyed the work - they were long days but the pay was good and I soon got back on my feet financially. The only downside was that it was not full-time work. During summer I was kept very busy but then the work dropped off and I was concerned that it would become a problem, so I started looking for something else. I found another job, again with a contractor, but he promised me full time work so I took it. The job didn't have the same amount of enjoyment, but it was work. All was good until I tried to lift something I shouldn't have and hurt my back. I was off work for some time and my thoughts went back to how I was feeling at college – that perhaps I should be working for a dealer. Working on a farm, driving tractors, mending things was probably not going to be a long-term thing for me as I would get very bored with it eventually. So while my back was recovering I started looking for a sales job working for a dealer. After all, I knew a great deal about farm machinery so why not try selling it? I talked to a couple of people without any luck, but then saw an advertisement at the local Ford dealer. The vacancy was for a junior sales trainee in the Ford Car dealership which also owned a Ford Tractor dealership. My thought was that I could apply for this then if I was successful, wait for an opening on the tractor side and move over. The interview went really well. They were looking for two people to start almost straight away with the idea being that one would make it and the other wouldn't. I got the job! As I wasn't working I was asked if I wanted to start early to get to know my way around the place and help them with a few jobs like transferring cars from dealer to dealer. This was perfect for me - it didn't pay very well but it gave me a feel for the place, and I got to know the other salespeople along with other staff.

The job started for real on the second of January 1983 and straight away there was a sense of competition between me and the other salesman who started the same day. I felt I had a bit of an advantage as I knew my way around the place, but success in the sales field did not come easily. My opponent got off to a better start than I did and I soon felt under pressure, but I stuck at it and eventually the sales came and we drew level. Then I had a piece of luck; my opponent was contacted by his previous employer asking if he would consider going back for more money. He accepted and I was on my own. It wasn't until May of 1983 that things really came together. For the first time I got into double figures for the month. I actually sold thirteen cars and had lots of enquiries to carry over. I was there! The thought of switching to the tractor side never entered my head again; cars were the love of my life and being able to make a living out of them was amazing.

Chapter 5

Maximum effort and the importance of PK

The remainder of 1983 had some ups and some downs in terms of sales but in general I was happy with my progress and so was the management. In August I was given my first company car, a two-year-old Fiesta which had just been traded and had some licence left on it. The car itself was nothing special but the fact that I had been given it to drive at no cost to me was very significant. Neither of the senior salesmen liked working Saturday afternoons. We worked every other Saturday and only a year before, the dealership had closed at 12 noon on a Saturday but as the bigger dealers were opening longer hours, eventually sleepy Driffield had to follow. I didn't mind doing the afternoons especially after I was given the car, as I could bring it into the side entrance of the showroom and give it a clean if there was no one about. After some negotiations I agreed to work every Saturday and at around 12:30, if I was working with Mark, he would leave and head straight for the pub. If I was working with Mike, in winter he would change into his soccer kit and head for the club for his weekly game and then in summer he would head for the golf club. Either way I was on my own. Saturday afternoons were a good source of leads. I didn't usually sell more than an odd car on the day but it gave me things to work on during the week which worked very well for me. Both the other guys had been there for many years so had lots of repeat business but for me, starting from scratch, every lead was taken seriously and with no competition it was a rich source of enquiries.

At the beginning of September, during one of our daily morning meetings, we were told of a national sales meeting to be held at the National Exhibition Centre in Birmingham. It was to be held over two days so that all the salespeople and managers were not away at the same time and it was scheduled for the following week. As we had a sister dealership 12 miles away we joined together so both sales teams were involved, but the showrooms were still covered. I was designated to drive as I was not, and am still not, much of a drinker and there would be plenty of opportunity when the refreshments came out. I asked what the meeting would cover and was given a very vague answer; basically wait and see. It was a very grand affair, seemingly hundreds of suited men and the odd lady all busy talking their dealerships up to their competition. I felt pretty out of place but Mike, who had been designated my mentor from day one, stayed close to me and kept me right. There were lots of young ladies walking around with trays full of glasses and Mike asked me if I wanted a drink. I asked him what was in the glasses and he replied, "Either gin or whiskey". The idea was that you took the glass of your choice then added a small bottle of either tonic or dry ginger. Now, I know this may seem naive but I had never tasted spirits at all. While I was deliberating which to take, he grabbed two gins and two tonics, passed one to me and said, "if you don't like it I'll drink it". The glass already had ice and a slice of lemon in it, I poured the whole bottle of tonic into it and took a sip, then another and I was hooked. I have drunk gin and tonic ever since, whenever the offer of spirits is made or I don't want beer. I left it at one drink as I was driving but enjoyed it all the same.

Shortly after, we were ushered into an auditorium. There was loud music, dry-ice smoke and a huge stage with two cars on it. We were shown to our seats and the music faded. As the smoke drifted off I could see a man walking onto the stage. He took the microphone and said in a very clear voice "ladies and gentlemen, we are under siege. There are lots of cars coming from the east (meaning Japan) and we intend to meet them head on". There was a series of pictures of Toyotas, Datsuns (now Nissans) and Hondas which were then being imported in great numbers. Eventually we were shown the new Fiesta. It was more rounded and much plusher inside, new engine options and the introduction of an automatic was planned although it didn't happen for some years.

The meeting ended and refreshments were served back in the foyer and we left. The drive home was pretty quiet as both the guys in the car went to sleep. The sales manager told me to drop him off and take his car home as he could walk to work the following morning. The next day we started making arrangements for the launch of the new model. New vehicle launches were big things in those days as there was no internet and very few leaked pictures, so it was usually the first time the public had seen the new model. Usually about twice a week a document was given to us called a status report. I always read it with interest as it told us the intended delivery date of all the vehicles heading our way. There were often vehicles on it which were allocated rather than ordered, for whatever reason. They were partly disguised so didn't mean much and at this particular time I was just interested in when our new Fiestas were arriving which was scheduled for the following week. This particular afternoon a Tollman delivery driver walked into the showroom and announced, "seven for you". I thought how strange as I hadn't seen anything on the report which indicated we were getting a delivery. I walked outside with the driver and looked at the cars on the transporter. My first reaction was that they were not for us as they looked nothing like one of our models, then on closer inspection I could see they had Ford badges on them, but I still didn't recognise the shape. The driver started to unload them. I opened the door of the first one; it looked like an Escort inside but it was a saloon/ sedan whereas the Escort was either a hatch or wagon. I went to the back and pulled the plastic off the badge; it said Orion. I'd never heard of the Ford Orion. I signed for the cars and went back to the showroom with the paperwork to show the sales manager. He was speechless, he shook his head and muttered "why on earth didn't they tell us about this at the meeting last week?". He made some phone calls and came into the sales office and said it has been kept a surprise so the motoring press didn't get to know of its arrival! It was launched at the same event as the new Fiesta and although slow to start became quite a reasonable seller. It's just a world away from the new car launches of today.

Shortly after the launch the sales manager came to me and said "the boss thinks you should attend some sales training to further your knowledge, so I've booked you on this course next month. It's for three days and it's being held at Ford's training centre just outside Romford in Essex". What I discovered later was that they were under pressure to do more training and thought I was a prime candidate. Ford produced a magazine every month with all the models in and features on any new ones or specification changes. I read them cover to cover, knew all the specifications and features, all the colour and trim options, all the prices and options. I was an encyclopaedia of Ford models and had become the go-to person for any queries requiring product knowledge. I lived and breathed Ford cars and no one could tell me anything about them that I didn't know. Unbeknown to me this was going to stand me in good stead for the upcoming training at which product knowledge was a big part. On day one I walked into the training room and took a seat. I had a quick scan round the room, there were twenty-two of us, mostly fresh-faced salespeople, twenty men and two ladies. After a short while the trainer came in and stood at the front of his desk and looked around the room, studying each and every one of us but saying nothing. When he got to the last one he looked up and spoke these words, "if you take only one thing back to your dealerships, let it be this golden rule. You have one mouth and two ears, be sure to use them in that proportion". I was impressed by his command of the room; he introduced himself and then went on to explain the format of the course. He asked if we all knew what PK was. Most nodded but some had a puzzled look on their faces. For some reason he looked straight at me and said, "what is it Robin?" I replied, "product knowledge Phil". He thanked me and went on to emphasise its importance. He then told us there would be a PK quiz every morning and after every lunch break and said there would be a spot prize for the winner of each quiz and then at the end there would be a big prize for the person who won the most quizzes. It started that very minute, 6 quizzes and I won 5 of them! I was actually really annoyed that I didn't win them all but 5 out of 6 is okay and I got to take home some cool Ford stuff. The big prize at the end was a Ford Motorsport package consisting of a range of Rallysport clothing, backpack and other small items. Ford were heavily into Rallying at the time and so was I, so it was all very gratefully received. I even got a well done from the boss when I got back to work. He said it was good to have recognition for a small dealership. It put the dealership on the map so to speak.

Not long after that, our dealership was asked to nominate someone to attend the regional PK quiz; obviously I was the first choice. It was to be held in Harrogate at a hotel close to the northern district office. There were dozens of salespeople, all thinking they would win. Once again there were some good prizes on offer and I intended winning them. There were four regions, northern and southern England, Wales and Scotland. The top three from each region went on to a head-to-head final and the top two of those got to go on the Dealer Principle trip which was to Thailand later in the year for a one-on-one final. I won the regional heat but came third in the national final so missed out on the trip but was very well rewarded for my efforts. I had more Ford and Rallysport clothing than I could ever wear and all the national finalists got to go on a track day at Oulton park in Cheshire where we were driving Formula Ford single seaters and Escort RS Turbos for the day. The experience was amazing and the best thing was that when I got back I was given my choice of company car to drive (up to a certain value) which made all the hard work I had put in for the dealership worthwhile.

At this stage I felt I had, for the first time in my life, some real direction work wise. I had always loved cars and the realisation that I was able to make a good living out of them as well as receiving recognition from my peers and management was a real bonus. It also went some way towards taking my mind off Stephanie, even though I still enjoyed a degree of crossdressing in the privacy of my home. Selling cars became the most important thing in my life; it was something I could really shine at and in the process earn good money and make some long lasting friendships.

Chapter 6

First shot at management

By the time 1987 arrived I was in full flight. Most months I either sold the most cars or came a close second to the Fleet salesman. Ford had some good products and keen pricing but there was an increasing number of foreign brands available and they all intended to have a slice of the market. The new registration letter on number plates came out in August and that year I was determined to reach 50 units for the month. I did that and so did the fleet salesman, so all in all, we had a great month. I'd never seen the compound look so empty. Shortly after the month-end I was asked to join the sales manager and dealer principal in his office for a chat. I was told that the senior salesman from our sister dealership was leaving and asked if I would be interested in moving over there to act as assistant sales manager in charge of sales at that branch. I replied in true salesperson style with "it depends what the deal is". Eventually a deal was struck and I started work there in late September. I had two other salesmen selling for me and soon built up a great rapport with them. We were a good team, had lots of fun and sold an impressive number of cars. It was nice to be included in management meetings and have my say. I probably said too much at times but I was intent on making my mark.

After a couple of years I realised that, even though I was doing a good job, the chances of progressing any higher up the management tree were very limited, as the Sales Manager wasn't going anywhere. Then, I received a call at home one evening from the Sales Manager of the local Volkswagen/Audi dealership. He explained that they had been taken over and were doing some restructuring which meant he would have a more General Manager role so wanted someone under him to run the showroom and sales operation and asked if I would be interested. I said I was, and we agreed to meet to talk about the role. We met early the following week and talked about the position and what I would hope to earn should I take it. He took it on board and said he would talk to the new owners and get back to me.

A couple of days later I was sitting at my desk when a call came through for me. A man introduced himself and said he had heard I was in the job market. I was a little taken aback as I hadn't discussed it with anyone at that point. It turned out that he ran the Volkswagen dealership in a town about twenty miles away, which was now part of the same group as my local one and my name had come up at a meeting he was attending. He asked me if I had accepted the job and said if I hadn't, would I be interested in talking to him instead. Now at this point I hadn't heard back from the first contact, so I said I was happy to talk. Once again, a meeting was arranged, this time at the dealership, which I must say seemed much more professional, and I got on really well with him. Again, I was asked what sort of package I would be expecting. I thought about it and on the grounds that there would be some traveling involved I asked for a little more than the local one. One of the things which was very important to me was a decent company car. I had worked my way up to getting an acceptable one where I was and wasn't going backwards on it, so I asked for a Golf GTi. To my surprise both the figure and the car were met with approval but he said he would need to get the okay from the owners.

This meeting had taken place on the Thursday evening following the meeting with the local contact on the Tuesday, whom I had not heard back from. The following day I was just bursting to tell someone, so I confided in one of the salesmen. He congratulated me and agreed that no matter how good I was I would not get the Sales Manager job there for a long time. Sometime in the afternoon a man, whom I had known for many years, walked into the showroom. He ran a small country garage in a village between our two Ford dealerships. He asked me if I had been contacted by the local Volkswagen dealer as he had given him my number. I thanked him and told him the story. At the end of it he asked me if I had accepted either job, I told him I hadn't yet had an official offer of a job but was more likely to go with the second one. He said he was pleased I hadn't accepted a job yet as he would like to talk to me about possibly working for him. My head was spinning; three possible job offers in the space of a week was unreal. We arranged for him to pick me up later and discuss what he had in mind over dinner. He had a Renault Autopoint which was basically a sub dealer working under a local main dealer. He very much wanted to expand it but didn't have time due to running the rest of the garage so wanted to know if I was interested. We discussed and agreed on a package; a deal was done and I left Ford two weeks later.

Chapter 7

New beginnings

I had been with Ford for almost seven years and had developed a reputation for myself as a hard worker and someone who would do what it takes to make a deal happen. Building my portfolio of customers had taken lots of late nights and long hours but it had been worth it to get established. The fact that I am still in contact with a number of my old customers to this day is, I think, a tribute to my policy of going the extra mile to get the deal and making lots of friends in the process. Unfortunately, it took its toll on personal relationships. I had numerous over those early years and most of them ended because I was unwilling to make any real commitment. The job came first or that was what I told people, to the extent that I actually believed it myself. The real reason for not wanting commitment was that I wanted time to myself, or to be more accurate, time to be Stephanie. I told some of my partners bits of my story and my longings but many I didn't, and I regret my decision not to do so. Another issue was children. I was very definite about not wanting children. The thought of bringing someone into the world as mixed up as I was, scared me to death. I knew the chances of that happening were probably low, but I just wasn't prepared to take the risk; especially as I didn't know why I felt the way I did.

During the first week in the new job I sold four cars. I was well pleased with myself, especially as I now had a much fairer commission structure. Also, in one way or another, I would be involved in any sales which the owner made, and I was paid commission on them too. I loved the relaxed way business was done and the fact that I could sell virtually any make of car. We also had a seemingly endless supply of used vehicles from one auction site or another. I loved going to the auctions; there was an atmosphere there which I so enjoyed being part of. It was good to mix with other dealers and we helped each other when it came to getting cars home. I also loved the fact that I didn't need to wear a suit anymore, although I did continue to wear a tie most of the time. It just felt right to do so.

I also moved to a new house late in 1989. I bought a three-bedroom detached bungalow in a cul-de-sac on a new estate. It was lovely making all the decisions on carpets and curtains and making the place look how I wanted it.

The following year I consolidated my position in the new job and continued to do well. Getting into the swing of selling used cars more often than new cars was easy. Every used car is unique and so cannot fully be compared with one at another dealer. I made it my business to ensure they were all prepared to a high standard and we established a good reputation for selling quality cars at competitive prices. I managed to hold on to a number of my customers from Ford. Like most selling jobs, if you build the right relationship with your customers you become their first point of contact when they need something, and I worked hard at keeping them. One such customer ran a hire car business in a nearby town. He had been my biggest customer for many years with Ford and changing his buying habits from new cars to nearly new was easy as it saved him thousands of pounds. I had also built up a close personal friendship with him and his partner and on one of our regular get togethers he mentioned that he wanted to visit Australia. My parents had lived in Western Australia for the last 10 years. I had been out once to visit and, on that occasion, thought I would like to return, but with either a partner or a friend and do a little more traveling while there, so this was the perfect solution. Plans were made and our flights were booked for New Year's Day 1991, returning some four weeks later. Andy said he fancied having a short stop over and as we were flying with Thai Airways, Bangkok was to be the venue. We were only there for about a day and a half and decided to book a scenic river cruise. Now I'm not massively keen on boats and boat trips but I was assured that the water would be calm. It certainly was - so calm in fact I slept through the whole tour! A complete waste of money but I must have needed the sleep.

In the last couple of weeks before setting off I had been out with a girl who had recently separated from her husband. I knew them both well (in fact I was best man at their wedding); they had two small children a boy four years old and a girl two years old. I was, at that time, not very child friendly to say the least but I had been asked for tea on Christmas Day and had an experience which would completely change my views. I arrived at the house about four in the afternoon and was greeted by Fiona, her two very excited children and her mum. I had met Fiona's mum several times before and found her to be a fascinating person to listen to as she and her husband had lived in Africa for some time and she had some interesting stories from their travels. The children were very keen to show me all their Christmas presents and the younger one, Natalie, was busy ironing some imaginary clothes with a toy iron and ironing board. When she had finished, she came over to me and wanted to sit on my knee. This was not something I had experienced before but I helped her up. The next thing that happened surprised me even more, she curled up on my knee, placed her thumb in her mouth and proceeded to fall fast asleep. We had some sort of special bond from then on.

On my return from Australia Fiona and I decided to make a relationship of it, and I saw them all on a regular basis. I couldn't believe how my new little friend took to me; it was indeed a very new experience for me. I also had an immediate connection with the older child Craig. He was very bright and advanced for his age and as I'd never really had meaningful conversations with children before it was all very new. It helped my relationship with Fiona a great deal too as she was understandably protective of them and happy that we had gelled from the start. The fact that I still have lovely relationships with both children to this day is, I think, down to those early days.

Fiona and I married in 1992. A friend who I had met through work had been telling me how they had married at Gretna just over the Scottish border and it seemed like a lovely idea, so it was duly organised. We kept it a secret from everyone except Fiona's mum, as she would be looking after the children while we were away. We planned the reception for four weeks later and posted very carefully worded invitations on the morning of the wedding so by the time they were received we were already married. We did the whole tourist thing whilst there, including, after the official ceremony, being "married" again over the anvil as it had been done for centuries there. It all went to plan and with a minimum of fuss which appealed to me a great deal.

Throughout our relationship I had spent hours deliberating whether to, and how to, tell Fiona about my mixed-up head but somehow just never had the courage. It was only a short time after the wedding before I realised that this put a huge problem in front of me because I immediately lost my time with Stephanie. The children were all-consuming when I got home from work until they went to bed. I loved the time with my ready-made family. As I had never wanted my own children, because of how I felt, this was the perfect solution and I had a great relationship with Craig and Natalie. They were both past the "scary" age when they can't communicate with you and both seemed to take to me. From day one I wanted them to call me Robin. I never wanted to be Dad as having two Dads would have only caused confusion for them and, above all, I wanted them to think of me as a special friend rather than a parent and it worked a treat. I still missed my time as Stephanie though, and it wasn't long before I was looking forward to nights when Fiona went out with her old school friend and I was left at home. The children were tucked up in bed and I cherished the time I was able to dress up in the underwear and clothes I had hidden in the bottom of the wardrobe. Sadly, it didn't bode well for the relationship and eventually I started to resent the fact that I couldn't be me.

Chapter 8

Ongoing confusion

A year on from the wedding and the confusion in my head grew worse and worse. I could see no way of dealing with it and eventually something was going to have to give. I probably wasn't being a very good husband, was definitely not as focused at work as I should have been and was basically unhappy. Work had somehow lost its attraction and I knew I needed a new challenge in that direction. The motor trade was what I was good at and so the time had come to move on. It was now 1994 and I was out one evening with a friend who I met in my last year at Ford. We were a similar age and had many of the same interests, so every couple of weeks we would head into town for a few beers and put the world to rights. On this particular night I needed to visit the cash point and was just crossing the road when a car pulled up beside me and the driver lowered his window to speak to me. I knew the driver quite well; he owned the local Citroen dealership. After enquiring how I was going, almost before I had time to answer, he asked me if I was interested in going to work for him. I was a little taken aback but said I would call him the following day to arrange a meeting. My friend who was waiting for me at the other side of the road also knew him and asked what he wanted. I think the look on my face probably gave it away, so we talked at length about the pros and cons of jumping ship as it were. I duly went to see him a couple of days later for what was a strange and very brief chat. There didn't seem to be any doubt in his mind that I would shortly be working for him so the only two things to discuss were how much he was prepared to pay me and when I would be starting.

Moving job gave me something to occupy my mind in the short term. There was lots to learn as it was predominantly a new car selling job rather than the emphasis being on used vehicles. I have always liked the Citroen product for some strange reason; probably because they are just that - strange! The good thing was they had a very loyal following and Citroen owners were very easy to sell to. The dealership had a good reputation and we were always busy. The downside was that we worked every other Sunday. I hadn't been used to working Sundays, but we did get a day off during the week to compensate, which worked well apart from the fact that I didn't get much time with the children.

I settled in well and had a great relationship with the boss. He had long been a person I admired as he had built the dealership up from very humble beginnings and took on the Citroen franchise when they didn't have much of a product range and were seen as very quirky. They had since gone on to be much more mainstream but still managed to keep their loyal followers. I think at the time Citroen had a National market share of about 3-4% but in our area we had close to 10% and were seen as a very high achieving dealership. The only downside was that this was the first dealership I had worked where there was no commission structure. We were just paid a fixed salary, so although the money was okay there was no opportunity to make more by working harder. This took a long time to get used to and by the time I had adjusted to it I was looking for a more rewarding structure. Also, the problem with my confused head was not going away. Changing employment had occupied my mind for a short time but the problem of Stephanie remained just that; a problem. I began to resent the fact that I couldn't go home, shut the door and be the person I wanted to be. Even if I could somehow explain it to Fiona it wouldn't be fair to the children; it would just have been far too confusing for them.

Then it happened again! I was sitting at my desk in the showroom when a man walked in, saw me and said, "oh I didn't know you worked here now". I had known him since I sold him a car for his son in 1986. I knew he owned a garage and that he had since taken on the Rover franchise. We sat and talked for a while, then the boss appeared and they went off together. A few days later, after a long day's work, I was sitting relaxing in the bath when Fiona opened the door and said there was a phone call for me. She handed me the phone and the voice at the other end was this man's son. I had spoken to him a few times since his father had bought the car from me but was surprised to get a call from him. After a few seconds I was quite sure why he was calling me but somehow, he seemed unable to just come out and say it. He eventually asked me if I was happy at Citroen and if there would be any point in my having a chat sometime about going to work for him.

Being approached and asked if you are interested in having a chat about employment is a massive ego boost whichever way you look at it and it seemed to happen on a regular basis with me. I made an appointment to see him the following week and was rather surprised when he said, "bring along your wife so we can meet her as well". An unusual tactic if ever I had heard one!

Once again it was not really an interview; it was apparently a given that I would be joining them and just a case of sorting out the finer details. This time though, I was better prepared and the package I asked for was a considerable improvement on the one I was on. It also included a performance element so I had something to work towards. He didn't even try to negotiate, just said, "That sounds fine. When can you start?". I immediately wished I had asked for more but there were a number of elements which I was unhappy with at Citroen that I had made sure I had included in the package. Firstly, the start time; I saw no point in being there at 8am as, in reality, customers don't come in that early; so the agreed start time was 9am. Secondly, although the job at Citroen included a car in the package, fuel was not included. I just thought that a salary package which included a car should also include fuel, within reason. This time I made sure there were no fuel limits and most importantly that there was the performance element to keep me interested.

At that time Rover was owned by BMW; a strange partnership I thought but could only be good for Rover. Like or hate BMW you can't deny that they are a quality product and hopefully some of that quality would rub off on Rover. That said, it was a completely different environment from working at Citroen. There was a desire to look after customers in a different way, like putting your arm around them and giving them an extraordinarily high level of customer satisfaction and I loved it. Nothing was too much trouble. The workshop was a place of calm and the emphasis was on helping each other and nurturing apprentices in a way I had never seen. It was like a big family and I immediately felt part of it.

The majority of products that Rover had on the market at that time were old and in need of some new models to update their range. This happened shortly after I joined them with the launch of the 400 series hatchback. This was the last model in the joint venture Rover had enjoyed with Honda before being bought out by BMW. It was basically the same body shell as the new Civic Hatchback but with some different engines and of course Rover's classic chrome grille which certainly did set them apart. Like most new model launches the pricing was, shall we say, a little ambitious and it wasn't long before there were offers and reductions, along with special editions to help things along. These measures certainly made a difference and with the upcoming British motor show we were promised a couple of surprises which hopefully would keep the sales moving. This particular year the motor show was held at Earls Court in London, so I didn't attend as the distance was too great to go there and back in a day. I wished I had, though, as there was a pre-production model of the soon to be launched new Rover 200. The response was incredible; so much so that the decision was made to launch it straight away instead of at the beginning of 1996. They had plenty of stock of three-door models on hand and the five-door version would be released about a month later. It was the right decision; we were inundated with enquiries and had a long list of people to contact as soon as our car arrived. Probably what was more important was that I immediately fell in love with the car. It drove really well, looked the part and it was priced to sell. Even more important to me was the promise of a hot hatch version to follow shortly which the range really needed to keep the momentum going. It didn't disappoint; our launch car was in the classic British Racing Green and while that probably wouldn't have been my first choice it certainly looked the part while being respectfully understated. I couldn't wait to get the car prepared and licensed for the road. I loved it from the start and had it plastered with decals proclaiming its credentials. The lettering on the back read "The all new Rover 200Vi, catch it if you can!" and not many did.

The other surprise at the show was the new Rover 400 saloon, this was a unique product to Rover as Honda didn't see the attraction. It was a bigger car than the hatch, both inside and out, and looked very classy indeed. I would be spoilt for choice in what to drive home each evening; so many options.

Chapter 9

The inevitable and Transformation

All in all, things were going pretty well work-wise. I liked the product, the dealership was a good place to work and I was well rewarded for my efforts. On the downside I was spending too much time there, in my wife's opinion, and being the best part of twenty miles from home there was a twenty to thirty-minute drive at either end of the day, depending on traffic. This led to a long day and coupled with the fact that I still resented the fact that I couldn't go home, shut the door and be the person I wanted to be, the end-result was inevitable. There are a limited number of times you can go home to an atmosphere and an argument about why you are late home. This came to a head in October 1997 when I decided we needed some time apart. I moved out and went to live with my parents in a little village called Setterington. It was a pretty little place; the house was small but I had the guest bedroom which had its own bathroom so at least I had my privacy. It was strange going back to live with my parents again; something I really never expected to happen as I thought when they emigrated to Australia in 1980 that they would stay there for the rest of their lives. They returned home in 1991, for a number of reasons but mainly because they now had two grandsons, and settled in Setterington.

Shortly after moving back I was sitting watching television with my mother. Dad had gone to bed, so there was just the two of us, and she said something really strange to me. We had never had what you could call a close relationship and that probably makes what she said to me even more strange. She said to me "We are really sorry that you and Fiona have parted; we like Fiona very much but, in a way, I'm glad you have come back to live with us as I think we have unfinished business". I asked her what she meant but she changed the subject and it was never revisited. I have thought many times since that it may have been about something that happened when I was born but I guess I will never know the full story.

After a few weeks and some negotiations, I agreed to move back in with Fiona and the children. I missed them very much and still loved Fiona, but the job at Rover was my opportunity to shine. It was a place where I could really make a mark and a name for myself. Opportunities like that, where you can set yourself up, don't come along very often so I had to take it. Over a lifetime you spend a great deal of time at work so you really need to enjoy what you do. This was that job; the one that just felt right and where I felt appreciated and looked after. Perhaps not surprisingly, going back to Fiona didn't last long and a few weeks later I had returned to live with my parents. This time I thought it was final. I decided to buy a house and found just what I was looking for in the village of Middleton on the Wolds. The house had everything I needed; it was only eight miles from work and I immediately enjoyed living there. I was given two kittens which I named George and Kitkat but sadly George was knocked down and killed by a car which left just me and Kitkat. He was a real character, black and white with a big fluffy tail and a joy to come home to.

The real joy of course was that I was free to be me again and for the first time I started fully cross-dressing; I even dared to wear a little makeup - mainly just mascara - but I enjoyed it immensely. Around that time I started having an evening walk, just around the block to start with but extending it further if the weather was nice. Slowly but surely I became braver and wore women's clothes, covered up by a coat when necessary during the winter months. I experimented more with makeup and often wore it when I went out for my walk. The more I cross-dressed the more I loved it. This was the perfect balance; a job which I loved and time to be Stephanie when I got home.

Whilst I was constantly questioning my gender at this time I was never in doubt about my sexuality – I have always been attracted to women. I soon started a relationship with a lady I had met through work and it was fun to begin with. After a while she asked if she could stay for the weekend. I thought I was okay with it but it meant leaving her in the house when I went to work (if it wasn't my weekend off) which I felt was a danger with all my female clothing etc. I told her I wasn't ready for that yet which caused a row. So I told her about Stephanie, well part of it anyway, and to my surprise she was pretty okay with it. It was a huge gamble, but I just couldn't risk getting into a full-blown relationship with her and then missing my "me time"; it would only end in tears and cause a lot of frustration.

About that time, while working one Sunday, I was in the forecourt shop at the dealership talking to the lady who ran it, when I saw an advertisement in one of the newspapers which were on sale. I bought the paper and took it home so I could read it and the accompanying article in private. The advertisement was for a business called "Transformation" and the picture showed a man's face which had been fully made up on one half to look like a lady. I was amazed by what had been achieved. The shop was in Manchester and was owned by a lady called Stephanie; she had once been a man and I was intrigued. There was an address to which you could write for more information and their latest catalogue of items for sale, specifically for male to female transformations including makeup, underwear and clothing. The thing that interested me most was the "he-to-she" transformation service and I immediately started to make plans for a trip to Manchester. I had a day off in the week, so it made this very possible. I couldn't wait but I was also very, very nervous. Another thing was that I had worn a moustache for many years and this obviously was going to be a problem; so the night before, off it came! It felt really weird after having it for so long but I wanted to look as authentic as possible. I found the shop in a very rundown area of the city, parked the car and went inside. There were two ladies behind the counter, one of whom asked if she could help. Rather sheepishly I enquired if I could be transformed. She asked if I had made an appointment. I had never even thought about it and said I hadn't. She replied, "We should still be able to fit you in as long as you don't want to be a bride". I had not even thought about how I wanted to be transformed or what the options were. I really wished now that I had phoned first but I was there, so anything would be better than nothing and I could always have a return visit if I really enjoyed the experience.

One of the ladies then took me into a room where we sat down to go through the options. I was so far out of my comfort zone it was bizarre, but I knew there and then I was going to have a good time. I decided on the evening dress - long and black with stockings and heels; this was going to be a very unusual day!

I was taken into a dressing room where I could choose the outfit. I had to rely on the lady as I didn't really have a clue what would look good. The one we chose was very glamorous and I was extremely excited to say the least. My transformer then chose a number of undergarments for me; I smiled to myself as she handed me some breast forms; I didn't say anything at the time but knew I wouldn't need them. She told me to go into a changing room and put on the underwear and to shout if I needed help. I put on the bra and pants but struggled with the waist clincher so asked for help. When she came in, she looked at me and then saw the breast forms on the seat; she looked at me again and asked if I had brought my own breast forms. I replied "In a way yes". I then explained that I had developed my own, like a girl, when I was in my early teens. She looked at me in a disbelieving way then touched my breast and replied, "they are bigger than mine!". She did her best to give me a feminine shape with the clincher and then put on the dress; what a feeling! It looked and felt amazing. The next step was makeup; I sat in front of the mirror and watched myself be transformed into a completely different person. I simply couldn't believe the miracle she worked on me; I had a lot to learn. Next step was a wig and shoes and I was done. I stood in front of the mirror, totally enthralled.

Once transformed I was taken up to an apartment above the shop, the idea being that you can spend time with like-minded people but as I was the only one being transformed at the time I just made myself a cup of coffee and sat outside on a little balcony. It was a beautiful day and I sat and read a magazine for a while. After about half an hour another lady came in and said she did the photography and asked where I wanted to sit to have my picture taken. I thought, as it was a nice day, out on the balcony would be good so she arranged the furniture and I sat in front of the camera. It was a Polaroid camera, so I didn't have long to wait. The picture was okay but the light was a little strong, so she gave me the photo and said let's try inside. The second one was much better. I thanked her for her patience, and she left. I went back to reading my magazine and shortly afterwards another transformed lady came into the apartment. We talked for a while and it was soon apparent that she was a regular customer; in fact she said she had lost count of how many times she had been transformed. She was younger than me and had a much better figure but was very pleasant and gave me some tips for next time!

Sadly, there never was a "next" time. I received a letter from Transformation saying the council had forced Stephanie to close the shop due to some bad press and complaints lodged by other shop keepers and homeowners in the area. In the letter she said she would find another area willing to allow her carry on with the business which in the meantime became mail order only. After a while I stopped getting flyers from her so I assumed the business was closed for good, however I have since heard that the shop did reopen in the same area and is still there to this day. What I do know is that my experience that day really opened my eyes to what was possible; but life gets in the way and for some reason I never revisited this wonderful experience. I thought about it often and kept the photo hidden in the front of a book. I remember many years later showing it to someone and telling them it was my cousin; her reply was "she is very attractive". I had never been called that before so the makeup must have been very effective! Given the direction my life has taken I would love to still have that photo but in the many moves I have undertaken it has sadly disappeared.

Chapter 10

An unexpected twist

It was now 1999 and we were rapidly approaching the new millennium. I had a query about some mail that I hadn't received and needed to contact Fiona. I hadn't been in touch for some time (since our divorce a year earlier in fact) and didn't know what sort of reception I would receive but I was very pleasantly surprised. We chatted for a short time and she in turn had a query about her car. After some discussion it was agreed that I would take it in for a service for her. I was going away for a few days with a friend, so made arrangements for when I got back. I had a fantastic, albeit short, holiday in Malaysia for the first Grand Prix there. My friend worked for a Proton dealer and as Petronas (who at the time were the majority shareholders of Proton cars) were sponsoring the event they gave a very special deal to Proton dealers. On my return, as agreed, I collected Fiona's car and took it in for a service. The following day was my day off so I did some jobs in Driffield and returned the car at the same time. Fiona and I spent a lovely couple of hours chatting and we arranged to meet again a few days later. She is very easy company and it was as though we had never been apart. Before too long we were back in a relationship which I hoped would be different this time. We saw in the new millennium together and as I have never been one for big parties we celebrated it, at home, with a glass of champagne, watching the fireworks.

As we both had a house there were some decisions to be made as to what we wanted to do regarding living arrangements. Neither house was really big enough; mine had the benefit of two bathrooms but neither Fiona or the children wanted to live in Middleton so it was decided that we would put both houses on the market and buy a bigger house in Driffield. We found a house which was about a year old, and it was a sad story really as the lady who was selling it had clearly spent a great deal of time and money making it exactly how she and her husband wanted it, but he had unfortunately passed away just a few months after moving in. It was far too big for just her so she decided to sell. Apart from the fact that it was a little bit pale and neutral for our tastes it was very nicely finished and she sold it with lots of extras; even the garden shed stayed put.

Sadly, before we were due to move my father passed away very suddenly. He was only 68 and it was a huge shock from which Mum never recovered. It left a big void with me also, as since they had returned from Australia my relationship with him was much stronger. We spent hours chatting about one thing or another and although he had very little interest in cars I think he humoured me when I was telling him about our latest offerings. He was a big believer in fate and had been heard to say that if he made it to 68 and three months he would be over the average age of his ancestors. He made it to 68 and five months.

Work was still going well and 2001 saw the inclusion of the MG franchise with every Rover dealership instead of about 15% of the dealerships. With this came the MG versions of all the current models, not just badge engineered like the models of the eighties but fully re-engineered with higher performance engines, better tuned suspension and full body kits and spoilers. This was right up my street as I loved the hot hatch performance cars of the eighties and nineties and had indeed spent most of my career driving something in that section of the market. We soon found ourselves even busier with two parallel ranges of cars to sell. We took on another salesman and were still stretched to meet the demand. Our local market share continued to increase but sadly it was short lived as there was no money going into developing new models for the future. But we made the most of it while it lasted.

While work was busy filling my days, it wasn't long before I was again missing my Stephanie time. I started to resent not having the opportunity to be Stephanie in my own home. I looked forward to any opportunity to be on my own and cherished any time as Stephanie that I was able to have. In my head I just thought eventually it would go away but it only got stronger as I grew older. I became better at hiding things at home and also braver in terms of wearing things while out. I restricted this to underwear but took every opportunity to wear a bra when I could. In winter I could get away with wearing one at work as I always had a coat of some description on. The showroom was quite cold and we were in and out dealing with people most of the day so it didn't look out of place; but I still wanted more.

Chapter 11

The attentions of a younger woman

There are things which I have done in my life of which I am certainly not proud and what happened next is one of them. In 2003 my home life had got back into a rut and I couldn't see an easy way out of it. I couldn't be the person I wanted to be at home and I resented it, so when I started receiving the attention of one of the female service advisors I think, at first, I was just flattered. After all I was an overweight and sometimes not very pleasant car salesman in my mid-forties who was married to his work. As much as I loved the job, it owned me. It wouldn't matter what time of the day it was, if the boss called me I would answer. He knew I would most likely know what it was that he needed an answer to, and it was much easier to call me than trawl through the pages and pages of bulletins which came through from the manufacturer every week. After all, that was what he paid me for, and pay me handsomely he did. We had a conversation a few years earlier, after I had been approached by another dealership to see if I was interested in joining them, and the outcome was that he didn't want to have the same conversation again so he would just make it so that no one else could afford me. I was happy with this arrangement and felt settled and appreciated.

The problem was that I allowed my relationship with Jayne to develop. I kidded myself it would be different being in a relationship with someone who is familiar with the motor trade. She would know how it works, how it's not a nine to five job, and if there was a customer wanting to be looked after the way our company did then it didn't matter what time it was, I was there to look after them. Also, before anything got out of hand, I would have to share my secret with this person, which I knew was a massive risk. The other thing was that she was married and I knew her husband who, seemed like a reasonable person. Then a bit of luck came my way as her husband got a job at Luton airport, to do with security, and they would be moving. Unfortunately, by that time I was smitten and knew it was going to end badly.

She left the dealership and moved to Luton with her husband and I know I should have left it at that, but I didn't, and we embarked on a long-distance relationship mainly over the phone. Then after about a week into the new job her husband was fired. There were several different stories but reading between the lines I think he had a fall out with another member of staff and thumped him so that was the end of that job! She on the other hand had landed a good job working for a truck dealership and was enjoying it. They had rented a house, so somehow the rent needed paying. He then found a job in the West Riding of Yorkshire and went to live with his mother for the time being. This gave me an opportunity to visit her, which I did at the first opportunity and decided to share my secret. It took a great deal of courage to tell her and, if I'm fully honest, I didn't tell the whole story but she said she was okay with the underwear as long as it was at home. I was relieved to say the least, as she was still in contact with several of the staff at the dealership. So if it hadn't been okay then I'm sure it would have been inevitable that lots of people would learn the truth about me.

It was only going to be a matter of time before the proverbial hit the fan and sure enough it did. Somehow her husband managed to read a text from me on her phone and the balloon went up, so to speak. I received a call from him threatening to rip my head off and she went into hiding until things had calmed down a little. I felt terrible for her, and rightly so, but it turned out later that he had been having an affair for some time so I didn't feel too bad for him. Now, what was I going to do about Fiona? I had to tell her and I know I hurt both her and the children who, by this stage were old enough to understand. A few days later I moved out of our home and went to live with my mother who had moved into Driffield after my dad passed away. This was only to be a very short-term arrangement as I planned to collect Jayne from Luton and set up home with her as soon as possible.

I bought a small semi-detached bungalow in Middleton which was tiny but did the job. The man who had lived there had passed away and his daughters, who lived in Essex, just wanted it sold as soon as possible so were happy to do a deal which suited me. When the time came for moving in they wanted to delay the date as they hadn't travelled up to remove his belongings from the house. In reality, they would have just taken his things to the rubbish tip as they had no desire to transport them back to Essex. I did a deal with them to send them a couple of items of sentimental value and a small cheque for the rest of the household items. As much as it was very strange to be living in the house with all his furniture and belongings, it suited us because we had virtually no furniture of our own. What I did find difficult to deal with was all his personal things which they didn't want. There were cards which had been sent to him when his wife died and ornaments which obviously meant something to them. The saddest thing was that the freezer was still full of food and there was still washing in the laundry basket!

Of all the places I have lived since owning my own home in 1980 this was the one I liked the least. It was very small and cramped, dark inside and had virtually no garden either front or rear. The garden at the rear of the house was at a steep angle up to a fence with a retaining wall, just one metre from the patio doors. This meant that every time it rained hard, a heap of soil was deposited near the doors. We planted some things which we hoped would bind the soil together with their roots. This helped a little but didn't solve the problem and I decided that it would only be a temporary home.

Jayne got a job as a service advisor with a Land Rover dealer, sadly not the one in the village but its sister dealership in Pickering which was a good forty minutes' drive. Unfortunately, she had two car accidents in the first few months which put her off the job and she decided to look for work in a different field. She took a position looking after "troubled" teenagers, but this was also a forty-minute drive but in the other direction. Either way I didn't think it would last long and sure enough it didn't. Thankfully she was able to get back into the motor trade at the dealership in the village. The pay was not particularly good, but the lack of travel made it a better option.

I have never been mad keen on holidays but one of the places I had always wanted to visit was Southern Ireland. We did some research and decided to give it a try. It was a lengthy drive to the west coast of Wales then a three-hour ferry crossing to Dublin. We both loved the place; the accommodation was excellent and apart from several days when it rained it was the perfect break. The dealership also qualified for the annual Excellence in Sales trip for dealer principals. This would not usually have meant anything to me as it would have been the boss and his wife who would have gone, but this particular year not many dealers had qualified and as we had easily made all of the qualifying levels, our area business manager asked me if I would be able to go if he could swing it with his bosses. I said he would need to ask my boss, but I was sure I would be able to go if the opportunity came up. As a dealership we were very well thought of because we held a much bigger market share than the national figure and looked after customers exceptionally well and so caused minimal stress to the manufacturer. Presumably they had budgeted for a certain number of people attending and might as well fill the places.

The trip was to Dubai, not a place I had ever thought to visit, but it was certainly a trip to remember. No expense was spared; we did all sorts of touristy things including a four-wheel drive trek through the desert followed by dinner in a mock Bedouin village. It was in the middle of nowhere, which amused me as it had flushing toilets and running water. Quite how that worked I never found out! All in all, it was a very enjoyable trip at the expense of MG Rover – one which we felt was well-deserved because of the massive effort we all put in. At one point, when the national market share was 5.5%, we had a share in excess of 12% for our area of responsibility which by any standards was a huge result.

On one of Jayne's and my nightly walks we noticed a sale board had gone up in front of a house which I admired every night when we walked past it. We talked about moving and decided to book a viewing before doing anything. We both liked the house, which was interesting to look at, set well-back off the road on a block of around 1000 square meters. I loved how private it was especially from the rear, it overlooked fields and no-one would be able to look in our garden as there were big trees at both sides. I immediately thought of the advantages this would have when I was there on my own and being Stephanie. We decided to take it a step further, but the owners wouldn't take an offer on it if the prospective buyers had a house to sell which of course we had. While this was frustrating, it meant that there would be no buying/selling chain involved as the lady who owned it was moving in with her partner. We set to work on selling our current house. The estate agent came around a couple of days later, a man I have known for many years who worked for the firm sharing my name. We talked about the valuation and agreed on a figure, two thousand five hundred pounds more than he thought but with a view to reducing it if we had no interest. We had no enquiries the first week but then three the following week with one booked for the week after. The last one of the week was booked for my day off, a single retired lady who was looking to move closer to her family. She was due to come at 4pm so I did my usual jobs for my day off which included changing the bed and doing the washing. At about 2pm I noticed a car pull up outside, a lady came to the door and explained that she had originally had three houses to see throughout the day, but one had been sold and the other one was not to her liking. She was heading home earlier than expected and wondered if it was okay to view the house then, rather than wait around until 4pm. I explained that I was in the middle of doing the washing but she was unperturbed and happy to look round anyway. I could see from the start that she was keen as it obviously fitted in to her budget and she liked the decor for some reason. She said she wanted to look in the loft space to see if it was possible to convert into a bedroom if needed. I offered to get my steps out of the garage but she said she would rather use her own and off she went to her car which was a tiny little thing and produced some steps from the boot. She brought them in and had a look in the loft. She thought that it would do the job and asked me what the lowest price I would take for it was. Bearing in mind that the estate agent wanted to put it on the market for £105,000 and I wanted to set the price at £110,000 and we had agreed to compromise at £107,500 I thought anything over £105,000 was a bonus. Before I could answer she offered me £105,000 which I told her I wouldn't accept as there were several people interested in it. She replied, "I'll go to £106,000 and will give you a cheque for the deposit now". On the grounds that I only paid £72,000 for it a year and a half earlier and the fact that a bird in the hand is worth two in the bush, I shook her hand and took her money!

Chapter 12

Station Road and MG Rover

We went back to the owner of the property we had viewed and negotiated a very acceptable deal and I felt happy that I could cover the increase in the mortgage with ease. That was, until about two weeks before our moving date when we were sitting watching a television show and my phone rang. It was certainly not unusual for it to ring out of hours, but I was surprised to see who was calling me. The call was from my area business manager from MG Rover; he sounded serious and with good cause. He called to tell me that it would be announced the following morning that MG Rover was to be placed in receivership. He went on to explain that all attempts to secure some funding from one of the leading Chinese motor manufacturers for a joint venture deal had fallen through and negotiations had failed so there was no other option. It was a huge blow for me, but he had just lost his job and the dealership had just lost its manufacturer so telling my boss was the next challenge.

I made the call and there was just a silence; he said he would see what he could find out and we would talk in the morning. He thanked me and bade me good night. I was a little concerned that it might affect the house purchase and my ability to obtain the mortgage but was assured the following day that I would be supported, so proceeded to settle on the given date. There was lots of confusion at work; after all we had many hundreds of customers and for many of them their pride and joy had just halved in value overnight. Many of them were on some sort of finance and most would now be in negative equity so there were going to be some very difficult conversations ahead. Warranty was an immediate problem because we wouldn't get paid for doing any warranty work so unfortunately we could no longer carry out warranty repairs, of which there were many!

There followed several months of negotiations and eventually a deal was brokered whereby the remaining unregistered vehicles could be sold with a two-year warranty backed by an insurance policy which manufacturers are obliged to have for this very occasion. This at least allowed us to sell the rest of the stock which was considerable. As was promised, I was supported and looked after. We expanded the used car side of the business and somehow my boss steered the ship through some very difficult seas.

Not long after we moved into the new house we were visited by my cousin and his wife who were over on holiday from Western Australia. I had spent a good deal of time with them back in 1986/87 while they were over in Yorkshire on a working holiday and had lived close to me. I had also spent some very enjoyable times with them on both of my trips to Australia while my parents were over there. On one particular occasion we had been out for dinner and returned to show them around our new home. We sat and chatted over a cup of coffee and somehow the subject of Christmas came up. As I have mentioned earlier I had never liked Christmas but now, being with Jayne, there were added complications. There was always going to be a problem as to who we were going to spend Christmas Day with. Since losing Dad, Mum obviously expected us to be with her. Jayne's parents were divorced and therefore we were expected to see both her mother and father separately, leaving no time for us to spend with each other. Out of the blue my cousin's wife said, "why don't you come over and spend Christmas with us instead?". It immediately appealed to me and Jayne was certainly open to the suggestion. We obviously didn't make a decision at the time, but thanked them for their kind offer and said we would give it some thought. I broached the subject at work to see what my chances of having four weeks off in December would be; to my surprise it was agreed to and in due course it was booked. The next thing was to look into flights; we did some investigation, found that they were not too expensive and so took the plunge.

December was never a busy month in car sales so I wouldn't be missing much there. Also we had taken on the Renault franchise to replace MG Rover and it would still be in its early stages at that time. I was quite a fan of the Renault product; it was always very innovative and certainly different. Renault were also heavily into diesel powered cars which I have always liked, and these were at the forefront of diesel technology and quite advanced compared with some of the MG Rover offerings, especially in their small cars.

As the year progressed we got more into the swing of the Renault franchise. While I couldn't ever see us selling the numbers of cars we had done with MG Rover there were lots of opportunities in markets in which we were previously not a contender so there was definitely the prospect of building it up to a very respectable number. Commercial vehicles were something which we had not been involved in and there was certainly the potential there. The Renault van range was highly regarded and well-priced, although it did take a great deal of product knowledge to get your head around all of the different options. Then there was the financing side of the franchise. The finance arm of Renault was huge, and the majority of their advertising was payment led (i.e. cars were advertised with a monthly payment rather than a cash price) which suited the way car buying was going. Also, Clio was a massive opportunity in a market in which Rover or MG didn't have a product. It was enormously popular with younger people which got them into the brand early and if you look after the younger customers you can keep them for life; so the earlier the better. This suited the dealership well as we looked after customers much better than the big dealers ever could, so the opportunity was there to be taken.

Then another curveball to get my head around; I received a call from the Citroen dealer I had worked for 10 years earlier to see if I was interested in having a chat with him. Citroen were putting him under pressure to employ a dedicated sales manager and of course I was the first person he called. He would have loved to have poached me back after all those years and I knew that was what he had in mind. By this stage it was November and only a few weeks before we were due to fly to Australia. We sat and talked at length about what he was looking for and he then asked me what it would take for me to join him again. We discussed several packages and methods of results-based remuneration and I was quite excited about the prospect of moving but said I wouldn't commit to doing anything until after my trip. He was happy with that and wished me a good holiday and we left it at that.

Chapter 13

An amazing trip and an unexpected bonus

By the time we were due to fly out I was more than ready for the break. The Renault franchise seemed to be more complicated and stressful, with less results, but I guess getting into a new way of doing things would always take time. A very good friend took us to the airport and looked after our car while we were away. The flight was long and boring but I was excited at the thought of visiting some of the places I had enjoyed on my previous two trips to Australia. I was also looking forward to some warm weather; it would be summer in Australia so it should be hot and sunny.

We were met at the airport by Heather, my cousin's wife; we were a little jet lagged but I was otherwise excited to be there again. My cousin Stephen arrived home from work shortly after we arrived and we talked the night away until we could hardly keep our eyes open. We slept in till about 11am the following day which seemed to dispense with the jet lag and spent the rest of the day planning our holiday. Christmas was going to be spent at my cousin's mum's home in Busselton, a place I had thoroughly enjoyed when I came over in 1991. Before that we were to do a road trip around the south west of the state, visiting more cousins and places of interest on the way. A truly wonderful time was had, and we stayed in some really weird accommodation such as a converted shipping container at Wave Rock, but they were all comfortable and enjoyable.

By the time we returned to Perth it was a case of pack your bags for the trip to Busselton. I was looking forward to seeing the place again and seeing Stephen's mum Pauline. She was a very hospitable lady who had been a part of the family for many years. It was indeed she who introduced Mum to Dad all those years ago. Christmas is probably not the ideal time to visit Busselton, as being a beachside town, its population doubles over the Christmas holidays. But it was still good to be back. All the family was expected at Pauline's house for Christmas; it was going to be crowded to say the least. Thankfully we were getting there early so had the pick of the bedrooms. Australian houses tend to have lots of space, so everyone was accommodated in one place or another; some of the younger ones actually slept on the veranda outside. I couldn't have fancied that; too many biting insects etc!

There was quite a lot of preparation to be done so everyone got involved. While he was in Busselton Stephen had arranged to take his car into the Holden dealership for a recall to be done and asked if I would like to accompany him. He was well aware of my love of anything on wheels, the faster the better; but I will look at anything! I went with him into the service department to drop off the keys, then he said he would see if the owner of the dealership (from whom he bought his cars) was in and available for a catch up. The man was available and we all sat down for a chat. He was very friendly and in the course of the conversation he asked me what I did for a living. I told him I had been in the trade for over twenty years and he was very interested in my responsibilities and my achievements. We chatted for some time then the guy from the service department brought Stephen's keys and we got up to leave. What the owner of the dealership said to me next will remain in my memory for the rest of my days. As we got up to leave he turned to me and said, "if you ever thought of moving over here there would be a job for you at my dealership". I was completely blown away. It was totally unexpected and I didn't really know what to say but after a few seconds I replied, "well I hadn't thought of moving but I'll bear it in mind". This posed a problem as firstly, I had told Jayne that it didn't matter how much she loved the place I wouldn't be moving here and secondly, I couldn't actually get the offer out of my mind. Talk about an ego boost; I had only known the man for about twenty minutes and he offers me a life changing opportunity.

After a while I asked Jayne what she thought of the idea, knowing full well that she would love to live in Busselton. She replied by saying that it had to be my decision as it was my job offer. I couldn't get it out of my head and decided I needed to talk to the owner again, but this time on my own. I got Stephen to call him and arrange a time. He was happy to see me again and was very friendly. We chatted for over an hour and he introduced me to a few of his team and we talked about what sort of package he could offer. It was going to be a lot less than I was used to initially, but he said the potential was much higher only he didn't want to promise the earth and then not deliver if things didn't work out as he planned. The position was to eventually run the Nissan side of the dealership as he was under pressure to have different sales managers for each franchise. Nissan was in an alliance with Renault so had lots of product similarities which I thought was promising. I have never been much of a fan of anything to do with General Motors so I wasn't too concerned about not having much to do with the Holden side if I did come over. At the end of our conversation he told me not to make a decision until I had returned home, then either to call him or email him if I was interested.

Christmas Day and the rest of the holiday were a bit of a blur really; I couldn't think of much else other than the job offer. We headed back to Perth the day after Boxing Day and started the long journey home the next day. Saying goodbye to Stephen and Heather at the airport was really tough. We had both so enjoyed our time in Busselton and it would have been easy to just accept the job offer there and then but he was right to tell me to go home and think about it. It's not an easy decision to leave all your family behind and start a new life in a different country. The flight home seemed very long indeed, and we had left beautiful weather back in Perth so the thought of returning to freezing temperatures and wet, miserable and dark days wasn't helping.

At last we touched down at Manchester after the pilot had informed us that the temperature was minus one degree. But instead of the aircraft taxiing to the terminal he took it to the perimeter fence and stopped. Nothing happened for a few minutes and then we were informed that there had been a death on the flight and we had to wait for the authorities to board the plane and remove the body. Eventually this was done and some steps were wheeled to the exit nearest to us. As we left the plane the ice-cold wind which greeted us was vicious, especially as we were not really dressed for it. We were transferred into buses and transported to the terminal. By the time we had arrived at the terminal my decision had been made. I'm not sure whether it was the cold or just a realisation that I had nothing to lose in giving it a go.

Chapter 14

Keeping the secret

My first day back at work was the day before New Year's Eve and it had been snowing. The main road was apparently very difficult to travel so I decided to go on the back roads where there would be next to no traffic to contend with. Unfortunately, snow brings out the worst in drivers and many of them should simply stay at home as they are both incompetent and scared to death of it. Most cars on British roads are now front wheel drive which has its advantages as the weight of the engine is over the driving wheels which generally makes progress easier. The downside is that once the front end gets out of control then all your eggs are in one basket so to speak, as the drive, the steering and the best brakes are all at the front. This makes it very difficult to recover once it's out of control. Thankfully I have had lots of experience and eventually got to work.

There was little chance of getting any walk-in customers on a day like that as, apart from the cars in the showroom, most of the stock was covered in snow and there was no point in clearing them as few people would be venturing out anyway but as it was my first day back there was lots to catch up on and lots of stories to tell. I was, however, determined not to mention the job offer as, at this stage it was not certain that I would be granted a visa allowing me to emigrate. That was the next challenge and a huge one it would turn out to be. I also hadn't yet spoken to Ray who, along with his wife Jan, owned the dealership in Busselton, about taking up his offer so didn't want to jump the gun in any way.

I decided to send Ray an email suggesting a phone conversation but he was happy at this stage to accept that I would see how big a job getting a visa would be before speaking to me again. He was, however, thrilled that I had made the decision to at least attempt to join his company.

At one of the many touristy places we had visited while we were away, Jayne had picked up a small brochure which was simply titled "Want to live in Australia?". It was a brochure advertising the services of an immigration agent so, as we didn't know where to start, we sent off an email enquiry to see what was involved. At first it seemed as though it was a no hope situation because I didn't fit into any of the lists of desired trades, but the immigration agent was more interested when we told her that I had a job offer as that opened the door to different types of visas. I sent her all the details of the dealership and who to contact and she said she would be in touch. After about ten days we received an email from her saying she had spoken to Ray, who was happy to sponsor me in order to get a 457 visa which would last for four years if approved. After two years we could then apply for permanent residency if we wanted to stay. She went on to explain her charges and what the whole thing was likely to cost. To my surprise Ray had already paid the first half for me, which I saw as a real commitment from him and for which I was very grateful. This was quite bizarre really, after only speaking with me for about 90 minutes, but he did say he always went with his first impressions and was rarely wrong. The following two months seemed like a constant battle to produce all the paperwork the immigration agent required.

We had some lengthy conversations at some really strange times of the day and night but she always seemed confident that we were heading in the right direction. The other issue was that we needed to have medicals for which we would need to get time off work as they were quite involved. We established where we needed to go and who to see and made an appointment. When the day came, I have to say I was more than a little nervous, but by this stage I really wanted to go to Australia, so it had to be done. On arrival at the hospital where the medicals were to take place we were both surprised as to how many people were doing the same. It was like a production line; X-rays, blood tests, urine samples, then wait to see the doctor. I went in first. The doctor was a man in his sixties, seated behind a huge desk covered in paperwork; he peered at me over his glasses and invited me to sit down. He started by saying, "So you want to emigrate to Australia?". I replied "Yes" and explained about the job offer. He made a comment about all the people with drive and ability leaving the UK as they saw no future in the place and said to me "If I were your age I'd do the same". He then said to me "We had better get the important thing dealt with first. Are you paying for just yourself or are you paying for your partner as well?". We had been told in the letter confirming the appointment that the cost of the appointment was one hundred pounds each and must be paid in cash, so I had gone prepared. I gave him the two hundred pounds. He counted it, folded it in half and pushed it into his back pocket. I was a little taken aback and asked if there would be a receipt. He scribbled something illegible on a piece of paper and handed it to me. On the physical examination he asked about my breasts and if I had ever seen anyone about them. I replied that I had seen two specialists when I was thirteen, but nothing had been done about it as I was told it was because I was overweight. He just nodded and said he would like a further blood test done before I left. He said it wouldn't affect his decision but thought he should follow it up anyway. He signed the paperwork and gave me a referral for the blood test which I had done while Jayne was seeing him. I never heard any more after that.

We couldn't really make plans until the visa was approved and I hadn't planned to tell anyone until that date but unfortunately one of the things the immigration agent wanted was a reference from both my current employer and a previous one. Given that I was talking to the previous one regarding going back to work for him it was going to be a strange conversation, as was the one with my current employer. As it happened both were very easy to have. My current employer seemed genuinely happy for me and agreed that it was an opportunity not to be missed. The owner of the Citroen dealership said that if it didn't work out there would always be a job for me with him, which was reassuring.

The three months after arriving back in the UK were a very unsettling time for me and I cherished every moment I could spend as Stephanie. I was not sure what the future would hold if we were to relocate to Busselton. There were several occasions when Jayne caught me out wearing women's underwear and she was not amused by it at all. After her initial reaction when I first told her, it had soon become clear that although she would tolerate it reluctantly at home, it was definitely not an option out in public even if I was fully covered up, which disappointed me a great deal. I spent every hour I could wearing whatever I could get away with, including makeup on occasions. It seemed like I was holding on to something which was likely to disappear if I was not careful and it concerned me a great deal. One thing I had never been able to do in the United Kingdom was to go in the ocean as Stephanie. It was always too cold anyway but even if it had been warm enough there would not have been the opportunity to do so. Having been to numerous deserted beaches in Australia I thought that it might be a possibility and it gave me something to hang on to in the meantime.

Having told both my current employer and a previous one we decided that we should probably start telling people about the job offer at least. It was going to get around sooner or later, so better that it came from us and people heard the full story. By this time we had the feeling that it was only a matter of time before the visa came through so we wrote down all the people we needed to tell and in what order. Then it happened; on 22nd of April 2006, we received an email from the immigration agent telling us that the visa had been granted. We were so excited that we danced around the house in joy. I was even late for work and didn't really care. Then came the task of organising freight, flights, what to do with the house and most importantly a farewell party!

We chose 9th July as our leaving date and worked back from then. I had quite a lot of holidays to use up, so I planned to leave work four weeks earlier and spend the last weeks sorting out all the loose ends and making plans for our arrival in Busselton. There was a lot to get through but we had assistance from a number of sources, especially the company who shipped our freight. They were super helpful in that they gave us a checklist of things to do both before and on arrival in Australia. Our freight left about four weeks before we did. It would need to go through customs so we knew we would be living with limited belongings for the first couple of months but it's surprising how you can manage with very little. The farewell party was organised for two weeks before our departure and our good friends from York did much of the work for that, including obtaining a marquee and erecting it the day before, as well as sorting out the catering arrangements which was much appreciated.

There was also the problem of how to tell my mother that we were leaving. I planned the day down to the last minute and went to visit her on my day off. We went out for lunch and did some shopping for her, then we went back to her house. I made her a cup of tea and told her that I had something to tell her. There was no easy way of telling it, so I just said "I've landed a new job and it's in Busselton". She was obviously surprised but said she was happy for me and obviously she would miss us both. She also said that she couldn't really say much as they had emigrated and left me when I was nineteen. I was pleased she saw it that way.

So I finished work, after over eleven enjoyable years, and felt I had left on good terms. The next few weeks flew by and before we knew it, it was time to leave. We said goodbye to everyone, the house, the cat (who was adopted by a friend) and set off for our new life on the other side of the planet.

Chapter 15

A new life Down Under

Heather collected us from Perth airport on Monday the 10th of July 2006. I was both excited and apprehensive but most of all I was convinced I had made the right decision in giving it a try at least. If I had just said to myself "I am in my comfort zone, why would I want to change anything" then I would always have thought "What if? What if it had been a great success? What if I had really loved the place?". I felt it was an opportunity not to be missed and I was certainly going to give it my all.

The first few days were spent getting our bearings and buying some essentials in Perth before traveling down to Busselton on the Friday. We organised a one-way hire van and travelled down in the afternoon. It took longer than we expected, so it was dark by the time we arrived at the house we were staying at temporarily. The house was owned by cousin Stephen and his wife Heather, from when they lived in Busselton a few years earlier. It had been rented out so was not in the best condition. It was clean enough, but the previous tenants had obviously had pets and it was full of fleas which wasn't a good start. But it was only temporary as we planned to buy a house the following week.

I didn't start work until the following week so we had some time to get to know the place, organise our Australian driving licences and sort out things like phones, internet, electricity and gas suppliers and find Jayne a job if possible. On the Saturday I picked up a car from my new place of work. I didn't know what to expect but was shown down to the used car site where I was to collect it. I had done some homework on what I was going to be selling and had dealt mostly with the Nissan side of things so this was a completely new thing. I was given a Holden Statesman. It was huge; about twice the size of the car I had been driving back in Yorkshire and had an engine almost three times as big. Jayne and I christened it "the General Belgrano" after the Argentine battleship which was sunk in disputed territory off the Falkland isles in 1982. The car was about as manoeuvrable as a battleship and handled with the same amount of finesse; but it did the job. It had obviously just been traded in as it was filthy; but in true Robin Ullyott form I gave it a wash and cleaned up the inside, so it was at least presentable.

We managed to get rid of the fleas in the house. I had a crash course in how to work a wood burner, bought a load of wood and soon had the place looking and feeling okay. It was mid-winter and it rained almost every day of that first week but we did have a little sunshine for the day we had chosen for house hunting. House buying is a completely different process in Australia compared to how it is back in Yorkshire. In Australia you find an agent you like and he takes you to as many houses as you would like to look at, then does a deal with which ever agent has listed it. As is usually the case, the budget we had set was not going to do the job so it was modified upwards a little and we started the search.

One complication was that, as we were not permanent residents, anything we wanted to buy had to be approved by the Foreign Investment Review Board (FIRB) which was going to slow the purchase process down a bit. We found several houses which we thought would meet our needs and settled on one in West Busselton. It was a four-bedroom, two-bathroom place, well established and in nice condition. We discussed an offer and put it to the owners. Sadly, there was someone else interested and as we needed to get a mortgage approved plus sort the FIRB out they opted for the other clients. Back to square one but we were not too despondent as there were lots of houses for sale. I was, however, concerned that this would happen again though. I need not have worried. The next day we were shown a house which we both liked; it was in a nice area, a little more expensive than we had hoped but it was basically brand new. It had only been lived in for about three months and was always going to be sold quickly, hopefully with a good profit to the owner. The agent we were using had done some homework prior to showing us through it and told us that if we offered the asking price the owner would be happy to wait until the approval had come through from the FIRB. We loved the house, and the area, so went for it. I was surprised, however, that the finance approval wasn't a foregone conclusion as it had always been for me in the UK. Here it was a much more rigorous set of rules and even though I was putting down almost two thirds of the price as a deposit, the first bank the broker applied to turned us down on the grounds that we had no credit history in Australia. I thought by 2006 they would have been able to go online and get a credit report from the UK but apparently it was not the case. The fact that they were never ever going to be financially exposed, due to the huge deposit I was putting in, didn't seem to make a difference. This was foolish really, as we had already set up bank accounts with them while still in the UK so we simply moved all accounts to another bank. I have remained with this other bank ever since, bought three properties through them and have had a great relationship with them.

We had bought a house! Everything went through and we were given a settlement date of August 30th. Not bad really as we had only been in Busselton for just over six weeks. Our freight had arrived in Fremantle and we had that delivered the following week. It was like Christmas Day. We sat in the main living area and unpacked everything that very night and I was quite touched by the fact that my new employer's sales manager took time out to come and see if we needed any lifting done which I thought was a lovely gesture.

We gradually got the house in order; there were lots of things to buy and we didn't have a massive amount of spare cash so some things had to wait. There was no form of heating in the house at all, so we bought a gas fire; thankfully the weather soon got warmer. The next problem was that the house had no cooling either. Our first lot of visitors from the UK were booked for the end of March when it would still be warm so it was going to need sorting out before then. But first, Christmas had to be dealt with.

My Christmas came a few weeks before the day. We had already had a change of Used Car manager only two months after I started, but the person who had taken his place had a personality clash with the service manager and gave his notice. This prompted Ray to have a re-shuffle and I was to be made Sales Manager, not just of Nissan as was the original plan but of Holden as well. With this came a huge increase of salary along with the responsibility I was used to. It made me feel very valued and would make me much more relaxed financially. One of the first jobs was to get a car sorted for Jayne. We both liked the Nissan Xtrail and would have probably bought a used one but with the improved salary I decided to go for a new one. Perfect timing as they were on a good deal at the time and just before we took delivery there was a further offer of $1000 of free fuel which made a good deal into an excellent one.

Jayne and I had now been together for just over three years and I felt it was time to make some commitment. I pushed Stephanie to the back of my mind for the time being and started planning when and where to propose. We had been asked to join some friends at a restaurant for lunch on Christmas Day so I decided to enlist their help in getting the ring organised and planning the proposal. I offered to drive to the restaurant so we agreed to pick them up, but we would have a drink and some nibbles with them before we left. A plan was hatched that I would somehow disappear for a few minutes and come back in my dinner suit, drop to one knee and do the deed. Everything went completely to plan and even the ring fitted perfectly. It was going to be a very memorable Christmas! I had already been in touch with Jayne's parents to ask their permission; it was of course granted. So, when it came to making the Christmas Day telephone calls they already knew what had happened. This was the one and only time in our relationship that Jayne was ever speechless.

Chapter 16

Settling into life in Australia and first guests

With Christmas over, it was time to really get stuck into my new role as Sales Manager. The paperwork involved in selling a car in Australia is very different from the UK where we didn't have "Contracts" or "Offer to Purchase" forms; we just did a deal on the shake of a hand. Here we have very elaborate forms by the dozen to fill in every time a car is sold. It took some time to get the hang of but eventually I got it. I very much favoured the Nissan product over the Holden equivalent as the vehicles just seemed better put together and more user friendly; but the Holden Commodore was still very popular and we sold large numbers every month. The latest one was released just after we arrived in Australia and it was certainly an impressive vehicle, if you like that sort of thing. But as a European person it just didn't do anything for me. I have always been into small-engined, highly-tuned front wheel drive cars; I had driven them for 25 years so to be put in a very averagely built rear-wheel drive car with a lazy V6 or V8 engine was quite a change.

December 2006 had been an outstanding month and we were well rewarded for our efforts. January, on the other hand, was a very tough month and I felt it in my pay packet. I guess it's no different from selling cars anywhere else; there will be good months and bad; I just had to learn how best to deal with them. I also got involved with used cars a little; again, it was a totally different process from the UK but the principles are the same, so I quickly became accustomed to the way things worked. The used car site was separate to the new car site which had its advantages; but it meant having to have more staff to cover the two locations. The downside, however, was that customers would often come onto the new car forecourt looking for used cars only to be told they had to get back in their car and drive down the street to somewhere else, which had limited parking and was not the most professional look-ing place. The offices were small and there was generally only one person there; so often the office was unattended if the salesman was busy with a customer. The other downside was that the salesperson could not do accompanied test drives as it meant locking the place up or calling the new car showroom for backup, which might not be available when needed. Thank-fully this would all change in the coming years when both sites were amalgamated.

Having now settled in, both at work and in our new home, my thoughts drifted back to Stephanie again. I longed to go to the beach and wear a feminine swimming costume, but just couldn't seem to get the time on my own or find a place where I would be able to be myself. I took every opportunity to be Stephanie at home but as I worked long hours there was little time when I was home on my own.

Jayne and I started planning the wedding. We chose the venue for a number of reasons, but mainly because the people were very genuine. They had only just started doing weddings and ours was the first one to be booked. The place was a winery called Knotting Hill Estate set in a beautiful area between Busselton and Margaret River. It was a very modern looking place with a deck overlooking a lake and a footbridge from the car park to the cellar door. It was everything we were looking for and I think, because they were new to the business, they were very flexible in terms of timing and numbers. They were also very competitive price-wise which suited me as I just couldn't see what you were paying for at some of the places we had viewed. One place which I didn't think was as picturesque as the one we chose was asking six times as much for a very similar package. The wedding was planned for March 1st, 2008 so we had plenty of time to get everything organised. We chose the photographer, a videographer, organised the catering and probably my favourite job was the tasting evening for the cake. The lady was amazing - I've never ever seen as many different types of cake let alone been asked to sample them all. We had planned to get a takeaway on the way home but neither of us could face anything else to eat!

2007 was a year of consolidation for us. Jayne had landed a job at the Ford dealership next door. She had originally not wanted to go back into the motor trade but it seemed like a good plan to start with as it was what she was familiar with. The pay wasn't particularly good but the job was okay. Then Ray came to me one day and asked if she would be interested in jumping the fence and coming to work for him. There had been some changes to staff in the service department and there was now a vacancy as a service adviser. Jayne and I talked about it and agreed that she would come in and talk to Ray about what was on offer. Ray didn't see it like that and went straight into the package she would be on and when he would like her to start; so she joined the family. It was good having her work at the same place and the money was better but the downside was there was even less time for me to be me; a situation I resented. I shouldn't have worried; one thing Jayne was well known for was getting bored with places of work and within six months she was talking to the service manager next door about a different package and a better job with them. Shortly afterwards she returned to Ford and I would at least have some time to myself again as she didn't always get time for lunch, so I was able to go home on my own. It was lovely during the summer months as I could quickly change out of my work clothes put on a bra and a pair of shorts and sit in the sun for half an hour.

We also had our first visitors from the UK in 2007; two lots in fact. The first were our very good friends from York. Since the day they dropped us at the airport we had spoken every week, usually on a Sunday depending on what each of us were up to, but always for a good hour. He had negotiated a very good deal with his telephone company and was usually the one who did the phoning. We had a lovely three weeks with them, did a tour up to Shark Bay and saw lots of our local area which we hadn't seen yet. The second set of visitors were Jayne's mum and her partner; what a difference between them and our friends! There were arguments, things broken and Jayne was in tears a lot of the time. "Never again" was our cry! And they never did come out again together; her mum did come out on her own for a couple of weeks, which was not too bad.

Chapter 17

The wedding and decision time

The build-up to the wedding was fast and furious. There seemed to be so much to organise, which is quite difficult when you work 50 plus hours a week and things are not like the UK where most shops open seven days a week. One of the few things we found difficult to get used to was that the supermarkets were not open long hours. The one we shopped at most in the UK was open 24 hours a day, every day, except Sunday when they had to abide by the Sunday trading rules. Thankfully we had time on our side and got the main things sorted well before the day. I decided that I would have a best man from England and a best man from Australia. Our friends from York had already said they would like to come back over for the wedding so that was an easy choice for my English best man and for the Australian I chose the man who had helped me mastermind my proposal back in 2006. He and his wife had become very good friends and done a lot to help us settle into our new life. They were a similar age to us and we went to their wedding only six weeks after we arrived in the country back in September 2006, so it was a natural choice. Jayne then followed suit and asked the spouses of the two people I had asked to be matrons of honour; it kept things very simple.

As the day approached our friends from York arrived and immediately took over the rest of the organisation which was a huge help as, from that point on, all I would have to do was to turn up on the day. The best men and I spent the night before the wedding at the Australian best man's house; we had pizzas and a fair bit to drink before turning in. The next day was going to be a big day. As the wedding wasn't until 6pm there was plenty of time to do the last-minute jobs and to take a car to the place we were spending the two nights following our wedding. It was a stunning place called Moondance Lodge just a few minutes' drive from the wedding venue with its own little restaurant and plenty of room to relax either inside or outside.

The best men and I arrived at the venue in plenty of time. The owners were busy rearranging the furniture after their day's entertaining of people at the cellar door. They were all smartly dressed for the evening's function and the place looked perfect. As the time approached, my best men and I were standing on the deck where the ceremony was due to take place, chatting with the celebrant when I saw the limousine arrive. It was difficult to see much as the view was obstructed by trees, but I caught a glimpse of someone getting out of the car; the surprise was that whoever it was had a red dress on. I hadn't seen Jayne's dress but had just presumed that it was a sort of ivory colour as she had shown me a small piece of material which she kept in her handbag. It had obviously been there to put me off the scent as I could now see her in a beautiful red wedding dress. Red has always been my favourite colour, but I was very surprised to see her in red. That was the only surprise of the day thankfully as the occasion went perfectly from start to finish; the reception was excellent and the food perfect. Even the speeches went well; not too long but entertaining. My English best man had been to see my mother, both Jayne's parents and my brother and had prepared a video which was a lovely surprise. He had a few dramas getting the thing to play but all was well in the end and we had a wonderful day.

After our two nights at Moondance Lodge we headed for the airport for the main part of our honeymoon which was on Hamilton island off the Queensland coast. I still can't believe that you can fly for over five hours and still be in the same country, but we eventually arrived in Brisbane for our connecting flight to the island. The climate was completely different from ours in the West; it was hot and humid and somehow the colours didn't seem as bright as they are at home. The resort was wonderful and we had our own little A-frame cabin, very private and nicely presented. As there are no combustion engine vehicles on the island except for a couple of courtesy buses, the only way to get around the island was on an electric golf cart which you could hire for a small amount each day as required. Unfortunately going in the ocean came with the risk of being stung by a jellyfish which can be fatal. It didn't bother me at all as there was no way I was going to take my shirt off and show off my breasts and Jayne wouldn't have let me wear a bikini, so it only really affected her. I was happy exploring the island on my golf buggy and we found some really lovely areas. Jayne wanted to have a massage and asked if I would join her; I was not comfortable, but did eventually end up having a neck, shoulder and hand massage to keep her company. Too soon it all came to an end and we were heading back to Western Australia. By the time we got back, our friends had returned to England and we were on our own again.

Before we knew it we had been in Australia for two years and the time had come to make the decision whether we wanted to stay and apply for Permanent Residency (PR) or go back to England. For me there was absolutely no contest; I loved it here and Jayne was much the same although, having more family back home was a big pull for her, and her sister had just had a baby which was another factor. We decided to see what was involved in getting PR and thought the obvious route would be to go back to the Immigration Agent who originally got us here. She had told us during the process of getting the first visa that once here, as long as we basically behaved ourselves, Permanent Residency was almost a formality; a statement which I took literally. I expected there would just be a few forms to fill in and all would be good. How far from reality that was! It was simply a case of starting from scratch again. There were lots of forms, medicals, interviews and a good deal of expense. Thankfully Jayne was good with paperwork and threw herself into getting the process started.

We were told the first thing to get sorted was our medicals. We had both sailed through them in England so didn't expect any problems. The first job was to identify which doctors in Busselton were authorised to perform immigration medicals. We found there was only one, and made an appointment to see him. Before the appointment though we were told to have chest X-rays done as well as a suite of blood tests. This we duly did. Thankfully we were allowed into the appointment together. After going through some paperwork the doctor began talking about the X-rays; he said Jayne's was fine but mine had shown up a problem. I was left speechless as he put the film up to the light box and pointed out a mass of something in my throat. He then said it wouldn't have been spotted but the person who did the X-ray did it too high and it had then shown the problem. He started talking about possible reasons for the lump and the possible treatments needed. He mentioned quite casually that it was possibly cancerous and that I would probably need surgery. The whole thing was too much for me to take in and I started to feel I was drifting away; the next thing I remember was waking up on the floor, not knowing where I was, and then being violently sick; it was projectile and it went everywhere. I had a massive headache and it was just as though someone had turned the power off; I couldn't walk, couldn't even lift my arms. I was a mess.

I was taken to the nursing station and laid on a bed. Jayne was horrified at what had happened and the fact that the doctor didn't seem at all concerned, just wanted me out of his office so it could be cleaned before the next patient. While I had been out, the doctor had given a referral to Jayne for me to see a surgeon in Bunbury to examine what the problem was and how serious it was. I was taken home and put to bed, still not really knowing what had happened or what the future had in store.

Chapter 18

Test after test and a very bad day

I made an appointment to see the surgeon in Bunbury the following week. Jayne didn't want me to go on my own so she took some time off work as well. My appointment was for 9am so it was an early start and we arrived at the surgeon's office in plenty of time. We sat in the car and talked for a while about the possible outcome of that day's appointment. At about 8:55 we walked into the reception and I introduced myself to the receptionist; she told us to take a seat and the surgeon would see me in just a few minutes. We waited for about twenty minutes before the surgeon came out and invited us into his office where he proceeded to sit, with his back to us, looking at the X-ray film which we had given him. He studied it for a few moments then said he would need to operate to remove the lump and there may very well be complications but nothing insurmountable. The whole time he spoke with his back to us. We were both very unimpressed by his manner; I don't think he once looked at us while he was talking. He then turned the light box off and turned to us and said he was going on holiday for a couple of weeks but his receptionist would be in touch.

I walked out of his office petrified; I didn't want him touching me never mind cutting lumps out. The moment we stepped outside Jayne looked at me and said, "we need to get a second opinion and he's not touching you". I was so relieved that we were of the same opinion. We hugged each other and went to get a coffee. That night Jayne spent the whole evening researching what our options were. She asked me if I wanted to forget it and go back to England and get it sorted there. We loved Australia; we were both getting on well in our jobs so there had to be an alternative to the doctor in Bunbury. By about 11pm I was ready for bed but Jayne wanted to talk about what she had found out. She had sent an email explaining our predicament to a lady in Perth who was a specialist thyroid surgeon. She read out some reviews of her and she certainly sounded to be much more patient-friendly than the doctor in Bunbury. At least I went to bed more hopeful. The following day the receptionist for the lady in Perth called Jayne to arrange an appointment for the following week so I didn't have too much time to worry about it.

I chose a nice car from the forecourt and we travelled up to Perth the night before the appointment. She wanted to see me at 8am, then if we were all agreeable she wanted to do some tests. What a difference to the surgeon in Bunbury; she was lovely, very understanding and couldn't believe that the other guy was just going to operate without first checking what the problem was. She explained that the tests she wanted to do would not be pleasant and that they involved some scans, then some biopsies with ultrasound-guided fine needles. I didn't really have much option but to agree to them. She also told me that there would be costs of around $1,100 to cover the tests. The day didn't get any better! The scans involved me being injected with a substance into my blood then a CT scan would be done. The surgeon said there was a small chance that this would be all that was necessary but if that were the case then surgery would be needed. I can honestly say that I have never been so terrified in my life; I cried like a baby. I've never been good with needles and I didn't know which was going to be worse, needing surgery or having the biopsies done. I would probably still need surgery anyway, the way my luck was going! I really did consider bailing out after the CT scan and deciding to move back to England but the problem would still need addressing when I got back so I might as well get it sorted here. But even if it could be sorted here I had no guarantee that we would be given Permanent Residency.

As expected, the CT scan didn't show enough and the surgeon came to see me and asked if I was still okay to have the other test; she held my hand and said it would only take 30 minutes to do then it would be over. Once again I didn't really feel I had much option but to agree. I was taken to a room and told to take my shirt off. The room was full of people; there were two nurses, the surgeon and a guy who was going to do the test. I asked if Jayne could stay and they agreed to let her but there were so many people she couldn't really get near me. The next 30 minutes were worse than any I have encountered in my life. I had a needle stuck into my throat 36 times. I can't tell you how much it hurt! One of the nurses held my hand and dried the tears which were rolling down my face. Finally it was done and the surgeon came to me and apologised for how many times they had to do it but she needed to make sure they had got into every part of the lump. She held my hand and said she would be in touch as soon as she received the results, which would probably be early the next week.

Then came a surprise and the best news ever. The surgeon called me on the Saturday morning to tell me that the lump was not cancerous and had probably been there for years, so it wasn't anything to worry about and she would write to the immigration doctor in Busselton and tell him the good news. I sat down and cried, again!

The following week I received a call from the surgery where the immigration doctor practised, asking us to go in again. He congratulated us for sorting things out and gave us the paperwork required. The next job was to lodge the case with the immigration service. For several weeks we heard nothing then I received a letter telling me that there were a number of points preventing me obtaining Permanent Residency, but mainly that the state no longer recognised my job as being one which justified giving me PR. We were both devastated, and so were Ray and Jan. I should point out that Ray is one who doesn't give up easily and immediately set to work to try and find a way round the issue. We went to several meetings with various officials and were quickly getting to the end of the possible routes to get it sorted and time was running out. Then I had a huge bit of luck. Ray had a meeting with the chairman of the Small Business Development Commission who had a keen interest in the motor trade and was doing some visits in our area. I saw him arrive from my office. Ray went out to greet him and proceeded to show him around the dealership. They eventually came back in and headed for Ray's office. Not long afterwards, Ray came into my office and asked if I could spare a few minutes. He asked me to explain to our visitor the ins and outs of my application for PR. Ray said that they had just been talking about how difficult it is to get fully trained staff and he had mentioned my case. The chairman was appalled by the fact that my case was struggling and said he would look into it as soon as he was back in the office on Monday.

After he had left Ray came into my office and said to me "I bet you have your PR by next weekend". I said it would be wonderful, but I wasn't as confident as he was. Ray explained that the Small Business Development Commission was in the government's sights and needed to be seen to be assisting small businesses so this was a perfect opportunity for him. The following Wednesday I received a call from the immigration department; a very curt lady who I knew had been my case manager simply said to me "It looks like you are staying. You seem to have friends in high places. Your visa will be approved by the end of the week" and then she bid me good day. I couldn't believe it and went straight into Ray's office; I think he had already spoken to the chairman but didn't want to jump the gun. He gave me a big hug and said (jokingly of course) "Congratulations. Now get back to work". It was almost lunchtime, so I went over to Ford and told Jayne the good news. We were elated to say the least and started planning a big celebration straight away.

Chapter 19

Celebrations and first visit back to England

Our "staying" party was to be held on our recently pur-chased three-acre block of land just outside Nannup, a small country town located 55kms east of Busselton. We bought the block for a number of reasons. Firstly, I love Nannup; it has a wonderful feel about it; it is very countrified and friendly and we thought it would be a lovely place to build a house to use as a weekend getaway or for short term rental. Secondly, we saw it as further commitment to Australia and building a life here. We organised a marquee, portable toilets and invited lots of people. It was a lovely evening and everyone had a great time. I made a short speech thanking everyone for coming and for helping us to settle into our new home and life. I presented Ray and Jan with a small gift for the huge part they had played in getting us here and keeping us here.

Shortly after the party Jayne received the news from Eng-land that her Granddad had passed away. She was very close to him and it hit her badly. We had talked about what we would do when someone close died and decided that we would only go back for parents or siblings' funerals but after giving it some thought Jayne decided she would go. It was late in 2009 and she booked her flights for about a week later. I didn't go as I had only known him for a couple of years before we came over here and didn't know him very well and Jayne said she was happy to go alone. This was the first time I had been on my own for any length of time here and I started thinking of things I could do and how I could maximise the time I had as Stephanie.

After taking Jayne to the airport I came home, closed the door and went to change into what female clothing I had. It wasn't much as I had to hide it in the bottom of my wardrobe, but I cherished the time I had and made the most of it. I made every excuse to leave work on time so I could spend the maximum time being Stephanie. As it was almost summer the weather was lovely and I could go outside in the sun. I didn't yet have the confidence to venture out in public but did wear my underwear at every opportunity without fear of being questioned about it and having to hide it all the time. Thankfully, our garden was very private. The couple who lived next door were lovely. They were a retired English couple who sadly Jayne had fallen out with over our cat Tilly. Tilly had a habit of catching birds and leaving their remains in their garden, which didn't go down very well. They were both small in stature so couldn't see over the 1.8 metre high fence between us and at the other side there was a vacant block so there were no prying eyes from that side either. I spent hours just pottering around in the garden or sitting with a beer in the sun. It was heaven and I realised what I was missing, but couldn't see myself doing anything about it at least in the short term. The day before Jayne was due to fly home was a Sunday so I had all day to myself to be me. I didn't venture out the front of the house all day and was determined to be Stephanie all day. The weather was warm and sunny so I spent most of the day in just a bra and a pair of Jayne's shorts which fitted me well. When it came to the evening I went to the bedroom to change for my evening walk and happened to look at myself in the mirror. I was horrified; I had really caught the sun and the print of my bra left very white patches on my otherwise red body. This was going to be a problem as it wasn't going to have faded much by the following evening when she arrived home and we were getting ready for bed. I was dreading it, but at the same time I said to myself, "this is who you want to be, perhaps it will bring on a conversation which might change things". I doubted it, but it did certainly bring on a conversation. The following day the redness had calmed down a bit but it still left very vivid lines and shapes and there was going to be no hiding it.

I left work a little early and headed straight up to Perth and to the airport. The flight was a little late but I bought a coffee and waited for Jayne to come through customs while rehearsing what I was going to say to her when she saw my body later that evening. When she came through she was pretty tired but pleased to be home. We spent most of the drive back to Busselton talking about her mum and her mum's partner and how they were already spending their inheritance from Grandad. By the time we arrived home it was late so we had a drink and headed to bed. Jayne went for a shower and I got ready and got into bed. I knew I was going to have to come clean about the sunburn so as soon as she came out of the shower I told her I had done a silly thing yesterday and worked in the garden most of the day with my shirt off and got sunburnt, and it got worse; I had been wearing a bra at the time. She pulled the covers off me and was not impressed at all. She made a big thing about someone seeing me; not that it would have been an issue for me, but how it would be embarrassing for her if someone told her about it.

I made the point about the neighbours being small and not seeing over the fence but she was seriously unimpressed with me. I turned over and went to sleep. If I'm honest, it was probably the beginning of the end of our relationship; but I had no idea how that was going to work so did my best to smooth things over for the time being.

It was now 2010 and we decided the time was right to plan our first trip back to England together. We had been away for almost four years and whilst we had had a few visitors they had mainly been our friends from York twice and visits from Jayne's parents. None of my family had made the trip which I thought was disappointing but it was early days I guess. The flight was booked for May of that year. I was very excited and looking forward to catching up with lots of friends and relatives. As much as I absolutely love living in Australia I do miss my friends. Modern communication methods certainly help in keeping in touch but it's not the same as seeing people. Also, having been away for almost four years I needed to buy some new clothes and I have to say that clothing in Australia is not of the same standard as in England; firstly, there are no Marks and Spencer stores!

When the time came we had made lots of plans to see people. My mother, by this stage, was in a nursing home and didn't get out much. I did however make the most of the opportunity and visited her five or six times during our holiday. Jayne's mum had paid for us to join them for part of their annual trip to Kefalonia, a beautiful Greek island which they had been visiting for many years. It was a nice gesture and we appreciated the thought, as we would probably never have thought to visit the place otherwise. Although Greece was struggling financially and had been bailed out by the European Union numerous times, Kefalonia seemed to run its own economy and was doing very nicely. I loved the fact that there was none of the "nanny state rules" which are so commonplace now. For instance there were no barriers at the harbour edge and no warning signs. The main strip of restaurants were only a few metres from the edge of the drop into the harbour, situated under makeshift structures at the opposite side of the road to where the food was prepared. I could imagine intoxicated patrons ending up in the harbour after a big night of drinking, so I mentioned this to one of the restaurant owners who Jayne's mum and her partner had befriended. His answer was very refreshing; he just said, if you fall into the harbour it's your own fault! He also gave us a few tips about driving on the island as we had a hire car. He told us that traffic lights on the island were more of a suggestion than an absolute rule and to proceed with caution even if the light was green and to always put a hundred euro note in your drivers' licence in case you are stopped by the police; it tended to lessen the amount of paperwork, which the local constabulary liked.

The rest of the trip to the UK was spent rushing from one lot of friends to another, to catch up with as many as possible. We had a few days away with Jayne's father who I particularly liked. We also organised a get together at a pub so people who we weren't going to get to see could come to us. It was a great success; about 30 people came and we spent a lovely four hours chatting to them all. We also hit the shops, so much so that we ended up having to buy an extra suitcase to fit in all the new clothes.

My brother Greg and his wife Lynne held a lovely get-together during the last few days of our visit, so that we could catch up with Lynne's family and some of mine who we hadn't been able to see. It was another lovely event but sadly, although he was invited, Nigel wasn't able to come. I had hoped to reconcile and reconnect with him but it was not meant to be.

Chapter 20

Back to work, head down and bad news

It took me quite some time to get back into the rhythm of work when we returned home. June is one of the busiest months of the year (as it is the end of the Australian Financial year on 30th June). The campaigns were complicated and I needed to hit the ground running. Nissan was hungry for a bigger market share and had an eye on a top five position so the proposed campaign was very effective. Holden, on the other hand, was struggling; lots of old models in the range and too much effort aimed at pushing a big sedan car when the market was moving towards smaller cars and SUVs. The Holden Colorado had recently been refreshed but it looked old compared with some of the rivals, including the Nissan Navara which had just won the Ute of the year award for the third year running. It was a good thing that we weren't just relying on the one brand. I soon got up to speed and the month turned out well.

The rest of the year went fairly smoothly and I took every opportunity to be Stephanie, although the moments were few and far between. Jayne was running a mobile coffee business which promised lots, but in reality I found myself working seven days a week doing my full-time job and helping her with events at the weekend. It was good fun though and we met lots of lovely people, especially at the fortnightly Sunday morning markets, many of whom are still good friends. One of the down sides of the coffee business was that we were not able to spend much time at the block and so decided to look for something else. I wanted it to be in Nannup, but was looking for something which already had a house of some kind on it where we could go and stay, even if it was a little primitive. After looking around and finding nothing I felt was suitable we visited the real estate people who sold us the block and told him what we had in mind. He took us out and showed us a few things but nothing really appealed until he showed us a very dilapidated house on a one-acre block just one street back from the Main Street. It was part of a deceased estate and was for sale for just under $400,000. This was much more than I wanted to pay but he said that the owners wanted it sold and would consider any offer. He told us that an offer of $250,000 had been turned down but they had received no other offers so something in that region might well be considered. We decided to put in an offer for $260,000 firm; if we got it then we would be happy but weren't willing to pay more. We also decided to put the other block on the market straight away. After a few days I received a call saying that the offer had been put to the Executors of the Estate and we would have an answer in the next few days, which sounded hopeful. I had a plan to develop the block as it had been zoned for subdividing into a maximum of four smaller properties, which I saw as a way of making a considerable amount of money. But I would need to sell the house in Busselton in order to fund the development. We managed to sell the first block quite quickly which helped financially and I was hopeful that the offer on the new block would be accepted. After a couple of weeks we had heard nothing so I followed up with the agent; he apologised and said our offer had been accepted but he hadn't got around to calling us. I was very happy indeed; Jayne, on the other hand, was not keen on selling our house in Busselton and we had many arguments about it. Eventually she agreed, but only if we could use an agent who she knew from her days at Ford. I was happy with this for the time being and the house was put on the market.

By this stage it was Christmas and we enjoyed a well-deserved, albeit short, break. The coffee business was slow as most of the businesses which Jayne visited in the industrial area had also closed down for the break. It gave me some time to spend at the new block and work out some plans. It soon became clear that Jayne had very little interest in the place so its upkeep and development would be up to me to deal with along with my full-time job and helping with the coffee business. All too quickly Christmas was over and we were back to work.

Then towards the end of January I received a telephone call from my brother Greg. He had never once called me since I came to Australia so I was sure it wasn't good news. I thought that maybe it was bad news regarding my mother, but it was far worse than that. My eldest brother Nigel had died suddenly from a heart attack. Greg could only get those words out before being overwhelmed and passed the phone to his wife Lynne. She and I had always got on really well and she was more composed. I couldn't really believe what she was telling me; Nigel had been quite scathing about me emigrating as he felt I was leaving Mum just when she was in need of looking after, so we had not really spoken since. We exchanged Christmas and birthday cards but that was about all. He made little effort to see us when we were over the previous year and I hadn't worried much about it then but now regretted it. I had no idea that he had been having treatment for his heart which involved surgery.

Immediately, I started making plans to fly back to England for the funeral but straight away came up with a problem; my passport was about to expire. Thankfully, the British Embassy and the airline were both very accommodating and I was allowed to leave Australia and whilst in England had an appointment at the passport office in Durham to take advantage of their same day Passport service so I could fly home again. The funeral was a very strange affair, held at Harpham church in East Yorkshire, then a wake at a local restaurant after the burial. There were lots of people there who I didn't know, as Nigel lived in London and rarely came up to Yorkshire. His life and business were very firmly based in London. He lived a very flamboyant life and mixed with some famous people but sadly did many things to excess which I think may have finally caught up with him. To this day I regret not reconciling with him or making more effort. For me, it was a valuable but sad lesson going forward.

I spent the rest of my time in England catching up with as many people as possible. England was just getting over a prolonged cold spell and there had been some issues with our house in Middleton which had been rented out since we left in 2006. The water storage tank in the roof had frozen, then overflowed and damaged the platform it was sitting on, which then collapsed and the water came through the living room ceiling in three places. There had been so many insurance claims as a result of the cold spell that getting it fixed was going to be a long wait. Thankfully I had taken out insurance to cover lost rental income so was not too badly affected in the end but I decided that, on the grounds that we were never going to go back to England to live, I would be better off selling it and moving on.

I arrived back in Australia mid-way through February and immediately started having a very hard time dealing with the guilt of losing touch with Nigel when I could have done more to maintain the relationship. It also didn't help that Greg and I went to the chapel of rest to see him. Nigel was dressed in his best Armani suit with his Gucci shoes and a cravat and that picture has stayed with me ever since. Whether it was connected I'm not sure, but I started getting really bad headaches, with the pain starting between my shoulder blades and running up the back of my head. They were completely debilitating; I couldn't focus on anything and was very worried about it.

Jayne had been to see an Osteopath some time earlier when she had been struggling with her back so I decided to give the Osteopath a try. I made the appointment for late afternoon so I could go home afterwards and rest. She seemed really nice; we talked for a while then she asked me to lie down. We hadn't discussed anything except the issue with my neck and head, so you can imagine my surprise when, as part of the treatment, she put her hands around my neck and asked me what was going on with my left knee? I was blown away; I had been having problems with my knee for a few months but only when I was in bed. I didn't limp at all so she couldn't have seen it when I came in. I asked her how she knew and she replied, "I can feel it". I said "You are nowhere near it so how can you feel it?". She explained that everything is connected and that she would sort it out later. Eventually she asked what else was going on in my life which could be causing stress so I told her about my brother. She was really sympathetic and recommended me to see another lady who practiced Emotional Freedom Technique therapy. I have to say I was sceptical but I made an appointment and I think it helped. I saw her three times and felt I was over the worst but not really fixed. I kept seeing the Osteopath and indeed still see her regularly now; she has been amazingly helpful to me so many times during the last nine years.

Chapter 21

An inevitable conclusion

Sadly, I received very little help or sympathy from Jayne and deep down I think I knew that our marriage was not going to be a long one. She sold the coffee business at a loss because she was bored with it and went back into the motor trade at a small mechanical repair business in Margaret River. As the job didn't start for three weeks or so, I suggested she went back to England for the time in between. Her sister had just had her second child and was struggling a bit so I said it would be a nice thing to do. I wasn't really thinking too much about her sister though, I just wanted the time to be myself; or to be more specific, to be Stephanie. She booked her flights and I drove her to the airport.

Part of me thought she might call me and say she wasn't coming back, but it didn't happen. I had just over two weeks on my own, I booked some time off and planned to spend time at the house in Nannup as well as a trip to Perth to buy some new Stephanie clothes. I had a truly lovely time, as I could come in from work, close the door and just be Stephanie; it was heaven. I think I knew then that it wasn't going to be long before Jayne and I parted, but I had no idea how that was going to work. All too quickly it came to an end and Jayne was back.

Later that year (2011) I was busy at my desk when Ray came in and asked me if there were good deals on the Nissan Xtrail range, particularly the "Ti" version which was the top of the range model. The deals and campaigns changed from week to week according to stock levels and what the opposition had on offer, so it was not unusual that he would ask for my help. Indeed sometimes it took all of us to make any sense out of the campaigns as they were very complex. However, he was in luck; that model was not massively popular and they obviously had lots of stock which they wanted to move. One of the surest ways of getting a slow-moving model going was to put on a huge demonstration bonus which was the current offer. We already had a white one as a demo as it was such a strong deal. He mentioned that there was a lady at the Golf Club, who was interested in one, and that he would give her a call and invite her to come in and have a look. The next day he took the white one to show her and a deal was agreed in principle but she didn't want white; it had to be blue. I checked the stock and to my surprise he said, "If there is one in pool stock pick it up and I'll do the rest". I duly did as I was told and the car arrived a couple of days later. Ray then told me that the lady wanted to drive the actual car before she would commit. I thought this was strange as they all drive the same and have the same features, but he said she was coming down the following day and could I look after her as he would be out. At the given time the lady arrived and I took her for a drive in the car; she was happy with it so I completed the paperwork and arranged a time for delivery to her home in Dunsborough.

When the time came I organised for a colleague to follow me and we set off to deliver the car. It was a wet day which is always good as if there are any marks on the car they would be invisible when wet; but the car was perfect anyway. When I arrived at the house she invited me in to finish off the paper-work; there was not much to do so I completed what was left and suggested we went outside so I could show her through the car and its controls. What came next was a very abrupt "It has an instruction book doesn't it". I said, "Yes it does but it's easier if I show you all its features and anyway you are going to get a survey from Nissan in three days time which will ask if the salesman explained all the car's features". She assured me she would say I had done so and said she didn't have time anyway, so I left. My parting shot was "If there is anything you don't understand please give me a call and I'll talk you through it". She assured me she would manage so I left it at that. I got into my colleague's car and we set off back to the dealership. I told him what had happened and made the remark that she would call me in the next 24 hours. I knew she would because there was a really weird trick to pairing a phone to the Blue-tooth. Sure enough I got a call the next day; she said there must be something wrong with the radio as she couldn't pair her phone. I asked her what type of phone it was, to which she replied, "An iPhone" to which I replied, "Oh we have lots of problems with them; can you bring it in and I'll sort it for you". She asked if it could be done over the phone but I said no as it may need the unit taking out. We arranged a time and she brought it in the following day. Now the trick with the Xtrail is that the handbrake must be on to allow you to pair a phone but I have yet to find that information in the handbook; it will be there somewhere. I took her phone and slid into the car, very discreetly raising the handbrake at the same time. The phone paired straight away. I just said "All done, you must not have been doing it right" and left it at that, thinking, if you had let me show you through the car I would have explained it to you but that is what you get for being clever! How ironic that this lady turned out to be my best friend, my soulmate and my partner not too many years later.

It was not long to Christmas and Jayne had a new interest; she joined the local bushfire brigade. I must say I was very supportive as they desperately need all the volunteers they can get; but, in true Jayne style, it became the thing she lived for until she moved on to her next favourite pastime. This too gave me some time on my own which was good. I even plucked up the courage to find a quiet spot on the beach and go in the ocean as Stephanie in a one-piece swimming costume. I had to be very quick, but it was worth it; I loved it. The other good thing was that she was no longer at home when I went home for my lunch, so, especially when the weather was good, I could get changed and sit in the sun for half an hour or so every day. It was a small thing but meant a lot to me to be able to do this. I started to experiment a little with makeup to see what I could get away with at work. I wore mascara most afternoons and became quite good at applying it. I did experiment with lipstick as well but it was rather too obvious. In fact, one day after experimenting, I got back to work and a colleague discreetly told me that he didn't think the lipstick was my colour and that I should probably rub it off. I was still struggling with both the headaches and issues inside my head, but this at least gave me some pleasurable "me" time.

Christmas was over pretty quickly. We didn't do much as we were having Jayne's father to visit shortly afterwards. I had always got on really well with Paul; he was an easy-going sort of man who I think appreciated the fact that I had rescued his daughter from her previous marriage which was to a man he most certainly disliked. We had planned a few days away in Denmark on the south coast. The weather was perfect and we had a great time. At one point when there was just Paul and me together he asked me if everything was okay between us. I told him that I was still struggling with my brother's death and that it had put a strain on the relationship but I thought we would be okay. He seemed to buy it but, deep down I think he knew there was more to it. I think one of the nails in the coffin came while Paul was still with us. It was a Saturday and I was at work in the morning. About halfway through the morning I started with a headache; it was a monster and I could hardly lift my head. I took some painkillers but they didn't touch it so I left early and called Jayne to tell her I was going to the emergency department at the hospital as I was in such a lot of pain that I thought there must be something seriously wrong.

She wasn't concerned at all; didn't seem bothered in the least and said she would see me whenever. I couldn't really believe what I was hearing so went to the hospital to see what could be done. They kept me there for three hours; there were no facilities to give me a scan of any type so they asked if I would be willing to go to Bunbury. I told them that I didn't have anyone to take me so would have to drive myself; so they kept me in for surveillance, drugged me up until I was feeling a bit better then sent me home to rest. It said it all really.

A few days later Paul went home and there was just the two of us. I did my best to try and keep the peace, but it was difficult and obvious that our relationship was going to come to an end pretty soon. Not long after, we had been out for our nightly walk after dinner and had sat down in the lounge with a cup of coffee to watch television. Jayne turned to me and asked if I wanted to watch it or if it was okay for her to turn it off. I had the strange feeling that something was going to happen, and I was not far wrong. She turned off the television and looked at me. She said to me "This just isn't working for me anymore; what are we going to do about it?". We had always said that if one of us wanted "out" of the relationship then the other would respect it and we would call it a day.

Inside I just didn't know how to feel; I knew she was right, but I still had feelings for her and I guess didn't want to admit I had failed again. I also knew it was the right thing to do as I so wanted to be on my own again, so that I could be Stephanie

more of the time. We talked about maybe going for some counselling but agreed that if our hearts aren't in it then it would
just be a waste of time. We agreed there and then to part and
she said she would move into the back bedroom. We hugged
each other and I thought that would be the end of the conversation. But by the time we had turned in for the night we
had made a basic agreement on how we would split things up
and how much I would have to pay her out. Eventually I went
into the bedroom and closed the door behind me. There were
tears rolling down my cheeks but I knew it was the best thing.
I stood with my back against the door and thought of the time
ahead. It was going to be tough financially but in the end it
would be worth it.

The following morning I woke, having had one of the best
night's sleep for a long time; it gave me hope and the feeling
that a large weight had been lifted off my shoulders. My original plan was to say nothing at work, but Ray seemed in a good
mood and so I asked if I could have a chat at some point in the
day. As always he was very supportive. He was sad for me, but
I think didn't have a very high opinion of Jayne as he thought
she would have given it a better go working for him instead of
returning to Ford at the earliest opportunity. He asked me if
I was going to be okay financially. We talked for a while and
he said he would sort something for me just to keep my head
above water for the time being. I was very appreciative but not
altogether surprised as he and Jan are some of the most loyal
and supportive people I have met.

I was a little unsure what to expect when I arrived home that
evening but there was a pleasant atmosphere and Jayne informed me that she would be moving out at the weekend. One
of the customers of the business she worked for had some holiday chalets which were mostly empty during the autumn and
winter months so she let them out for a very reasonable rent
just to keep them occupied. I was quite surprised that she was

leaving so soon but it made sense; after all, the decision had been made. After working Saturday morning I arrived home to find her gone. It was a strange feeling which soon evaporated when I changed out of my work clothes and into Stephanie clothes; I felt at home.

Chapter Summary - Part II

Searching for answers 2012 - 2015

40. Last few weeks in the UK
41. Canada, Canberra, Melbourne then home
42. The bombshell

Chapter 22

Time to get my life in order

Even though Jayne had moved out we kept in touch and met up once a week for dinner. Six months earlier (towards the end of 2011) we had befriended a Canadian pilot who was based in Busselton, flying one of the water bomber helicopters which were contracted to help control bushfires in the region. Quite why Western Australia would employ a Canadian company is still a little beyond me but they were in the second year of a three-year contract. They were based on the outskirts of town at the State Emergency Services depot and lived in apartments near the centre of town. He was a friendly sort of guy; didn't take offence when we made fun of his accent and we spent a good deal of time with him. When he flew back to Canada in early April he said if we ever wanted to visit Canada we would be more than welcome to stay at his house, as he was away most of the time. We would be able to borrow his car and treat his place like home. He was very disappointed when we told him we had parted and reiterated his offer for either one of us if we felt we needed a break. As Jayne was now cashed up she decided to take him up on his offer and to cut a long story short, she is still there – with him. Whether or not there was any sort of relationship before we split I don't know and quite frankly don't really care as our separation would have happened sooner or later. I'm actually pleased she is at least with someone reliable.

When Jayne first left I decided that it was time to get my life in order or, more importantly, get my health in order. The first thing on the agenda was to lose some weight. I had been overweight to various degrees all of my life but it was now getting out of hand and having lost Nigel, to a heart condition at the age of 53, I made the decision to do something about it. I weighed in at 105kg which at 177cm tall was not good and I had in my mind to get down to 89kg or 14 stone (the weight I was when I left school in 1977). I didn't mention it to anyone but it wasn't long before people were noticing that I was losing the kilos, which was very encouraging. Living on my own, I found it easy to step up the exercise and limit what food I ate. Although I had never been one for eating healthy food, I did cut down on the unhealthy stuff as much as possible. I have always loved grapefruit and started eating at least one a day. Grapefruit is said to be a superfood; packed full of vitamin C, plenty of fibre and virtually no calories. Whatever they are, they certainly made a difference. They also have a downside in that they are full of phytoestrogens; whether or not that had an effect on me I'm not sure, but I certainly ate a lot of them.

I managed to reach 89kg without too much trouble and felt so much better for it. Every single day I allowed myself one chocolate biscuit which I ate after my evening walk, with a cup of tea, savouring every mouthful. On one of my weekly visits to the block at Nannup I hurt my back whilst lifting the lawn mower off the back of a Ute. Thinking it was just a twinge I didn't really worry about it, but as the day went on it didn't get any better so I went home early and had a hot, relaxing bath. The next day I was still in a lot of pain so I thought I should make an appointment to see the Osteopath. Fortunately, she was able to fit me in later that day; her last appointment actually, so I didn't need to leave work too early. While she was treating me she asked if I had ever had my thyroid checked. I said I hadn't and she suggested that I should do so, as it looked swollen. It probably looked different rather than swollen, as, by this stage, I was down to around 85kg so it was probably more prominent than when she had seen it before. When she finished with me I sat at her desk and we chatted for a while about my weight loss; she was very encouraging and said I looked so much healthier. I asked her about the thyroid check and what it would entail. Having had 36 needles stuck into me only a few years earlier, for what I thought could be a similar reason, I wasn't going to let that happen again. I also told her that, at that time, I wasn't actually registered with a GP and wouldn't know which one to go to. What happened next has had such a positive impact on my life, it's hard to imagine how a single recommendation could turn out to be so significant. She reached over to her handbag and pulled out a GP's business card; she gave it to me and said, "Go and see this lady; she is my GP and is the best in Busselton".

The Medical Practice was on my way to work, so the following day I called in to make an appointment. I was immediately struck by the friendly, calm and empathetic atmosphere in the waiting room and the lady sitting behind the desk was equally lovely. There was a feeling of informality and professionalism - instead of the usual counter, with a receptionist sitting behind, this was just a desk; it was very patient-friendly indeed. She gave me a laminated form to fill in; it was weird to write on, but she explained that after my details had been entered into the computer the form was simply wiped clean, thus saving paper. I was impressed!

My appointment was the following day and I had been allocated a long appointment as it was my first at the practice.

The doctor was running a little late but I didn't mind; it shows that you are treated as a person not a number who is rushed through in order to get to the next patient. The doctor was about my age I thought, very slim, short hair and had an air of calm about her; I immediately felt at home. I told her I had been recommended to her by my osteopath; she nodded and said what a lovely lady the osteopath was. I of course agreed. I told her that I had lost quite a lot of weight for which she congratulated me and had a look at my thyroid. She asked lots of questions about my health history and my parents health. She gave me a referral to get some blood tests done and asked me if I intended losing more weight. I said I would probably like to get down to 80kg which she agreed was a sensible goal. I thought she was going to send me on my way, but she looked at me and asked, "Is there anything else you want to tell me about?".

I thought for a few seconds then for some reason I blurted out that I had gynecomastia and had had it for almost forty years. She looked a bit surprised, then asked, "Would you mind if I had a look?". I had a feeling that this would be the case but felt completely at ease with her and so took off my shirt. I could see the shock on her face straight away. She asked if she could examine me, and I agreed. After a few moments she said, "Well you certainly have gynecomastia, not just fatty tissue". She sat down while I got dressed and asked me if I had ever been to a specialist to try and get to the bottom of the issue. I told her the story about going to the one in Leeds all those years ago but that nothing ever came of it. We chatted for a little while longer then she said we would have to leave it there as I had been with her for almost an hour. She said that the receptionist would give me a call when the blood test results were back. Then she took the referral off me and wrote even more things on it; I've never seen such a list of tests.

I headed straight to the hospital to have the bloods taken; it's not something I enjoy as I hate needles at the best of times, but somehow I knew that this lady wanted what was best for me. A few days later I received a call from the receptionist asking me to make another appointment to discuss the results of my blood tests. I scheduled it for a couple of days later and again couldn't get over the lovely calm atmosphere in the place; it was unlike any doctors' surgery I'd ever been to. When it was my turn I sat down in the Doctor's office and she started to go through the results. There were very few results in the "normal" range but my thyroid was on fire and my oestrogen level was three times what it should be. After a short discussion she said I should see a specialist; an endocrinologist who would look at both the thyroid issue and the oestrogen/gynecomastia problem as well. She asked me if I would like to see a male or female endocrinologist. I thought female, as I was sure I would finish up taking my shirt off again, so she gave me a number to call and the name of the specialist. She asked me to make an appointment then let reception know and they would fax off a referral. This was the start of two long term relationships; one with the doctor and the other with the endocrinologist, both of whom have looked after me with such care and empathy I don't know what I would have done without them.

One of the highlights of 2012 would have to be the dealership winning a trip, with Nissan, to the Gold Coast in Queensland. Nissan had been incredibly successful for most of 2012 and had recently introduced an excellent finance deal of 1% on their whole range which was bringing in lots of customers. They ran a program called the "Platinum Dealer" in which all the key elements of the dealership were measured, including the hitting of sales targets, customer satisfaction and parts and accessories sales. We had always done well in the program, and in 2012 had excelled. There was a gala dinner at the event, where all the departmental managers went up on stage to be presented with the award by the current CEO of Nissan Australia. It was held that year at the Palazzo Versace, the only seven-star hotel in Australia at that time and it was certainly a grand affair. As I didn't have a partner I was allocated a single room but in reality it could have housed a whole family. In fact a whole family could have lived in the bathroom alone; it was huge. I've never seen a shower with so many options or jets in it; it was truly magnificent! We had also been awarded the State Dealer of the Year award which was a great accomplishment given the size of our dealership and the population of our town. It was certainly a memorable trip, which is fortunate as I can't see me staying in a seven-star hotel ever again!

Chapter 23

The uncomfortable zone

Lots of people talk about "their comfort zone" and how they don't like to step outside of it, but I have mixed thoughts on this. On the one hand, being in your comfort zone is very safe, no risks attached and no uncomfortable moments to deal with; on the other hand I've heard it said that all the best things in life, the excitement, the adrenaline pumping moments and the best rewards are in the uncomfortable zone and I tend to agree. I have always been the one who took my fair share of risks and someone else's as well. I've always driven on the limit, the limit of the car that is, not the speed limit. I've always tried to get from A to B in the shortest possible time and have the most fun into the bargain, but I can't tell you how much time I've spent completely out of my comfort zone for all the wrong reasons in the last eight years.

I made my appointment with the endocrinologist and planned my trip to Perth. The lady's name was of Asian origin but I was surprised when she came out of her office and called my name. She only looked about 15 years old, was very tiny and had quite a brusque, no nonsense type of attitude but was pleasant all the same. I was dressed in a black shirt and black ladies' jeans as, regardless of my wanting to be a girl, they have actually always fitted much better than men's ones. She asked me to take a seat and began to go through my blood test results. She covered the thyroid first; she explained that because I had lost so much weight quickly my thyroid was still working for a 100kg person, when in fact I only weighed just over 80kg; and it could have possibly become toxic, and needed dealing with as soon as possible. She then moved on to the gynecomastia and asked if she could examine me. She had a press here and there and asked me how long I had been like this. I told her since I was twelve and she just looked at me in disbelief. She said she would like to sort the thyroid out first and then see what could be done about the hormone issues and the gynecomastia. She asked me if I was willing to have a scan today if she could arrange it. I thought that as I was in Perth I might as well get it over with, so I agreed. She called a nearby hospital and spoke to the Imaging Department; I was treated to one side of a conversation while she negotiated with them to fit me in. She was successful and put the phone down with a satisfied smile and proceeded to give me directions to the hospital. It was well within walking distance and she said it was easier to leave my car where it was and walk, as parking was an issue at the hospital. She sent me on my way and told me to come straight back to her office with the results when I'd finished so she could make a decision on what action to take.

I made my way to the hospital and found the Imaging Department. The curt nature of my conversation with the Receptionist left me fully aware that my hastily arranged appointment had put them out. She pushed a clipboard with a form on it across the counter and told me to fill it out. Before I had finished, another lady came into the waiting room and asked if I was Robin; I said "Yes" and she beckoned me to follow her. I mentioned that I hadn't finished filling out the form to which she replied, "You can do it later, we have squeezed you in so we need to get started". She took me into a room and told me to undress and put on a gown then to lie down on the bed of a machine. I was terrified. She told me I would need to lie perfectly still for twenty minutes while she did the scan as she couldn't keep stopping. I did as I was told; she must have taken images of every millimetre of my throat from every angle and then moved the camera down to my genitals; I was too scared to ask why. Afterwards, she came into the room and said she needed to take images of my arm, so I would have to hold it out straight and keep it perfectly still. Again, I was too scared to ask why she needed images of my arm; I just wanted it to be over. Eventually, when the scan was finished, she told me to get dressed and finish filling out the form before seeing the receptionist on the way out to pay the bill. I asked how I would get the images and she glared at me and said they would be mailed to me in due course. I mentioned that the endocrinologist asked me to take them back with me, to which she replied, "She will have to wait until I've had time to write the report". I said okay and left the room. I paid the bill and made my way back to the endocrinologist's office.

Upon arrival I sat in the waiting area and a few minutes later she walked down the corridor, saw me and invited me into her office. She looked at me and asked where the report was. I told her that they wouldn't give it to me and that had said I would have to wait until the report had been done. She was not impressed! She picked up the phone and gave the receptionist an earful, telling her that I had to drive back to Busselton tonight and she needed to discuss the results before I left. Eventually they agreed to email the images to her but said she would have to wait for the full report. She put the phone down and looked at her computer. After a while the images started coming through and she asked me to come around the other side of the desk so she could show me. It didn't mean much to me, but she pointed out some irregularities which she identified as toxic nodules which needed dealing with. I asked how that was done, to which she simply replied, "We nuke them". Now I was already well out of my comfort zone and this wasn't helping much. I asked how this was to be done and she replied "There are several methods. The first method would involve injecting the radioactive isotope directly into the nodules but this would be very difficult in your case as some of the nodules are on the back of the thyroid". I was pleased to hear that! She then said, "It can be given intravenously". I thought this sounded better but not altogether enjoyable as I guessed it would still involve a needle. Her final option "Or you can simply take a tablet" sounded much more appealing to me so I said I would go with that. She picked up the phone to the nuclear medicine department and spoke to someone. Once again I was treated to one side of a conversation; one which I wouldn't have wanted to have been on the other side of. This lady took no prisoners at all! She argued that, as I lived in Busselton, it was not realistic for me to come up to Perth for a further consultation then back for the treatment. Eventually the person at the other end of the phone agreed to do the consultation over the phone a few days before the treatment was due. I liked this lady a lot; she really made me feel she was working for me and that she had my best interests at heart.

I drove back to Busselton and was very pleased to get back to the house, shut the door and immediately head off to bed. It had been a very long day; not a pleasant one, but I did feel it was a step in the right direction and hopefully a step on the way to me being fixed.

I didn't hear anything for a couple of weeks and was starting to get a little anxious about it as the thyroid was really giving me some grief by now. I had dropped to 74 kilos which meant I had lost almost a third of my body weight in less than six months and a number of people had mentioned that they thought I looked ill. I had so much energy though; more than I ever remembered having, but that caused a problem in itself. I couldn't sleep at all, so the GP put me on Temazepam in the hopes that it would help. It certainly did; but I found the best way to get to sleep was to go for a run on the beach before bedtime. Thankfully I only lived about 500 metres from the ocean. It was all so foreign to me; I had never had any interest in getting fit before, but now it was a real possibility. Another change was that I just couldn't sit still for five minutes or hold my hands still at all; they just trembled constantly.

Then at last I received a call from the specialist who would be giving me the treatment. He had a Scottish sounding accent but an Italian sounding name. He was pleasant enough though, and was very interested to know how I would be getting to and from Perth. I thought he was going to say I couldn't drive after the treatment, but it was almost the opposite. He said I must be on my own in the car after the treatment as I would be partly radioactive and so couldn't be in such a confined space with anyone for that length of time.

The treatment was booked for a Monday and I remember thinking "Seriously, how difficult could it be to take a tablet?". I wondered how big it would be but wasn't too concerned. He had also told me to put the cat in a cattery for a few days as it wouldn't be good for her either. A couple of weeks before the treatment was to begin Jayne returned from Canada with the helicopter pilot as it was bushfire season again. We had been in touch several times since she had returned as she wanted to buy a car to use for the four months she was going to be here. It was at this point that she told me that they were in a relationship. I was neither surprised nor bothered. It was agreed that, as they were based in Perth at the time of my treatment, I would travel up the day before and stay the night with them. It was good to see them both, although I had already seen Jayne when she came to pick up the car. They weren't far from the airport and it would be much better having a short drive in the morning, rather than having a full round trip from Busselton the same day, especially if I wasn't feeling on top form. They agreed to come with me to the hospital and wait there until I had finished the treatment, which was comforting.

I drove to the hospital and arrived in good time. We found the Nuclear Medicine department and sat in the waiting area. A nurse came for me and took me to a very small room where there was a chair, a small table and a pile of magazines to read. They all had written on them in big black letters, "DO NOT RE-MOVE, RADIOACTIVE". It didn't do much for my feeling of being scared, so I didn't touch them. Before the nurse left, she went through what was going to happen, asked me if I knew how serious a treatment it was and how I was getting back to Busselton. Not long after she left, the Scottish sounding man came in and asked the very same questions; he seemed happy enough and said he would be back in five minutes. When he returned he was fully suited up in a white overall, mask and gloves and was carrying a stainless-steel canister which he put on the table. He removed the lid and took out a smaller canister from inside; he then tipped the contents into a white cup and handed it, and another one with water in it, to me and said, "Take this now". I looked in the cup; the tablet in the bottom resembled any other tablet, quite big but didn't look overly difficult to swallow; I took it and then drank all the water. He didn't hang around - he left immediately, saying that a nurse would be along in about fifteen minutes to check on me. After about ten minutes the door opened; a nurse came in and asked how I was feeling. I said "Fine, how should I be feeling?" She queried whether I was feeling nauseous and when I answered in the negative she said she would be back in another ten minutes to check on me again. I didn't really know what I expected to happen but I felt absolutely fine. After a while she came back and again asked me how I was feeling. When I said I felt good, she handed me a card and said, "If you vomit in the next twelve hours you need to call this number as these people will need to come to wherever you are and clean it up". I asked if I would glow in the dark and she smiled and said, "Everyone asks that - no, but your urine will". She then said I was free to go and that I wouldn't be radioactive for the first hour but after that I needed to be careful not to get too close to anyone for a few days, especially small children and pregnant women. She reminded me to pay the bill on the way out.

I headed back to the Reception area where Jayne and Bill were waiting for me. I went to the counter, gave my name and I was presented with a bill for $1,060! I could hardly believe my eyes. The receptionist said I would get about $600 back from Medicare so it wasn't too serious, but it was an expensive morning all the same and an experience which was well and truly out of my comfort zone.

Chapter 24

Ups and downs and a second encounter

The nuclear medicine treatment had done nothing for my mental state of mind which was not in a good place. I had never imagined that I would ever be 'underweight'; it just wasn't something I thought I would ever have to deal with, but I was getting uncomfortably close to 70 kilos. My first blood test, three weeks after the treatment, revealed that nothing had changed; my thyroid was still on fire and still toxic.

There are all sorts of issues resulting from hyperthyroidism, including Graves' disease and thyroid cancer, so consequently the lack of improvement was certainly not helping my mental health. It all came to a head on 1st December 2012. It was a Saturday, and I was at work in the morning. On Saturdays we opened up all the cars on the forecourt and gave them their weekly run. We started them all and did some straightening and moving round to put fresh "faces" in prominent places. I then settled down to a cup of coffee and to read any new emails I had received. Unfortunately, there was one very abusive email from a customer who felt we should renew his vehicle registration as it had been a demo vehicle and only had about five months of registration left on it when he bought it. When I sold him the car I made sure to write on the contract the expiration date of the registration. I should also point out that, in buying the demo vehicle, he did in fact save over twelve thousand dollars from the list price; so the three hundred or so dollars for the registration was small compared with his saving. Anyway, he felt very disgruntled about it and threatened all sorts of things which upset me a great deal. Then I found an email from Nissan saying that we had missed out on November's incentive by 0.2 of one percentage point. This also upset me and the day just went downhill from there.

We closed up around 1pm, as per the Saturday trading hours rules, and went our separate ways. I headed into town and did some shopping then went home. I didn't see another soul after that and just couldn't get off the downward spiral into deep depression. I decided to have a bath, hoping that it would relax me, but it only made things worse. I emerged from the water and found myself going through every drawer in the house looking for any sort of painkiller. There was quite a pile on the kitchen bench, and it would probably have done the job; but around 9pm I heard a text come through on my trusty Nokia phone. On opening the message I saw it was from a fellow Yorkshireman who I had helped when he first arrived in the country saying, "Thanks for all your help, can't believe it's been a year since I arrived here". Strange as it may seem, and thankfully so, it was enough to stop the downward slide and just lifted me out of the danger zone. I will be eternally grateful for that message. Some years later I discussed it with the said Yorkshireman and thanked him.

There was something else weighing on my mind; Christmas 2012 was looming and there was an added problem; lots of people had asked me what I was doing for Christmas and I had made up something to suggest that I would not be on my own, but the reality was that I was indeed planning to spend it alone. After the episode on the first of December, I was now dreading it even more. Throughout the previous month after the thyroid treatment Jayne had kept in touch and I knew that sooner or later she would ask what I was doing for Christmas and she didn't disappoint. They were now down in Busselton where they were based while Bill was "on call". She had already told me that they were spending Christmas in Perth with friends unless there was a bushfire to deal with but she sensed the hesitation in my voice and before I could speak she said, "You're going to be on your own aren't you?". I had to own up and agree and so she asked if I would like them to spend the day with me. I couldn't hide my relief and burst out crying. Ten minutes later she was knocking on my door and I ended up telling her about the tablets episode; she was really cross that I hadn't told her before and immediately started planning Christmas. It may seem really weird that I was relieved to be spending Christmas with my estranged wife and her boyfriend, but in reality we had never fallen out, never had a bad word since we agreed to split and I got on really well with Bill. He was fun to have around and I was quite looking forward to making fun of his accent again. I must say that being forced to decorate the house and put up the tree was very challenging; but, in the end it was going to be better than being alone, even though I could have spent the day as Stephanie.

Sometime during early December, Jan had come into my office and mentioned that there was a lady she knew through the golf club looking for someone to spend time with, go out to dinner or the movies with and asked if I was interested, as I was on my own. I asked who it was and she replied, "Denise, the lady who bought the blue Xtrail from us". I immediately recalled in my mind the experience of delivering her car and how dismissive I thought she had been. I had been in touch with her several times since on follow up calls and she had been okay and in fact had needed my help in sorting an issue out with the car only a couple of months earlier. However, I wasn't really excited about the proposition, so I said I would think about it without any serious intention to do so.

Well, it was about to come up again. Ray came into my office and asked me to write down for him the current offers on a couple of small SUVs, one Holden and one Nissan and the features and benefits of each. He had a lady, Maggie, from the golf club coming down to see him later that day. I did as he asked and when I took the details into his office he mentioned that he would probably get me involved as I knew more about the cars than he did. I thought to myself, "I've heard this before", but didn't mind as I truly appreciated that he valued my knowledge and salesmanship and acknowledged the fact that no one in the dealership knew more about the range than I did. When Maggie came in he brought her straight to my office and introduced her to me and basically then just left me to it. I talked to her for some time then showed her through the two cars. She asked me which one I would buy. On paper the Holden was a better deal; a bigger car, bigger engine, more power etc but the Nissan was in my view a better car; it was built in Sunderland in the UK, a better build quality, more economical and plenty big enough for what she wanted. But I didn't want to put her off the Holden if she liked it more. She decided that she would take home all the specifications and pricing and call me the day after to organise a test drive of the one she had chosen.

The following day, true to her word, Maggie called me with her decision and indeed had decided on the Nissan, subject to driving one and it being comfortable. We made arrangements for the next day for the test drive. I have a very specific route for test drives and I always drive first. We swapped over just outside town and she asked if she could call in at the golf club as we were driving past so she could show her friend; it seemed a harmless enough proposition so I agreed. As we pulled into the golf club she said, "I think you know my friend, you sold her a Nissan Xtrail". As we pulled into the carpark I saw Denise and the penny dropped! It occurred to me that Denise was not what I would have regarded as being a "car savvy person" so couldn't really see the point of showing her the car. She didn't seem very interested in it anyway, but did make a point of speaking to me to thank me for sorting out the issue with her car a couple of months earlier which I thought was progress.

We got back into the car and continued the test drive. Maggie then said to me, "So, Jan tells me you're single". I was a little taken aback and was working out how to reply, when she went on to say that Denise was looking for a man and that I would fit the bill perfectly! I was flattered, and she then said something to me which no person had ever said before; she told me I was hot! I made some joke about the car's air-conditioner not working very well, but I could see this was going to be an interesting sale. We arrived back at the dealership and she announced that she was happy with the car and that she would like a white one. I took her into the office to do the paperwork but before she would sign it there was one further thing I had to agree to; I had to call Denise and ask her out!

Chapter 25

Christmas, the worst meal & New Year's Eve

Christmas went very well. It did feel strange having Jayne living in the house with her new partner, but we had a lovely time considering the fact that I dislike Christmas at the best of times. In the meantime I had done as I was told and called Denise to ask her if she would like to have dinner with me sometime. Perhaps not surprisingly (as I'm sure it had been discussed between her and Maggie at length), she accepted my invitation. As it was only a few days before Christmas when I asked her, we agreed to get that over with first, and the date was set for December 28th 2012. I chose the venue; it was quite local to her house and as I had agreed to pick her up seemed like the perfect place. We had both eaten there before and had good service and good food so I had great hopes for the evening.

I had chosen the most expensive car on the forecourt to pick her up in but was conscious not to talk about cars all night; she asked what the car was and I gave a very brief description and left it at that. We arrived at the restaurant and were shown to our table. Neither of us were drinking alcohol at that stage, so we just ordered a bottle of sparkling water and went straight to the main course. She ordered a seafood risotto and I ordered a chicken dish; both were extremely disappointing to say the least. I think the chef forgot to add the seafood to the risotto and the chicken in my dish was definitely overcooked and tough. We talked non-stop through the meal though, and I learned that Denise was actually born Welsh. It hadn't registered with me that she wasn't a native-born Australian but it gave us something in common and we talked a lot about our upbringing in the UK and family back there. Neither of us wanted desserts so ordered coffees to finish off the meal; they even managed to get these wrong. It was whilst we were waiting for the coffees to arrive that I made a comment that, at the time was bizarre, given that it was a first date, but which proved to be deeply significant. The comment was, "If I had been born a girl, I would be a lesbian". To be fair, Denise took it in her stride (despite thinking it was a strange thing to say on a first date) but years later reminded me how truly prophetic the comment had been. The coffees arrived and were dreadful; cold, too strong and mine was spilled into the saucer just to complete the disaster. In fact, her coffee was so bad Denise complained and received a replacement which was better, but not by much. I paid the bill and we headed back to the car.

On the way home Denise asked me if I would like to go back to her house for a (hopefully better) coffee as she had a nice coffee machine there. I felt the evening had gone okay apart from the meal itself so I agreed. It was a balmy warm night so we sat out in her alfresco area and chatted over two cups of lovely coffee until well after midnight. I noticed that she had a spa and sauna and asked if she used them often. She said she didn't but I was welcome to come and try them out. Now, I was a long, long way from taking my shirt off in front of her or anyone for that matter. That was a privilege only on offer to medical people at that stage as my much-reduced weight had made my breasts more prominent. It came time for me to leave and we said good night with a hug at the door. I told her that I had enjoyed the evening, thanked her for her company and if she wanted to see me again I would be happy to, but would leave the ball in her court. She immediately asked me what I was doing for New Year. I was a bit taken aback and said I wasn't sure but thought Jayne was organising something so would be busy and left with the thought that she was a little bit too keen and pushy as I was not looking for a full-blown relationship at this stage.

The following day Jayne called me to ask how it had gone and if I was seeing Denise again. I said I had really enjoyed the evening and that I would like to see her again at some point. I also mentioned about the New Year's Eve comment and Jayne was straight on to it and said I should call her and invite her to my house and we would do some food there for the four of us. I had explained all about my relationship with Jayne and how it might sound a little strange but thought I would give Denise the opportunity to meet them. She accepted without hesitation and asked what she could bring. I thought we could sort the main course out pretty easily so asked her if she would bring a dessert. She was happy to do that so the date was set.

New Year's Eve came and Jayne, Bill and I had prepared the savoury part of the meal and did our best to get into the spirit of the evening. Denise arrived and I made the introductions. She had made a pavlova for dessert; one of my all-time favourite desserts which I considered a good sign. We had both lost a considerable amount of weight since I sold her the car back in 2011 and I for one vowed I would never get to that size again. The Pavlova was excellent and even better, at the end of the evening, she persuaded me to keep what was left!

I was beginning to think "I like this lady a lot". One of my favourite things to do on New Year's Eve is to walk down to the beach and celebrate the New Year with a glass of champagne overlooking the ocean. I've done it lots of times since being in Australia and hopefully there will be lots more of them. Once we had seen in the New Year on the beach we made our way back to the house and decided to make coffee. I didn't have an elaborate coffee machine like Denise, but Bill had brought his grinder, his beans and a coffee plunger, which was a nice end to the evening.

Denise announced that she would head for home so I accompanied her to her car. We had a long hug and a very brief kiss. I think she was disappointed that I wasn't more forthcoming but I was really only treating this as someone to go out to dinner with or maybe to the movies and thought, at the beginning, that this was all she was looking for. My parting shot was similar to the one at her house - "If you would like to see me again let me know and I'll let you organise it". She smiled and with that she left.

I went back inside where Jayne and Bill were tidying up. Jayne remarked that she thought Denise was really nice and seemed to like me a lot! Although I played it down, I had to admit there was something special about her. When Jayne and I first parted and I got into the swing of having the freedom to wear what I liked and be whoever I wanted, I made a vow to myself that if I entered into another relationship it would be on one of two terms. Either it would be just a weekly outing of some sort and kept at arms-length, or the person had to know the full story about me and accept that I was different, and not in a small way. As I went to bed, I pondered how this possible new relationship was going to progress.

Chapter 26

A third and fourth date and a plan hatched

A few days later I received a call from Denise asking if I would like to go to the outdoor cinema at one of the many Margaret River wineries. I am fairly particular about what I watch so I asked what the movie was. It was the latest James Bond film so I immediately accepted and Date number three was planned. It was on a Thursday night and being in Margaret River I decided I would drive, as my normal work car had a bull bar on it and, given the time of day, there would probably be some kangaroos about. Better to be safe than sorry I thought.

We had a thoroughly nice evening. The film was good, Denise had pre-ordered pizza for the interval and we had both enjoyed the snacks which Denise had packed along with a flask of coffee. On the way home Denise said she would like to cook me a roast and asked if I would be free on Saturday? I said that I was, and would love that. I couldn't remember the last time someone had cooked a roast for me. She asked if I would prefer beef or lamb; so as I'm not much of a lamb fan, I opted for beef.

I asked if I could bring anything but she said no, she would have everything sorted. There was a part of me which was a little scared that this was moving way faster than I had intended. I really wasn't ready for a full-scale relationship and I felt that Denise had that in mind, so I decided to ask the question after dinner.

Saturday came and the roast was delicious, cooked to perfection and with all the accompanying roast potatoes and vegetables I like, including the all-important (for a Yorkshire man) Yorkshire pudding. It was as though she was going all out to impress and it definitely worked. After we had cleared away the dishes she made me a coffee and we sat down in the games room. I waited for a break in the conversation and asked her where she wanted our relationship to go? She thought about it and replied that she was happy for it to become more serious, even physical if that was what I wanted! I was shocked, I hadn't expected that response at all and said I wasn't ready for that yet, but was happy to keep it going in the way it had been for the time being. I explained that before the relationship would ever move to the next level there would be something I would have to show her and discuss with her. I also said that once that moment had happened there would be no going back. I think she was a little surprised and even a little embarrassed, but we got past it and enjoyed the rest of the evening.

On the way home I started planning how and when I was going to approach the subject of my breasts, my love of wearing women's clothes, especially underwear, and my feelings. It was going to have to be handled very carefully as there was a risk of her just saying she didn't want anything further to do with me and then potentially telling people about my secret. The tricky part would be judging when she liked being with me enough to put up with my female tendencies and not dump me on the spot. Over dinner I had told her all about my property in Nannup and she said she would love to see it, so I made tentative plans to show her on the following weekend. Sunday morning I did my usual chores early and headed off to Nannup with the lawn mower. I liked to keep it tidy so as not to get in bother with the Shire over not having an official "fire break". The lady whose job it was to check that fire breaks had been done had agreed to let me off not having one at the front as long as the grass was kept short so I went most weekends at that time of year to give it a trim. It was quite a job; being about half an acre at the front and only having an 18-inch-wide lawn mower, it was hard work but I loved the job. The garden and lawn had been so overgrown when we bought it back in 2010, but it was now a very tidy property. I didn't want to be too late back as I had some ironing to do when I got home. So when I had finished cutting the grass I quickly tidied up, locked the padlock on the house door and headed home. It takes about 40 minutes to get back to Busselton and as I pulled into my driveway I remembered leaving my house and work keys on the bench top in the house at Nannup. Thankfully I had a spare house key hidden so I could get in but as my work keys were in Nannup I was going to have to drive out and pick them up the next day and somehow manage at work for a day without them.

This, however, gave me an idea. I sent a message to Denise telling her what I'd done and asked her if she would like to come to Nannup with me after work to recover the keys. She replied saying she would love to, so I started hatching my plan to tell her my secret. She drove to my house and we then took my car to Nannup. The road is quite notorious for kangaroos and emus, especially at dawn and dusk, so it's best to use the car with some frontal protection (i.e. a bull bar). We chatted nonstop on the journey and soon arrived at the property. Time always passes more quickly when there is someone else in the car. She was excited when she saw the house; quite the opposite reaction to what I expected. She seemed genuinely happy to come and help me there. On the way back we discussed the numerous redevelopment opportunities the property offered, but the problem was that I didn't have the funds or the ability to develop it and in my heart I didn't want to live there. If I was going to live in Nannup it would be out of town, not one street back from the Main Street.

When we arrived back at my home I made us some sandwiches and we sat and chatted. I had devised a plan to tell her my secret and it was time to put it into action. I asked her if she trusted me. She said it would depend what it was I wanted her to do. I had dropped lots of hints that I was going to tell her something about me which could change the way she viewed our relationship; but she seemed unperturbed so I asked her to stand up, give me her hand and close her eyes. She was obviously, and understandably, very nervous! I quietly and carefully unbuttoned my shirt and put her hand on my breast. She was surprised but not shocked and asked me to explain. I told her she could open her eyes and I gave her a long hug. I said "You have no idea how hard that was for me to do. I have just shared my deepest secret with you. Thank you for not freaking out and heading for the door". We sat down still holding hands. I was quite emotional.

I explained that the condition is called gynecomastia and that I have had it since I was twelve years old. I also made the point that they were not "man boobs", they are real breasts and as yet no one had been able to figure out why I had them and why my oestrogen level was so high. She was very understanding and, I think, thought I had made a big thing out of it when it wasn't really important. So I said, "there's more to it though". I then told her about my love of wearing women's clothing especially underwear, and that I often wore a bra because the support made my breasts less painful. At this point she said she wouldn't be completely comfortable with me wearing women's underwear in front of her but wasn't fazed by what I had told her. We talked at length about the difficulties I have faced over the years. I even gave her the option to call it a day if she no longer wanted to see me. But if our relationship was going to go anywhere then I didn't want it to be a secret and it needed to be out in the open. She thanked me for my honesty and asked me where and how I bought my women's underwear. I said I usually went to Perth or brought it with me from England. She asked if I had much of it so I took her hand and led her to my bedroom and opened the bottom drawer of the dressing table. There, neatly stacked in rows was a drawer full of bras, sorted by colour and style. I think she couldn't believe her eyes, firstly that I had so many, and secondly for the OCD way they were arranged. She thanked me for sharing my deepest secret with her and gave me a big hug. For both of us that evening saw us move on to the next level in our relationship.

Chapter 27

More tests & our relationship develops

It was now three months since my thyroid treatment and time for another blood test. I hadn't really noticed any change and felt the likelihood of a second round of treatment was looming; but the results showed a small improvement which was encouraging. Sadly my hormones were well out of range and my GP now focused on them. It was decided that I should see the endocrinologist again so I called to make an appointment, only to find that the lady I had seen had gone on maternity leave but there was a man there who I could see if I was happy to see a man. I decided I didn't have much choice so made arrangements to see him about three weeks later.

Meanwhile, my relationship with Denise was coming on in leaps and bounds. I introduced her to four-wheel driving and she loved it. We were soon on the lookout for a vehicle of our own which we could adapt specifically for taking off-road. From a feeling of being very wary of getting into anything serious I was now thinking that maybe Denise would become a long term partner, hopefully more permanent than any previous relationships. I felt it had great possibility, especially after her reaction to my secret; and I was determined to push the boundaries to see how far I could go before she was uncomfortable with it. I was even more pleased when she asked if I would like some company when I went to see the new endocrinologist and I accepted without any hesitation. I knew it would mean taking my clothes off again, but in front of a man this time which I wasn't sure I would be at all comfortable with. I needn't have worried; he was lovely with me - very sympathetic and caring - but it made a great deal of difference having Denise with me.

One of my hormone problems was a lack of testosterone which was affecting me in a number of ways including a lack of energy and stamina which I had enjoyed since losing the weight. He decided to try me on a testosterone supplement which was applied though a transdermal liquid under my arm each morning and night. It was quite a messy procedure until I got into the swing of things but it certainly made a difference to my energy levels. The downside to it was it didn't improve my personality at all. It made me more arrogant and aggressive; two qualities I dislike about people at the best of times. So I reduced the dosage from twice a day to once a day in the hope that my personality would improve.

I was always on the lookout for some sort of four-wheel drive vehicle for us. We originally thought we would buy something around $15,000 but the gap between a relatively new car and a car of that price is huge in terms of age and condition. We didn't want to spend much more than that as it would be a second car and one which wouldn't be used much during the week - Denise had her car and I had a work car. After some thought I mentioned to Denise that we had an ex-demo Nissan Navara which had been driven by the Accountant and was, I thought, very good value for money; less than a year old and in excellent condition. It was very basic but because it was almost new it had the latest safety equipment including stability control, which appealed to both of us. It was agreed that I would talk to Ray and negotiate the price and we would then discuss it that evening. In the end I felt the price on offer was so good I agreed to buy it there and then.

Denise was pleased with the decision and we began to plan what adaptations we were going to make in order to equip it for our needs; it was an expensive process but one which gave me pleasure. I had spent lots of hours building up cars for customers wanting to create the perfect off-road vehicle; so it was good to be doing it for us. I had a very particular view on which accessories were worthwhile and which were not, either from a value point of view or practicality. At the end of the process I felt we had a very well-equipped four-wheel drive which would give us lots of hours of enjoyment in the future.

My next set of blood tests from a thyroid point of view were perfect, which was a massive relief. The levels had stabilised and were sitting well within the acceptable range and I felt much better for it. I persevered with the testosterone treatment until the bottle was empty, then decided to give that a rest as well. The endocrinologist had written me a script to get more but as I felt as well as I had done for some time, I decided not to fill it for the time being.

One of the highlights of early 2013 was meeting Denise's mum, Doreen, who was over from Wales. We had already spoken numerous times on Skype and had got on really well. Sadly, she had been ill on the flight so wasn't at her best when she came through to the Arrivals hall. But once into the car she came around and was soon chatting away. I have real respect for anyone travelling alone half-way across the world at the age of 83. Airports are not my favourite place at any time, but for someone that age I think it is a fine effort. Doreen was a real battler; she was about 4 ft 10 inches tall and around six stone in weight but was very active for her age. As Denise was in a golf competition shortly after Doreen arrived, I was designated the task of entertaining her for the day.

I planned a mini road trip around some of my favourite places - including showing her the property at Nannup, having lunch at my favourite cafe in the town and a visit to Donnelly River Mill town where you can hand feed kangaroos and emus if you dare. I had to watch her carefully, as sometimes the kangaroos and emus get a little over excited and as most of them were bigger than she was I was concerned that she might get knocked over. But all went well and she enjoyed the experience. She wasn't complimentary about the emus though; she didn't like them at all! On another occasion we took her four-wheel driving and she loved it! At one point Denise was quite worried - I had asked her (Denise) to spot for me which means getting out of the car and guiding me through a very tricky part by telling me which way to steer. She actually took a photo of the car delicately balancing on two wheels as we went over some deep ruts with Doreen holding on in the front seat. It's a classic photo, definitely a keeper! Doreen called it "rough roading".

Late in 2012 I had booked a trip back to the UK for May 2013, which came around very quickly. It seemed like a long way away when I booked it but was now just around the corner. Denise also had a trip to the UK booked for later in the year so in order for us to keep in touch she suggested we buy an iPad so we could Skype while I was away and then Denise take it to the UK on her trip. In reality, sharing the iPad was never going to work as no sooner had I come to grips with it I fell in love with it and there was no way she was taking it from me when she went away. We subsequently purchased another one and they have been comprehensively used by both of us.

My trip to the UK was my first on my own apart from the brief trip for Nigel's funeral. I was very much looking forward to catching up with as many friends as possible and enjoying some serious retail therapy. Somehow clothes always seem better in the UK and fit me better. There is much more choice as there are more people to clothe and the prices are very competitive. I also hoped to top up my Stephanie clothes drawer if the opportunity arose. The plan for most of the trip was to stay with my brother and his new partner. He had recently split from his wife of many years and set up home with a lady I had known since 1997. I really liked her when I met her then and was looking forward to getting to know her more. I was probably closer to Greg at that time than I have ever been before and since, and felt that it was time to share with them part of my secret. They had been very supportive of me while I had been going through my thyroid treatment and seeing the various specialists, so I wanted to explain a bit about why I was seeing these people. I chose a night where we were all at home and sitting comfortably after dinner and told them I had something to tell them regarding my health which was difficult for me to talk about. They were both very supportive and very surprised when I opened my shirt. We talked for some time and overall I felt happy in how it had gone. They both assured me that they didn't love me any less and were keen to see how things progressed.

The rest of my trip went really well, I caught up with lots of friends and family and did plenty of shopping. As it was my first visit since losing weight and also now having Jayne's side of the wardrobe available to me, I had lots of space for new clothes. Part of me liked the idea of using Jayne's side of the wardrobe for Stephanie's clothes when I had enough, but there was work to do in my headspace before I was brave enough to go and try things on.

Chapter 28

Bad news at work and first trip together

I returned home at the end of May and was straight back into work as June always had the potential to be the biggest month of the year. There had been a few changes since I left, but nothing too serious. I got the usual pep talk on how things should be done but heard nothing I didn't already know. The new campaigns were significantly enhanced from May and we were up and running from the first day of June. We had a good month overall, exceeding both Holden and Nissan targets; Nissan with ease and Holden only just; but we got there anyway. Then came the bad news; General Motors, Holden's parent company in the USA, announced that they would cease manufacturing cars in Australia in 2017. It was a huge blow to the Holden workforce both at the factory and out in the field. At that time Holden produced both the Commodore and the Cruze in Australia. The Commodore had recently had a model change and was probably the best yet and the Cruze, which was the only small passenger car built in Australia, had been a strong seller for us and was indeed a good car, but the factory had lost money for many years. The Government was tired of propping it up financially and the end of the line had come.

The bad news hurt Holden a great deal, with enquiry levels dropping noticeably. The Holden district sales manager and I sometimes had dinner together after our monthly meetings and it was interesting to hear his point of view outside of work. The State office had one senior district manager and one graduate who generally looked after us; he was a nice young guy who told me he didn't see much of his future with Holden as he thought there would be staff cuts to come. His tenure in the job came to an end shortly after that and his replacement was a lady with whom I immediately had a connection. Throughout my career in the motor trade I have endeavoured to build a good relationship with the representative of whichever manufacturer I've been dealing with. You just never know when you might need some help, and a good relationship always stood me in good stead for that. Indeed, I have had hundreds of favours over the years which most likely would not have been forthcoming had I not had the right kind of relationship. Over the years it has, on numerous occasions, got me into trouble with the business owners who I don't think like sales managers getting too close to the manufacturer for some reason; but I kept on doing it anyway. Rachel and I got on really well and rather than go out for dinner she started coming to my house and I cooked a meal for us. It was a big test for me as, at that stage, I was not much of a cook but I did my best and she never complained. It led to a much more relaxed relationship and we spoke at length about our work and personal life. We are still great friends today which speaks volumes. She left Holden in 2015.

At this point Denise and I started to plan our first trip together. She had not seen much of Western Australia so we planned a road trip, taking in some of my favourite places.

The trip was planned for late October when the weather would hopefully be warming up. The first stop was Hyden and a look at Wave Rock - I've seen Wave Rock numerous times and never tire of its enormity. Not far from Hyden is the start of the Holland Track which was cut through the bush many years ago to create a link from the wheatbelt to Coolgardie. We planned to stay at the motel in Hyden for a couple of nights before heading out along the track and, on arrival made our way to the Motel Reception. I have stayed there before; it's a little tired but friendly and clean. The restaurant is quaint - you buy your meat from the butcher's counter and cook it yourself on a huge stainless-steel barbecue - so if you ruin it you can only blame yourself! Once in the Reception we gave our names and were handed our key. We turned to leave but before we reached the door I was accosted by a lady demanding to know if we were visitors to the town. I said we were just there for a couple of nights and she proceeded to tell us about a dance being held in the town hall that evening and how we must attend it. I told her I had two left feet to which she replied, "That's okay we can step on both of them!". She then bid us good day and said she would look forward to seeing us later. I looked at Denise and she asked the lady, as we were leaving, what sort of dance it was, expecting her to say country dancing. We were both a little surprised to hear her say Ballroom. My first reaction was "not a chance". Neither of us had clothes with us for ballroom dancing and I wouldn't know where to start anyway; but over dinner we both warmed to the thought and said we could always go and if we were not enjoying it we could leave. Dinner was not a long affair as there were not too many people in the restaurant, so we made our way to the town hall; me in trainers and jeans, Denise a little less casual. We were greeted at the door by the same lady who relieved us of ten dollars each and introduced us to some friends of hers. It turns out that people travel for miles to go to these events and they were mostly from farming backgrounds. This was a help to me as I was immediately engaged in a meaningful conversation with a local farmer about the year's harvest and how good the crops were looking that year. He actually said to me that, barring disaster, that year would yield the first profit in ten years and, with any luck, it would pay off the money they had borrowed to exist for the last decade as well. It struck me what a difficult life they had, having to wait for a good year before they could survive without living on borrowed money.

There was a man on the stage playing a saxophone. He had an easel next to him with a list of tunes/dances on it and as he finished one it was moved to the bottom. Before too long I was propositioned by a young lady who almost dragged me onto the dance floor. Denise had already been invited to dance with a friendly local and came back grinning and said I should try it. This lady had a bigger task on her hands than she thought, as I really do have two left feet. This is how it works - the leader (man on stage with saxophone) plays three tunes in sequence all of which have the same dance steps. After that he moves onto the next run of three, the idea being that by the third tune you have the dance steps nailed. Each time it took me until the end of the third one and I was still struggling, but I did my best. My partners and the other dancers were very accommodating and forgiving, which was just as well.

Then the leader stopped playing and everyone left the floor. I thought to myself that it must be over; he had reached the bottom of his list of dances on the easel, so I thought that was it for the night. I was wrong; what happened next was quite remarkable. Some people carried trestle tables onto the dance floor followed by the most amazing array of cakes and desserts. I was in heaven; there was so much to choose from and such small bowls. Thankfully, you could visit the table as many times as you liked - and I did. I was so pleased I hadn't overeaten at dinner as the desserts were to die for. I could just imagine all these farmers bringing their family's favourite dessert to compete with the neighbours' offerings. It was truly epic!

Then about an hour later the tables were removed and the man was back on stage with another list of dances and off we went again. I was still hopeless but made an effort anyway and it was very much appreciated by the locals that we had actually attended. We eventually made our way back to our room. Thankfully we had a very relaxing itinerary planned for the following day; just a walk on Wave Rock and a visit to a few of the other attractions in and around the town. Hyden is very small, so you can see all it has to offer in one day but it's a very friendly place and one I will return to one day I'm sure.

Chapter 29

The Holland Track and the rest of the trip

Day three started with an early breakfast and the 40kms drive to the beginning of the Track. It's a very inauspicious entry to the track and quite easy to miss, but I remembered it from the last time I did it with Jayne in 2008. There is a small sign at the entrance, informing you about the people who keep the track open and when it is passable and what times of year to avoid. We set off down the track, very excited at the prospect of seeing very few other cars or people for the next two days and camping in the middle of nowhere that night. The going was fairly easy for the first few kilometres and the vegetation quite low, but after that the track became rough pretty quickly. There had been some rain recently so there was a bit of mud around, but in general we had no issues. We had equipped the car with some good all-terrain tyres and lifted the suspension by two inches to give us more clearance, so I wasn't expecting any problems.

To stay on the track we needed to closely follow some pace notes and rely on arrows and signs, which at times were difficult to see, but on the whole it was great fun. We stopped regularly to look at various points of interest on the way and enjoyed the variety of different trees and vegetation. Eventually, we found a lovely little clearing to set up camp for the night and got opened up the rooftop tent. Dinner was steak and salad, and very enjoyable at that. There is something very special about camping in the middle of nowhere with no one around or at least you think there is no one around because you can't see or hear anything. In reality, there may be someone just a few hundred metres away; but being hidden away in thick bush is very private indeed. We woke early the next morning as it was light at about 5am. By six we were up and ready for breakfast, which was my now famous scrambled eggs with bacon and tomato and an instant coffee. I've not yet figured a way of having a real coffee when out in the bush but I'm sure it will come. After packing up the tent we headed in the direction of Coolgardie; or at least I thought we were. We had driven about a kilometre when Denise said to me "Are you sure we are going the right way?". Our campground had been off the beaten track and I thought I had turned the right way. I said I thought we were, and kept going. Denise was less sure and tried to get the compass on her phone to register where we were. Then the car hit a low branch as I drove underneath it. Thankfully I have a good memory, if not a good sense of direction, as I remembered hitting the same branch shortly before we discovered the campground. I found a place to turn around and again hit the branch. It was just as well I hadn't knocked it down the night before or we could well have found ourselves back in Hyden!

Finally heading in the right direction, we soon picked up the pace notes again. There were lots of points of interest on the second half of the track, and both the terrain and the vegetation continually changed as we approached Coolgardie. By 2pm we were pulling into the service station on the Main Street. I had remembered this from the last time. There's not much going on in Coolgardie nowadays but the service station did excellent hot chips and as we hadn't stopped to eat on the track they were very welcome.

After lunch we drove the 37kms into Kalgoorlie. I have quite a love of the place; it's not somewhere I would want to live but it's very interesting all the same. We found the motel and checked into our room. I had stayed there several times before; the place is a bit tired but clean and quiet and each room has a parking space outside so I could keep an eye on the car. We did lots of the touristy things - went to the Super Pit, to the Museum and had a drive round the old part of the town. There are still houses which date back to the gold rush days; lots are not lived in but are still intact and worth a look.

Next on the list was a drive due south to one of my very favourite places in the world - Esperance. It was quite a long drive but the view at the end of it is worth it. Esperance is a lovely small town on the south coast which is world famous for the beaches at the near-by National Park, Cape Le Grande. They are unforgettable - the whitest sand, the bluest water and kangaroos on the beach. If I was ever in the position to have a holiday home on the coast it would be here. It's a long journey direct from Busselton - about 700kms - but it's easy driving and well worth it when you arrive. We had booked an apartment at a place called Island View, which we had found on the internet. It didn't disappoint - it was clean, well equipped, had views over the ocean and the owner was just delightful. Nothing was too much trouble and he gave us lots of advice as to what to see and do during our stay. The weather was bright, albeit not that warm, but I was determined to go into the sea before we left.

There are five stunning beaches in Cape Le Grande some of which you can drive on; some you can't as there is no access. The most famous beach of all is Lucky Bay. It was voted Australia's top beach one year I believe and it's easy to see why. The pristine white sand is very firm and it's quite possible to drive on it without being in four-wheel drive, and we did just that. There were a few cars parked up near the entrance, taking advantage of the coffee van which goes there six days every week in the high season. They do very good business; I have been lots of times and don't ever remember not having to queue for my coffee and this time was no exception.

At the end of the road is Rossiter Bay and, compared to the other four beaches, its entrance looks very ordinary which would deter a lot of people from venturing further. However, if you drive the nine kilometres along the beach to the end of the bay then you are treated to a beautiful piece of Western Australia. The sea is relatively sheltered and due to the long drive on sometimes challenging sand very few people actually go to the end, which is another bonus. We stopped the car and marvelled at the view. I said to Denise that I wanted to go for a dip to see how cold the water was. This was a big moment for me, as I took off my shirt revealing my black bra and walked to the water. It was very cold but also very refreshing. I cannot begin to tell you how it felt to be in the ocean in a bra and swimming shorts, which were ladies shorts anyway. It felt amazing; a freedom which I had not experienced before. After a while when I was thoroughly cold I returned to the car for a towel. Denise had paddled, but thought it was too cold for a swim. I half expected some disapproving comments when I got back in the car, but all she said was "I bet that felt wonderful". I agreed and thanked her for her understanding; it meant so much to me.

The next couple of days were spent doing some of the touristy things in the area. There is a full-size replica of Stonehenge just outside the town. It has been erected with all the stones positioned to align with the winter and summer solstices, in the same way as the original in England only this structure is all intact and very majestic. It feels really weird when you stand at the altar - it made the hair on both of our necks stand on end; quite a feeling indeed. I can understand why they don't allow ceremonies there but it is great to look around. It must have cost a fortune to erect. There is a small gift shop and the owners are really nice people, so it's well worth a visit. The coastline on the western side of Esperance is dotted with small bays and beautiful beaches but for me they don't have the attraction of Cape Le Grande or the slightly more remote Cape Arid, but are lovely all the same. The only downsides to the south coast are that firstly it is often very windy and secondly the ocean water comes straight up from the South Pole and so is icy cold most of the time. But it's still one of my favourite places to visit.

From Esperance we headed west to Bremer Bay; not a place I had visited before but several people had told me it was a really pleasant place to visit. For me it was probably the least enjoyable part of the trip. We had booked a camping site in one of the caravan parks, something I had not done before and with a bit of luck won't do again. The sites were too close together and it was generally noisy, even though there are signs asking people to be respectful and not make too much noise. Bremer Bay itself I thought was nothing special compared with Esperance; the beaches were certainly not as picturesque those in Cape Le Grande and it was very windy. It was all part of a learning curve though, and I won't be going there again. It did, however, break up the journey home, which would have been a very long one.

Chapter 30

More tests and more specialists

We arrived home from our trip very much looking forward to the next one. It had been a great success. We had got on the whole time without a single disagreement and I was, in my mind, planning an even bigger one as soon as the opportunity arose. There are tracks all over the State and some very challenging ones at that. I felt that our car had performed well; the only disappointment was that with the tent on top it used an inordinate amount of fuel and with only 80 litres on board it did limit how far we could go without a fuel stop. There is always the option of carrying fuel cans in the back of the Ute, but it's not the perfect solution and fitting a long-range tank is a very expensive exercise; so a bit more thought would be needed before planning a long trip.

Work-wise the rest of the year went pretty well; both of our manufacturers had good campaigns and their products for the most part were well received.

Health-wise I had more tests and saw yet another endocrinologist. My oestrogen level was still far higher than normal and up to now nothing had been found which could be causing it. I had so many tests and scans that all came up as being normal. I had a CT scan of my adrenal gland, an ultrasound of my testicles and a blood test to determine the condition and operation of my pituitary gland all of which were clear. It was suggested that I see the endocrinologist again so I called to make an appointment only to be told he had returned to the UK to work. Back to square one and finding someone else. I was beginning to think that I was too hard for them to sort out, so none of them wanted to treat me.

Eventually, I found a man based at one of the hospitals who was willing to see me. First appointments are always the same; I end up taking off my clothes for them and getting poked and squeezed which is extremely unpleasant and this one would be no different. He was a strange man, had a bit of an accent, was dressed in a suit and didn't show a great deal of warmth. He asked me to undress and lie on the bed. Then he came over and asked if I was allergic to latex which scared me to death. I told him I didn't think I was, so he put on some sterile gloves and had a good look at all my bits and pieces. After he had finished he asked me to get dressed and come and sit at his desk. He asked me several questions then told me he was going to speak with the head of endocrinology at Melbourne University; a lady he said he knew well and whom he considered the best endocrinologist in the country. I was then treated to one side of a conversation while he sent photos of the scans and other test results to her, occasionally asking me questions along the way. I must have sat there for 15 minutes waiting for him to finish. After he put the phone down he looked at me and said "She is of the same opinion as me. All of your tests have come back negative, so there can only be one reason for your huge oestrogen levels and that is that you are self-inflicting". It took me a while to digest what he had said and I asked him what he meant. He said, "You are obviously taking some sort of supplement which is pushing your oestrogen level almost off the scale". I asked him if he thought I was doing this deliberately to which he said "Well you must be, for it to be that high". I was furious. I asked him if he had treated many Yorkshire people. He said he didn't understand what that had to do with it, so I gave him both barrels, as it were. I told him that Yorkshire people do not give up their hard-earned money easily and I had just paid $300 to see him. Why would I do that if I was causing the problem myself? He didn't have an answer so I stood up and left.

I returned to my car and was shaking. How dare he accuse me of causing the problem. Firstly I wouldn't know where to start and secondly these supplements would presumably cost a lot of money; something I was pretty short of at the time. A few days later I received a call from him; I had his number in my phone so I knew who it was and considered not answering but in the end I did. He half apologised for what he had said then went on to say he would like me to have another scan; a PET scan. I asked him what it was for and he told me it was just to make sure the other scans hadn't missed anything, as I was so adamant that I wasn't self-inflicting. I asked him what was involved and how much it would cost. He explained that a radioactive isotope would be injected into me and then I would have a scan similar to the CT scan. He also said it would be around $600. I said I would think about it so he said he would send me the details and a referral and would call me in a couple of days to see what my thoughts were. The following day I called him and told him I wouldn't be having the scan and wouldn't be seeing him again. He wished me luck and I've not seen him since.

I went back to my GP and told her the story. She was horrified and asked me if I wanted to see anyone else or just monitor the levels with regular blood tests for the time being, along with my thyroid levels which were seemingly perfect now. I decided to give it a rest for a while and do as she said. It had been a very unpleasant experience and I was not keen to see someone else and potentially deal with more of the same accusations because they couldn't figure out where the oestrogen was coming from. I was still concerned though, as some days my breasts were so sore that they really hurt. It helped to wear a bra for support but that was not always possible, especially at work. At least when I went home I could wear whatever I liked and I wasn't looking to change that arrangement anytime soon. I thoroughly enjoyed living on my own. Catering was a bit limited, as I hadn't had much experience in the kitchen. I stuck to the basics and I felt I did pretty well in the circumstances. I often ate the same meal three or four times in a row, as I would make a large quantity and live on the leftovers for the subsequent nights. I never got bored as I didn't make anything unless I really liked it so was always happy with my meals, even if they lacked a bit of variety.

Denise and I were looking forward to our first Christmas together in 2013. I had already told her it was not my favourite time of year so she was hoping to change that view. She had recently sold an investment property in Perth and was looking for something local to put her money into. I enjoy looking at houses, so went along with her to view possible purchases. I had recommended a real estate agent who had looked after me and who also bought his cars from me. It's good to have some reciprocal business; it helps build friendships and loyalty when either of you need each other's skills. Around the end of October we arranged to see a house not far from mine. It had been a rental for some years and needed some work, but the agent said it had potential so we agreed to have a look. We arrived before the agent so I went through the side gate to have a look around the back; he had told us it was vacant so I knew I wasn't going to be upsetting anyone. Once through the side gate I was blown away by the size of the place; the block was almost 900 square meters, one and a half times as big as mine, and it showed. The alfresco area was huge; it needed a bit of tidying up, but it was a lovely area. There was also a big shed on the property, split into two parts. Unfortunately the agent only had a key for one side but it was impressive nonetheless. The inside of the house certainly needed some work. Every room had a coloured feature wall; purple, lime green, bright red and dark blue. They were also badly chipped, gouged and marked so there was a lot of painting to be done if Denise bought it, but the agent was right; it had huge potential and I fell in love with it there and then.

Chapter 31

A new house and a passion discovered

After some negotiations Denise bought the house. We went there a number of times before it settled just to have another look and the more we saw it, the more we loved it. Denise lived in Dunsborough which was only twenty minutes' drive from my house, but that property needed lots of work and, to be honest, did nothing for me. After a few visits to the new house she decided she liked it more than her current home, so would do the work on it and then rent out or sell the one in Dunsborough. An empty house is the perfect blank canvas to transform and it wasn't long before a plan was made as to what needed doing. All the carpets and blinds had to go (the carpets stank of dog and the blinds were black and mostly broken). This made the place look very bare but easy to work on. The dining room was the most presentable of all the rooms, so Denise bought a new bedroom suite which we set up in there so that we could stay at the weekends and work in other areas of the house. She purchased a new fridge/freezer and brought some spare cutlery, plates and utensils from her home so we could get by.

I have always enjoyed painting but while I was with Jayne didn't have many opportunities as she would always take over the job. Here I could paint to my heart's content. Some of the dark coloured walls needed many coats before the colour underneath stopped bleeding through. The front room, which was an "in your face red" needed five coats before I was happy that there was no red showing through. I so enjoyed doing it and learned a lot; we had chosen a neutral colour (Berkshire White) for the walls, and all the skirtings, doors and frames were to be white gloss. One of the guys at Bunnings advised us to use a light tint called Lexicon Half in the gloss paint - this has a very small amount of black in it which stops the paint going yellow over time.

The house had real soul; something my house just didn't have and although it was older than mine and the bathrooms were a bit dated it was somewhere I felt I could possibly live. Over the Christmas period we absolutely transformed it. We stayed most nights and weekends and I stayed a few during the week on my own. While painting I wore only a vest top and shorts and, for the vast majority of the time, a bra. I felt such a freedom; it made me feel closer to Stephanie and Denise seemed to be growing a little more comfortable with it. For the first time in our relationship I could see us living there together. The partial acceptance of my choice of clothing went a long way towards this. I had made a pact with myself when Jayne left, not to get into another relationship in which I had to hide my love of being Stephanie. It was however to be some time later that it happened.

There were seemingly dozens of jobs which needed doing; but I was determined to make the place homely. Replacing the blinds was not a cheap job, but along with the carpets really finished it off. I replaced the toilet cisterns, the wash basins, the mixer tap in the kitchen and all the tap-wear in the bathrooms. There was a built-in barbecue and a non-functioning water feature in the alfresco area; a new pump fixed the latter and the resident goldfish (which came with the house) seemed very happy!

During this time my mother, back in the UK, was deteriorating in health and had been in hospital a few times. Then my brother Greg had a brain bleed which was very serious indeed. He went on to make a full recovery but it would take some time. Denise asked me one day what would happen if Greg wasn't able to take care of our mother's affairs. I said I would probably have to go back to the UK for a while. This brought up the subject of my visa, which was a Permanent Residency visa. The problem with this visa is, if you leave the country for an extended period of time, then you may not be given permission to re-enter afterwards; so she persuaded me to apply for Australian Citizenship. She was a big believer in making a commitment to the country you considered home and had become an Australian Citizen in the mid 1980s. I had always been proud of my British Nationality, but in reality did not want to go back there to live, so I made the decision to get naturalised and have dual citizenship. It's quite a long drawn out process but thankfully Denise was there to help me through it. There is paperwork galore and also a test of your knowledge of Australian history and values to complete, which, after studying some online questions, I thankfully passed first time. The next step is the ceremony, which is normally held at the Shire administration offices. I decided to wait a couple of months and be presented with my "Certificate of Citizenship" at a special ceremony on the Busselton foreshore on "Australia Day" - 26th January; it was a grand affair. Our local MP was the one presenting the Certificates. I had met him before as he lived in Busselton and came into work sometimes to see Ray. It was a day I will never forget; we asked lots of friends to join us for the ceremony and then cooked a breakfast for everyone back at Denise's house. We decorated the alfresco area and the whole place looked lovely - there was still no furniture in the house but it was the perfect venue on that special day.

Denise moved into her new home in February 2014 and her house in Dunsborough was rented out for the time being. It was good having her nearer to me and I found myself spending much more time with her. I had so enjoyed working on the renovations; it had revealed a huge passion for painting and general maintenance jobs and made me decide to paint my own house in order to get rid of all the coloured "feature" walls. I wasn't in a rush, as we were spending time four-wheel driving and there were still a few jobs to do at the new place.

By April, my mother's health had deteriorated further and it was clear that she wouldn't be getting better. She passed away in early May, so arrangements were made to go over for the funeral. Thankfully, Denise had no hesitation in saying she would join me. Traveling halfway round the world for a funeral is always hard and I had already done it three years earlier for Nigel's, but it was something that needed to be done. The funeral directors were happy to delay it until we could get over to the UK. We both had to arrange for pets to be cared for and to have the time off work. We stayed with Greg and his partner for the first week while we attended the funeral, and then went down to Wales to stay with Denise's mum. I hadn't been to that part of the UK before so it was to be a new experience. On the way to Wales we spent a couple of nights with some friends of Denise in Guildford. They live in an idyllic stone house set in beautiful countryside next to the Surrey Downs; again, another part of the UK I'd not seen. They are truly lovely people and I took to them straight away. I loved the house even though I banged my head on the low doorway into the bathroom several times. At the bottom of the property's garden there was a heated swimming pool which I longed to go in, but was too embarrassed to. Denise knew how I felt so she suggested that I mention to them about my gynecomastia and how I had never been able to go swimming because I was too embarrassed to take off my shirt in front of people. He was a Dentist, and so had a medical background, and they both said they would not be fazed if I wore a bikini in the pool; I was so grateful to them and was in the pool like a shot. As I've not had much chance to practice, I am a very poor swimmer; but after a while I developed a little more confidence and swam across the pool. The freedom I felt was much the same as when I was painting, only better. The problem was that I knew I was just going to want more and more exposure as Stephanie even though I hadn't told a single soul what my femme name was or that I had chosen it way back when I was twelve.

Denise was really supportive but still had boundaries which needed to be adhered to and respected. I was more than happy to do this as I was just thankful to have the opportunities that I had. It was more than any other partner had ever given me and it made me realise how lucky I was that she wanted me to be happy.

We spent some time in Wales and I was able to do some basic maintenance jobs for Doreen. I was a bit restricted as I didn't have much in the way of tools, but I loved being of assistance and being useful. I had a real bond with Doreen, much stronger than I ever remembered with my own mother. I think it was a mutual respect more than anything; we just got on.

Doreen hadn't been out to visit Denise that year because she had struggled with the flight over the previous year. So it was agreed that she would fly back to Busselton with us. It would be the first time she had seen the new house and I was looking forward to some more "rough roading" with her. For some reason she always got on better with the flight home than the one coming out to Australia. That may have been to do with the time of day, but I still think she did amazingly well for a person of her age.

Chapter 32

Back to work and lots to think about

We arrived back at the beginning of June and I was immediately under pressure to make the month a good one workwise. Neither franchise had been enjoying much success during 2014. For Nissan, the Navara was now looking old and was only ever going to sell on price; I still liked the car and pushed it at every opportunity. It was by far the biggest seller of the range for us. The Xtrail had recently been replaced with a new model which had been very well received but it had changed from being a fairly useful all-wheel drive car to very much a soft roader and had some market realignment to do. As for Holden, the news of the factory closure had seriously dented the enquiry numbers. It was as though the public had come out in sympathy for the workers who would be made redundant when the factory closed its doors in 2017. The month went satisfactorily but not as well as we had hoped. Both manufacturers' campaigns were messy, not as straightforward as they could have been, and it doesn't take much to confuse the car buying public and make them defect to another brand.

At the end of the month I was aware that there could be some changes coming and was wary of the outcome. I was called into a meeting and told that there were to be some changes to the structure of my department in that the General Manager was going to be Sales Manager and I was to be made assistant Sales Manager. Now I don't really care what title I have but I could see it having a potential effect on my pay packet, which I was concerned about. It was a Friday, so I said I would take the information about the new structure home and peruse it over the weekend and give my response to it on Monday.

Denise and I discussed it at length over the weekend, and on the Monday I gave Ray a letter explaining how I felt. In true Ray fashion he asked me not to do anything rash and he would put some thought into finding a compromise. A couple of days later, while Ray was away at a franchise meeting, I received a call from him apologising and saying he wanted to have an off-site meeting the following morning - just the two of us - to sort things out; which we did.

In September of that year I had my first taste of the upper north of Western Australia as we had a few days in Broome. I had heard much about the place and when Denise suggested going there I was very keen. We decided to fly there, not drive, as we only had one week off work. We hired a car and had a bit of an argument with the hire car company as we had hired an all-wheel drive but their representative tried to put us in a two-wheel drive version of the same car. I got into it and couldn't find the control for the drive train so looked under the back only to find there were no drive shafts at the back indicating two-wheel drive. She had chosen the wrong person to try that one on with! She apologised and rectified the mistake. I really loved Broome - the climate was perfect in late September; the water was warm and our apartment was very comfortable. It even had an outdoor shower, something I had not experienced before but in that climate it was perfect and I vowed to go back again as there was lots to see and do.

Both Denise and I were already keen on spending some more time traveling, but after this Broome trip it was even more-so in our minds. Firstly, there were lots of places here in Australia which we would like to visit. I love the outback and doing the Holland track the previous year had whetted our appetite. Secondly, even though I spent forty-five years in the UK, there were still lots of places there I hadn't seen, as well as a few places in Europe that I would love to visit or revisit. So we started planning when, where and how. We decided 2015 was going to be the year of travel.

With a view to selling my house, I painted it from top to bottom, replaced a couple of carpets and generally made the place look the best possible. I approached the same real estate agent through whom Denise had bought her house and asked him to come around and give me a valuation. I had in mind how much I wanted to get for it and his valuation was pretty close, so I put it on the market. I had discussed with Denise about moving in together and she was very happy to do so. It would be a massive thing for me not to live in my own house but our relationship was now such that we spent most of our time together when not at work, so it seemed the logical thing to do. It's pointless running two houses when you want to be together and as I had such a big input into making Denise's home the place it was, it was definitely the right way to go. As expected, my house sold pretty quickly and I didn't need to drop the asking price much to get a deal, which was satisfying. One problem was that the house title was still in joint names - Jayne's and mine. Due to some recent cases of properties being sold by people who didn't own them, completing the seller identification process was going to be a problem. As Jayne was in Canada, the house was in her maiden name and her "Identification" could only be done by the Toronto Australian Consulate (she was in Vancouver) it was easier for me to fly her back to Australia, be formally identified by the Settlement agent and to fill in and sign all the necessary paperwork.

We decided to get Christmas over with and then gave our resignation letters to our respective employers; Denise worked as a Bookkeeper for a Dunsborough Accounting firm. The house was due to settle in early January so Jayne came over the first week of 2015 in order to do the necessary paperwork. One complication was that since my mum had died I had been in regular contact with my first wife, Fiona and after numerous times of asking she decided to visit us and she was arriving the last week of January. To put it simply, it wouldn't have done to have both of my ex-wives here at the same time as there would have been a murder on my hands. I knew they wouldn't get on so it needed careful planning. I bought a cheap second-hand car for both of them to drive and hoped everything would go to plan. Jayne arrived and by that time I had moved out of my house and gradually started moving the contents over to Denise's home. Jayne wanted to take some things back with her and I was happy for her to do that. She packed them up and booked some extra luggage allowance; a win all round as it meant that I didn't have as much to move. Denise, Jayne and I travelled to Perth to see the Settlement Agent in order to get the identification sorted for both properties, and I immediately put the Nannup home on the market. Properties don't tend to sell as fast in Nannup so I wasn't expecting a miracle, but thought it was time it was sold. There was a considerable amount of maintenance work required each year, so if we were planning to travel then it would be a problem when we returned. I was sadder about selling the Nannup property than the house in Busselton, as it had been a place I could go and immerse myself in. The house was very ordinary, had no electricity but did have running water and a toilet. I had rigged up an outside shower in the bathroom – a bit unorthodox but it worked for me and gave me some hot water so I left it there.

Jayne came and went, and a few days later Fiona arrived. I was now into my last week of work, so definitely winding down to the finish. My last day at work was one of mixed emotions; I had never been out of work in my life and although we had sorted the bones of our traveling, we had nothing booked and it felt weird.

During my last week Denise's mum was taken into hospital, which was a considerable worry; she lived on her own and would struggle to get the help she needed when she came home. She had fallen, or been blown over, while putting the waste bins out one night and chipped her pelvis. There was some concern that she may have done more damage in the process but thankfully not. She was, however, going to be laid up for some time. Denise decided to travel back to the UK with Fiona so that she could spend some time with her mum and hopefully get her on the road to a full recovery. As we had planned to spend a considerable amount of time in the UK that year we decided that, rather than hire a car, we would buy one. Nothing elaborate, just something which would be good on fuel, reliable and comfortable and we found it in the shape of a 2011 Renault Scenic. It was an ex "Motability" car which had only done 13,000 miles and had been reasonably well cared for. My friend, who bought it for us from an auction, was happy to meet Denise and Fiona at Manchester airport. They would then drive him to his house and carry on from there to Yorkshire where Denise would drop off Fiona, stay with Greg and his partner for one night before making her way down to Wales the following day.

Chapter 33

Home alone, unemployed and R U Handy

Since moving in with Denise towards the end of 2014 I hadn't really had any time there alone until she left for the UK.

One of my concerns about moving in with Denise was my cat Tilly. She had been used to having me all to herself for the last two and a half years and, before that, being spoilt by both Jayne and me (we got Tilly in 2007). We had left a cat with a very good friend when we left the UK and had not planned on having any pets, but a colleague's daughter brought Tilly into work one day to see if anyone wanted her. She was the last remaining kitten in a litter and I fell in love with her at first sight. I was concerned that in the move she wouldn't get on with Denise's cat Baloo or her dog Bella. But she is a tough character and very soon was the boss of the dog, who learned to give her a wide berth. Baloo was a different matter. He was old and wily and took every opportunity to have a go at Tilly. She didn't give in though, and eventually there was some sort of truce between them, although Baloo often tried to assert his authority over her. Anyway, I was there, and she was with me so we both had to get used to new surroundings.

Denise and I had talked at length about what I was going to do for a living once we came back from our travels, and the favourite option was to start a small business doing general maintenance, but mostly painting. I had put a considerable amount of thought into what to call my new venture then, while out one night walking the dog, it came to me - R U (my initials) Handy. It stuck and no sooner had I thought of it I was asked to do a painting job for a friend of Denise's. My business was up and running and I enjoyed every minute of it. She was a lovely lady who had bought a house with her new partner and moved in but hadn't sold the old house yet. The real estate agent told her she needed to lose the feature walls and generally tidy the place up and that's where I came in. Having the freedom to come and go as I pleased was wonderful. There were lots of little jobs to do as well as the painting, so I could pick and choose what I wanted to do, and when. The weather was amazing, so I often started early then left about 4pm and headed to the beach. I had found a place where I could have a swim in a very private area which was usually deserted, so I could wear a bikini or one-piece ladies costume and not have to worry about being seen by anyone. If there happened to be someone else on the beach I could just walk along a little further and swim there instead; it was heaven to me. While painting I could wear whatever I wanted and my favourite was the same attire that I had worn while painting both Denise's and my house - a black vest top and black shorts with a bra under the vest top, of course. One day, while I was busy painting and was half way up a ladder, the owner of the house came in. There I was, wearing a bra and a vest, and she was looking right at me. I did my best to keep my arms over my front in whatever way I could and nothing was said. It was actually quite weird. It happened a couple of times after that and each time I got a little more courageous and showed myself off a little more; but still nothing was said. I was beginning to think my breasts were invisible!

Since the two ex-wives had gone back to their respective countries, the little car was now surplus to requirement so it was time to give it a real clean and sell it. Also, Denise was thinking of selling her car and getting something better. The Xtrail had been fine but it was certainly not engaging to drive and not very good on fuel, so I had suggested several alternatives which I thought would do her better. We decided that I would advertise both cars and see which one sold first. I have always loved detailing cars and spent almost the whole of one day doing both of them and putting them on the "Carsales" website. This meant taking lots of photos and writing a glowing report for each car, something I have had lots of practice doing over the last thirty plus years when preparing the advertising for the various dealerships I've worked for. By night, both cars were up on the website. The next morning I had an enquiry on the little car and by lunchtime it was sold! I was over the moon. I hadn't been greedy with it but had made enough profit to make me happy. I didn't get any enquiries on the Xtrail apart from an obvious scam, so we kept it for a while longer and decided to look at it again when we returned from our travels.

Denise arrived back having helped restore Doreen to a state where she could look after herself. She had amazing resilience to come back so positively after a fall like that; for many people it would have been the end of them but she soldiered on and we planned to spend some quality time with her while we were in the UK later in the year. It was now time to seriously plan our upcoming trip.

The initial plan was to go up to the north of Western Australia early April and see some of the countryside, eventually heading over the border into the Northern Territory and to Darwin to meet up with Denise's friends from Guildford who were over for a holiday. The idea was for them to hire a fully equipped four-wheel drive vehicle and explore the Kakadu and Litchfield National Parks with us, which would be great fun. I spent a good deal of time preparing our car for the trip. We had the roof-top tent on top and the back was packed with everything we could possibly need. We set a date for leaving and organised a house sitter to look after the dog and cats, as well as the house, for us. She seemed very capable and we felt they would all be in good hands and then disaster struck; the day before we were due to leave she sent us a message saying that she was in hospital and told us that she wouldn't be able to house-sit.

We were very disappointed to say the least, but not beaten. Denise put an advert for a house sitter on the local "Buy and Sell" site and within hours we had a number of applications for the job. The next problem was deciding which one to choose. Out of the seven groups of people interviewed there was one stand out candidate and two possibles, if for some reason we decided against the first one. After a second conversation we were both very happy with our choice. She was a single lady, our age, very hands on and outgoing and we are still great friends today!

We finally departed and headed north. Our first stop was about 400kms north of Perth so we had a long first day's drive. We found an excellent place to camp and our adventure had begun. The roof tent was okay but not the easiest thing to get in and out of, especially if you are desperate for the toilet in the middle of the night. The following morning we were up early, packed up the tent, had breakfast and were on our way before seven. We had both had a pretty good night's sleep considering how basic the tent was but we headed north again and had another big day. Night two, we were just south of the town of Denham; I had been there before in 2007 and really liked the place but wasn't able to have a good look round. The problem with that part of the west coast is that it is usually windy and this was no different. We had booked a beach side camping ground but it was so exposed that the wind sounded as though it would tear the tent off the roof. I stood it for so long, but the canvas of the tent was flapping in the wind and there was just no way I was ever going to get to sleep so I climbed down from the tent, got into the car and tried to get to sleep again. After about half an hour with no luck, I saw some headlights coming towards us; there were several other vehicles parked on the site but I hadn't seen anyone about. The car drove past us very slowly giving us a careful once over in the process and then pulled up next to one of the other vehicles. Two men got out and started transferring packages from one car to the other. It was all very weird. The next thing I knew, Denise was joining me in the car. She said she had also been watching the men and thought it was very suspicious. They were far enough away from us, so I wasn't worried for our safety, but it was about nine thirty and I couldn't see me getting any sleep there so we quickly packed up the tent and headed into town. As soon as she had a phone signal Denise started calling all the accommodation in Denham (even though by this time it was approaching 10pm) hoping we might get a room for the night. The first one she called was fully booked apart from a room with a storm-damaged veranda roof. The only reason it wasn't occupied was that they were concerned the veranda roof might be noisy in the wind. We decided to take a chance with it - anything would be better than getting no sleep and they let us have it at a discounted price so it suited us perfectly. We both had a good night's sleep - the bed was comfortable and we didn't hear the roof so it was a good result all round; so good in fact that we decided to stay another night before heading further north.

Chapter 34

Some long drives but worth it in the end

After leaving Denham we continued north. We had hoped to stop at Coral Bay but when we arrived it was throwing it down and very windy. Rather than get the tent set up and then struggle with the wind, we opted to find somewhere to stay the night. Again, we found a room at a motel which was pretty basic but clean and dry and with plenty of power points so we could keep the car-fridge cold and charge the two battery packs we carried with us. There didn't appear to be much to do in the evening so we took something out of the freezer for dinner and had an early night. The following day we packed our things back into the car and went to find somewhere for breakfast. One of the problems we had encountered was that there were lots of flies around, which was very unusual for that time of year. Unfortunately, there had been some unseasonable storms and rain which had caused them to hatch and become a problem. I had been badly bitten by sand flies on our first night, causing lots of itching, but the pharmacist in Denham sold us a product called Itch-Eze which worked very well and thankfully had just about cleared them up.

Our next stop was Exmouth; not a massively long drive for a change and we hoped for better weather and the possibility of a dip in the beautiful waters around there. Again, we decided to play it safe and book some accommodation in a hotel on what used to be the American base. Although it was a bit ordinary to look at, the room was quite nice. We had booked for three nights as there is quite a lot to see around there. Before we left home, Denise had been having some problems with her knee and the physiotherapist had strapped it up for support. The stick-on strapping had become very tatty looking so she decided to take it off and re apply some more. She went into the bathroom and came out ten minutes later with blood pouring down her leg. The strapping should have had baby oil or something similar applied to it before pulling it off or there is a danger that it might strip the skin off with it. The problem was that no one had told us this and now there was a big patch of skin missing from her knee so she couldn't re strap it. She cleaned it up the best she could then put a makeshift dressing over it.

The next day we headed out to Turquoise bay which is famous for its warm water and its beautiful colour. I was very excited as it would be the first time I had been able to swim since we left home. We changed in the car and I had decided to leave my bra on which was black and just put on some swimming shorts. I wrapped a towel around my shoulders and we headed for the beach. It was quite busy but we found a quiet spot, laid our towels down and went into the water. I felt such a freedom again; I loved it. The water was warm and the beach very sheltered. Denise did some snorkelling while I tried to swim a bit and floated around. After a couple of hours we decided to head back. The weather was lovely and warm so I just tied my towel around my waist and set off back to the car. There were lots of people on the beach and after we had walked about 100 metres Denise stopped me and said she was not comfortable walking with me dressed like I was. I was very disappointed and asked why; after all no one would know me so what was the problem? I felt that I looked pretty feminine, with the shorts and the towel covering my bottom half I couldn't see what the problem was. I didn't want a scene so I put the towel round my shoulders and marched off to the car. I told her I didn't understand what the problem was and she explained that it was obviously not a bikini top I was wearing - it was clearly underwear, and women just didn't do that. I couldn't really see what the difference was, but put it down to experience and nothing more was said about it.

The following day's weather was not so good so we went to the Ningaloo National Park and visited the visitor centre. Having had a couple of disappointing days weather-wise and a problem with the large number of flies, I suggested leaving the coast and having a look at the Karijini National Park which was about 500kms inland from where we were. At least the wind would be less of a problem there than it was on the coast. The only accommodation we had booked in advance was at an amazing place we found when we visited Broome the previous year. About 100kms south of Broome, the luxurious Eco Beach Resort, was booked for about ten days away, so we needed to find places to visit between now and then.

The drive to Karijini was not pleasant at all; it rained most of the way and was cold as well. We hoped once we had moved away from the coast the weather would improve, but we arrived at Tom Price at about 4.30pm in torrential rain, so the tent was again not very inviting. We went into the tourist centre but the only thing they could suggest was a rather expensive hotel which was owned and run by one of the big mining companies. Our room was cold and there didn't seem to be any form of heating, but we managed. After dinner we went back to the room to decide where to go to next.

Until now, the whole trip had been a bit of a disappointment, mainly due to the weather. So somehow we needed to change our fortune and get to where it was warmer. After some discussion the best option seemed to be driving to Broome. It was a huge drive; about 1,100kms but fairly easy going and there would not be much traffic. Rather than arrive there and then have to find somewhere to stay we did some homework and found an excellent offer on a suite which had cooking and washing facilities for a very reasonable price, so we booked it there and then. The only problem would be the time of our arrival as it was going to be a long day driving. Breakfast was all part of the deal at the Tom Price hotel, as was a packed lunch as it catered for the mine workers. We filled our pack-up boxes to the top and hit the road. We were on our way by 7:30am and, apart from stopping to refuel, it was a case of pushing on as fast as I dared. I sat the car at about 120kph and hoped I didn't get stopped. The kilometres flew by and we hoped to be in Broome by about 6pm. We had to stop again to refuel as the car could only do about 550kms to a tank. It gave us chance to stretch our legs and visit the toilets before getting back on our way. We were a little late but had phoned the hotel to let them know and they were fine.

After checking in we were shown to our room. It was perfect; a king size bed, good kitchen area and bathroom with a spa bath; what more could we ask for? The only downside was that it was up several flights of stairs and we had to carry the Waeco fridge up there somehow. Eventually we managed it and looked forward to a well-deserved, good night's sleep.

I had really enjoyed Broome when we visited it the previous year so we knew where things were, and the weather was perfect. We planned a visit to the pearl farm and found a good place to swim. Unfortunately Denise's knee wasn't looking so good - the swim in Turquoise Bay had infected the open wound. The seawater down in Busselton would have probably helped it, but due to the water in the North being warm there are all sorts of organisms living in it and it looked as though it was going septic so we needed to find a hospital. It always surprises, me when traveling around our beautiful country, how accommodating the medical profession is, and Broome was definitely no different. We were taken to a waiting area with a bed for Denise to lie on and a seat for me, in order to wait for a doctor to come and see her. He was a lovely chap. He asked us where we were heading and told us some great places to visit if we were up to some pretty heavy four-wheel driving. He then dressed Denise's knee with silver leaf as it needed treating as a burn and told us to come back a few days later to have it checked. He also advised her not to go in the water and not to strap it up for the time being until it had healed.

After our stay at the hotel had ended we had two spare nights before moving to our accommodation at Eco beach Retreat so we decided to book a beach top camping site at the Kooljaman Cape Leveque resort. It was a two hour drive north of Broome and was definitely a four-wheel drive only road. There were interesting places to visit along the route, so we set off in good time to give us time to see them. Cape Leveque is almost the most northerly point of Western Australia. The resort is the most northerly settlement and while the camp sites were basic it was perfect for what we wanted. Each site has a wooden structure covered in hessian for a sun shelter; we parked up next to it and set the tent up. There was a short climb down to the water which was almost bath water temperature. Our first night was perfect; we both slept well and got up early the next morning. Denise was a bit restricted as to how far she could walk and the water was out of the question until her knee healed but she sat on the beach and watched me in the ocean. The second night was a little windy but not really a problem. I had just about exhausted myself in the water so slept pretty well again. Denise had been up a couple of times and getting in and out of the tent with a painful knee was becoming quite an issue; but she struggled on. The next morning I had one more swim then packed up the tent and headed back down to Broome and on to Eco Beach.

Chapter 35

Eco Beach Resort and the Gibb River Road

We arrived at Eco Beach Resort and checked in. This would have to be one of my favourite places and one I hope to re visit soon. The well-appointed chalets are perched on the cliff top overlooking a beautiful beach. There is a lovely dining room and spa to provide the necessary experiences to enjoy while there. We unpacked the car and took our things to our chalet. This was pure luxury in my eyes; there was nothing but a twenty or so metre area of natural low scrub between the chalet and the cliff top and only a window with the middle slightly frosted between the shower and the same. It did feel a bit strange being in the shower and looking straight out to sea, but was very special.

Neither of us is competent at fishing so we booked a morning with the Aboriginal cultural elder, which included a fishing lesson. We met at 7am and he took us along the beach to a couple of places where he said we would be sure to catch fish. He taught us how to catch live bait by throwing a net and how to cast. Unfortunately, the fish were very shy that day and it took attempts in several locations before Denise, with his help, caught a sizeable fish which we were allowed to take home and cook for dinner.

That afternoon was extremely pleasant for me, being able to swim in a very sheltered part of the bay just out of sight of the main beach area in water which was lovely and warm and reasonably calm. It was such a pleasure for me not having to worry about being seen by someone who might know me and then having to explain why I was wearing a bikini or similar. The emotion I felt is something that I just can't explain; it made me feel closer to Stephanie than at any other time for some reason. Maybe it was the fear of being caught or seen by someone? I can't tell you how much the opportunity meant to me. Sadly, Denise was unable to join me in the water due to her knee but she watched me from the beach, enjoying how much pleasure it gave me.

The following day we had our spa treatments - I had my first ever pedicure and Denise had a massage. The girl doing the treatment was lovely; she spoke in the most sing-song voice I have ever heard and explained everything she did, as she knew this was my first. We had a lovely chat about where we were heading next and about her family and hopes and plans for the future. I knew then it would not be my last pedicure; it was too good an experience.

All too soon our time there came to an end and we were on the road again. First back to Broome, then east to the start of the Gibb River road. Denise had done this on an organised camping tour in 2012 but it was all new to me and I was excited to get started. Our first stop was a camp site just a few kilometres from the start. It had been a long drive and we wanted to get a good start in the morning, so turned in early. Denise was not having much fun climbing in and out of the roof tent with her painful knee but we were going to be in it for some time so she was making the best of it. The following day's plan was to get to Windjana Gorge where there was a nice camping ground and the Gorge itself is spectacular. It does, however, require a good level of fitness to walk/climb the five kilometres to the end and back. Sadly I think this was where it all went wrong for Denise. She told me not to wait for her and to go on in front as she thought she was holding me up; so I did as I was told and marched on. There was a considerable walk back to the campground (and our car) once out of the Gorge. Fortunately we hadn't set up the tent so as soon as I got back I filled my empty water bottle and set off in the car to go and get Denise. She was just at the entrance when I arrived and the look on her face said it all. She was just about shattered; out of water and it was still in the high thirties. She was very relieved to see me to say the least; we drove back to our camp site and set up the tent. Another early night was the order of the day, but I could see that Denise was very concerned about her knee. Not being able to strap it was a problem and it wasn't getting any better.

The following day we decided to head off the track and go to Fitzroy crossing. Denise had called there on her last trip and we were fairly sure there would be some sort of medical help there. We booked into a chalet at the caravan park, the downside of which was that they were all on stilts; so, up several flights of stairs with the car parked underneath. Once checked in we headed for the hospital. Fitzroy Crossing isn't a particularly large town; it is mainly inhabited by indigenous people and is not an affluent place but turn the corner into the street containing the hospital and you could be forgiven for thinking you were in a different world. The hospital was a pristine new development, opened in 2008 as part of a State Government push to rebuild/upgrade all the hospitals in the Kimberley region. There was a surprised look on the faces of the receptionist/triage lady when we walked in; I don't think they saw many non-indigenous people there. We explained what the problem was and were asked to wait for a nurse to come and take a look. A junior doctor then appeared and took us off into a treatment area. She took a thorough look at the knee and said probably the best she could do was to strap it as there was no Physio due in town for two weeks. She was very kind and gave us lots of her time but sadly she was only really experienced in strapping sports injuries which wasn't the case with Denise's injury; however she did her best.

We went back to our room and had an early dinner. As there was a laundry on the site I decided it would be a good idea to do some washing. It was a fair old walk to the other end of the park to the laundry but I enjoyed seeing all the fancy rigs which were visiting. There were caravans there which must have been worth hundreds of thousands of dollars and the various types of vehicles towing them were also very elaborate. When I arrived back in our room I asked Denise if she wanted to come with me for a gentle walk just to give the knee some exercise. She thought this would be a good idea, so after a cup of tea we headed back to the laundry together. We picked up the washing and headed back to the room. Up to that point Denise had been quite optimistic about how the knee was going, but sadly when it came to going back up the steps it all went wrong. I could almost hear the crack at which point Denise let out a shriek and slumped onto the steps. She was obviously in a tremendous amount of pain. I suggested going straight back to the hospital but she thought if she could get to the room and rest the knee there was a possibility that it would improve over night. We hobbled back to the room.

After dosing up with painkillers she finally got to sleep but when the morning came she was certainly not going anywhere except back to the hospital. This was a problem as I didn't know how I was going to get her down the steps to the car, so I asked for help from Reception and shortly after I got back to the room there was a knock on the door. I opened it expecting some strong person willing to give me a hand but she said after I left she decided that it was too risky to try and get Denise down the steps so she had called an ambulance. We were a little surprised but thought it was probably the safest solution. About fifteen minutes later there was another knock on the door. It was a small indigenous man who we had seen the previous day, emptying bins in the hospital; he was a happy, smiling man and we had both commented how lovely he was. He was obviously the ambulance driver as well. With him was a female doctor who was so petite that I thought this is going to be interesting; if they were planning on lifting Denise onto the stretcher it was going to be a challenge. Eventually, with my help, she was loaded onto the stretcher and taken the long way round to the ambulance avoiding the steps and taken off to the hospital. I followed in the car and watched as they wheeled the stretcher inside. I wondered where we would be heading the following day as our chances of meeting our friends in Darwin were looking slim to say the least.

Denise was taken into an emergency ward and settled into a booth where she was seen in due course by a doctor. The way we were looked after on both occasions was wonderful; there seemed to be people all over the place being tended by nurses and doctors, all in a very calm and professional manner. We were both blown away by the place. Eventually a doctor came to see us and asked if he could take a look at the offending knee. He attempted to see what movement there was but as he could move it very little without causing extreme pain he gave up. He was of Chinese origin and quite difficult to understand but a very pleasant man indeed. He went off to get a second opinion and was away for some time but eventually came back with another doctor who listened as he explained what he thought was the problem. They both left to consider their verdict.

Chapter 36

Rocked knee, clutches and a long drive home

The Chinese doctor returned and what he said next was absolutely classic. He looked at Denise and said "What has happened is that your knee has rocked and you're going to need clutches". I thought for a while, then the penny dropped. Denise's knee had locked and she was going to need crutches! How I kept a straight face I don't know. Bless him - he was a lovely man, so helpful and kind.

My mind was racing, trying to work out how far we were from home and how long it would take to get there. Could I drive non-stop? How would Denise go with so much time in the car? After a short while the doctor came back into the booth and said it was most likely Denise would need some sort of surgery and offered to speak to her GP or preferred surgeon. Denise thought for a while, then remembered the name of a surgeon, back home, who several friends had consulted with and had given glowing reports. She gave the doctor the surgeon's name and he went off to make the call. Within a few minutes, another doctor came in and said he understood that we were going to drive back to Busselton to get the knee sorted. We confirmed that was the case and he said he would show me how to inject Denise with a drug called Clexane - it would prevent blood clots which could happen when sitting in one position for such a long time. Denise took a look at me and obviously my face spoke volumes. She said that wouldn't work because I would be in a heap at the side of the road if I did it, as I am prone to fainting at the sight of a needle. She asked him to show her how to do it instead. He looked a little surprised but did as suggested. I was very relieved to say the least; I just couldn't have done it!

After the demonstration the doctor left and Denise's phone rang. She answered it and it was the surgeon's rooms in Bunbury. They had been given Denise's number by a Doctor but that was the only thing they could understand due to his accent, so they were wondering what the story was. Denise gave them a quick run down and they made an appointment for her a week after we expected to arrive home (it was the first available). Denise would need some medicines for the journey home but as the pharmacist at the hospital didn't work full time, the doctor had advised it would be easier for me to come back later in the day.

Leaving the hospital we went back to the room to start planning our route and where we could stop for the night. It was around 3,000 kms to home so we figured we could do it in three days. Fortunately, there were towns conveniently placed to make the days fairly even, although I expected the last day's drive to be a long one as the traffic could play a part going through Perth. So while I busied myself packing the car, Denise made some reservations in motels along the way. I checked the car over thoroughly and we were all set for an early start the following morning.

Later in the afternoon I returned to the hospital to collect the drugs for the journey home. When I arrived the pharmacist was busy so I waited in line. He was quite a while and, as I waited, the doctor walked past and asked if I needed help. I said I was fine and thanked him for asking. He interrupted me and said, "Stop being so nice, we're not used to it" and smiled and walked on. Eventually my turn came and the pharmacist handed me a huge bag full of drugs for Denise. I gave him my credit card expecting a huge bill to go with them. So I was shocked when he said that everything was free there, and wished me a safe journey home. I returned to the room and we had an early night so we were well-rested for our departure the next day.

The following morning was bright and sunny. I put the rest of our gear in the car and Denise slowly made her way round to the entrance - the long way, avoiding the stairs. I met her at the front of the motel after paying the bill and we set off on our long journey. I had purposely not been in the room when Denise did her injection; I thought it a wise decision not to watch!

The roads in the far north of our state are long, straight and pretty boring, but we made good progress. The car was comfortable but its very nature meant it was not like driving a sedan car and with the all-terrain tyres it wasn't the quietest of vehicles; but it was going to have to work hard for the next three days. The tank held enough fuel for around 550kms so we would have to regularly visit fuel stations; a costly exercise, as some them have little competition so are able to charge just about what they like.

Unfortunately, there is no route south from Fitzroy Crossing, so the day was spent mainly travelling west. Our first stop was South Headland, a distance of just under 1,000kms. The traffic was virtually non-existent so it was a very easy first day and we arrived at our night stop at pretty much the time that

I had predicted. We checked in to the motel and while Denise sorted a few things out in the room I checked the car over. It had performed well and I was pleased with how easy the day had been. We had dinner in the restaurant attached to the motel; it was fairly basic but did the job. Denise then did some work (she was still handling the accounts and payroll for one of her clients whilst away) while I went for a walk. Having spent almost ten hours sitting in the car I felt I needed to have a good stretch of my legs before bed.

The next morning we were up and off early again. This was going to be the biggest day, distance wise, but probably not time wise and at least we were heading due south now. We had a number of stops for fuel and food, not wasting any time though, and made good progress. Our next stop was in the town of Cue; I was sure I'd been here before but couldn't remember the place. Again, the room was basic but clean and it was attached to the Tavern so we had dinner there which was excellent. Once again, Denise went back to the room to do some work. Meanwhile I checked the car over and then went for my walk. It was very quiet and there's not much to see in the town, but I was surprised to see a Ute driving up and down the streets fogging mosquitoes; it all seemed a bit drastic and I kept well out of the way of it but guess it must work. We both slept well and woke refreshed for the last day of our travels.

Once again we were up and away early on what I expected to be the longest day but I thought it would also be good getting back into more familiar territory. The downside of the last leg was that we were encountering more traffic which at times held us up, but we were soon seeing signs for Perth which was encouraging.

Although we had experienced lots of mobile phone reception dead spots all the way home, she luckily had a phone signal when the surgeon's office called. The lady on the phone said that they had just had a cancellation for the following

Monday (three days' time) which she could have if she wanted to see the surgeon earlier than the following Friday. She accepted, as the sooner she saw him then in theory the sooner she would have surgery and the more time she would have to recover before we headed off to the UK. Unfortunately, we hit the city at rush hour; but as we were going around the east side it wasn't too bad and it was a good feeling getting onto the freeway south. There was another unexpected complication and that was the house sitter, Betty. We had called her and explained the problem and told her that instead of coming home at the end of May, staying a couple of weeks then heading off to the UK as planned, we would now be home for about seven weeks. Although we had both really taken to Betty when we interviewed her and knew she was the right person to look after the house and animals, the reality of living with someone we didn't really know for seven weeks was a little daunting. It would seriously dent my ability to be Stephanie at home – something I had grown used to in terms of wearing little but a vest top, bra and either shorts or jeans. But she had nowhere else to go and we needed her for the second and biggest leg of our trip.

We arrived home around six-thirty, very tired and ready for our own bed. Betty had made us a lovely meal to come home to and within a few hours I was sure that she would be fine to live with for seven weeks. She was easy-going and down to earth which suited us both and we are still great friends to this day. So, disappointingly (for our UK friends and us) we never did meet them in Darwin. They did all that had been planned, on their own, which was a phenomenal achievement given they were in an unfamiliar, fully equipped off-road vehicle exploring two National Parks. We would still like to go and experience that part of Australia at some stage.

Chapter 37

Knee surgery, Nannup and off again

Denise and I went to meet the surgeon on the Monday. He was lovely and explained what the problem was (a torn lateral meniscus) and what he could do. He then shocked us by fitting Denise into his operating "List" the very next day, which was excellent news. She would just be a day patient so we were up early the next morning to get to the hospital in Bunbury for 7am. I left her there, went home and waited for the call to say she was okay. The hospital called just after lunch and told me I could collect her at 3pm and I was surprised to see her up and walking - albeit slowly and with a little assistance - but it was encouraging all the same. The operation had been successful and she would be fine for the next part of our trip.

While we were away I had received an offer for the Nannup property and accepted it. It wasn't quite as much as I had hoped, but I decided it was the best thing to do. I had made a profit on it so was happy with that, and it had given me a great deal of enjoyment, especially during 2012 when I was in need of something to occupy my mind. As the settlement date was while we were still in Australia it gave me a chance to empty the house and shed, and say my goodbyes. I was sad in a way because I have a love of the town and hoped that I would someday maybe buy another property there. This came along much sooner than I expected.

Casually looking through the property guide which was in a rack outside the real estate agent's office, I saw a property on the same estate that my original block was on. It was the same size as the one Jayne and I had owned a few years ago, but was about half the price we sold ours for. I was intrigued and showed it to Denise. She suggested we go and have a look at it the following weekend. We could then see what, if anything, had been done at my old block in town and visit my favourite cafe for lunch.

The drive to Nannup is a pretty one at any time of the year, but it's best not done at dusk or dawn as there are lots of kangaroos just waiting to commit suicide on the front of your car and do a whole lot of damage at the same time. We drove round to where the old house was, and there was a caravan behind it. I had a set of spare keys that I wanted to drop off so we stopped at the side of the road and walked onto the block. Once there we met the new owners who were busy trying to find the leach drains as they planned to connect to the deep sewage which ran right past the gate. I introduced myself and gave him the keys; he asked a few questions and we went on our way. As it was lunch time we decided to make the cafe the next place to stop. Lunch was excellent and we were soon on our way to look at the block for sale.

The estate on which the block was located was about four kilometres out of town along the Brockman highway. Since Jayne and I sold the first block, there had been a lot of development, so it looked much more inviting as you drove in. I had a pretty good idea where Cockatoo Drive was and found the block easily. We parked the car on the side of the road and went onto the block for a closer inspection. What we found was a mainly treed block with a few small cleared areas. The remains of the clearing were piled up in big heaps which I thought was pretty strange but I thought maybe the owners had started preparing a building envelope and grown tired of it halfway through. There were some enormous trees on the property and it had an untouched feel to it which appealed to both of us. We decided to follow up with the agent on Monday and get a feel for what the owners would accept for it. We were in a pretty strong position as we both had the funds readily available if we decided to take it further.

I had a conversation with the agent who I knew quite well as he was the one who sold the other property for me. He explained that the couple who owned it just wanted it gone as the prospect of building on it was out of their reach. He advised that the asking price was very close to what they were prepared to accept. We decided to go in ten thousand less and in the end we bought it for five thousand less than the asking price, which we were both very happy about. So my time not being a Nannup property owner was to be very short-lived, although the new block wouldn't settle until after we had left for the UK. It was, however, something exciting to come back to.

We left for the UK in early June 2015. Sharing the house with Betty had been much less hassle than I expected and I had really enjoyed having her as a house mate. We all took our turn in cooking and cleaning and got along really well. Our first stop once we arrived in England was Guildford. Denise had left our Renault car parked at her friend's house where we had stayed the year before. It was the first time I had seen the car and on first sight I was impressed. There were a couple of things which needed sorting out but on the whole I was very happy with our purchase. I had always liked French cars; they have a certain flair and individuality which I enjoy. The other thing was that the engine, which had been around for many years, was well known to me. It was very economical yet had plenty of power to get out of trouble if you needed it. I had taken with me a few basic cleaning things as I didn't know if I could get them while over there. As the car was black it looked so much better once I had given it a good polish.

Before we left Australia we had joined a website called "House Sitters UK" and had our first booking confirmed before we left. Our idea was to find house-sits in places we hadn't visited before and it soon became obvious that it was going to be relatively easy. Before we did any house-sitting we had arranged to meet up with Rachel my district sales manager from Holden who was currently touring Europe. We met in one of my favourite places, Prague. We had booked an Airbnb place, close to the centre of the city, which turned out to be amazing. The first night we were on our own and then met Rachel at the train station the following day. We had a most wonderful time visiting all of the amazing sights in the city. I went there on a business trip with MG Rover back in 1999 and loved it. It was so good to see Rachel; she had been very supportive of me and the dealership before I left. We talked at length about Holden and the predicament they seemed to have got themselves into and the reasons why. As it turned out, she didn't return to work for them as the corporate way of the business clearly didn't sit right with her. There was a culture of just keeping your head down and not making waves, instead of using your initiative and making things work better and I was not surprised that she didn't go back.

Our first house-sit booking was in Huddersfield which, while it is still in Yorkshire, was a place I had never been. The house was on the outskirts of the town in quite a rural setting. There was a dog to look after which could be quite a handful but the house was nice, clean, comfortable and well equipped.

The weather was excellent for the whole six days we were there but it did break the day we left. We caught up with my brother and his partner one day. The friend who I had helped when he first arrived in Australia was visiting the area at the same time so we were able to meet up with them as well.

It was then down to Wales to stay with Denise's mum. Before leaving Australia when we were speaking to her on Skype, I would remind her to make a list of jobs she wanted me to do while we were over; and this week was my time to get on with them. There was painting to be done, a washing line to sort and numerous jobs in the house. All little things, but the sort that just don't get done but bug you every time you come across them; like the airing cupboard door which didn't close properly and drawers with sagging bases. I really enjoyed doing the jobs for her and she was so appreciative, which made all the difference. It was good to see her and enjoy some day trips with her.

Our next house sit was in Northern Ireland. I had been to Southern Ireland a couple of times and so loved the place, but never to the north. We drove over to Holyhead in North Wales to catch the ferry over to Ireland. It departed at three in the morning and arrived in Dublin port at six. The plan was to get over there then find somewhere to park up and get some sleep before driving up to the north.

Chapter 38

Northern and Southern Ireland

By the time the ferry arrived in Dublin I was really tired. I had tried to sleep on the ferry without much luck. It was a glorious morning so the plan was to get out of the city and find somewhere we could park the car and sleep for a while. We weren't due at the house-sit until the following day so needed to find somewhere to stay for the night. Denise located guest house which looked nice and gave them a call. The lady said that she wasn't taking any bookings that day which was disappointing, but luckily the lady called us back a few minutes later and said she could have us after all if we still needed somewhere. We accepted and made our way there. It was a beautiful house; quite rural but perfectly kept. There wasn't a weed in the garden and the lawns were beautifully manicured. Even the grass verges outside the property were well maintained as were most of the verges in the area. We had both commented on how well kept the whole area was; very different from both Wales and England.

The lady greeted us at the door and immediately I could smell she had been baking; a good sign I thought. It was about two in the afternoon and she showed us to our room - which was beautiful - and offered us a cup of tea. We accepted and said we would just get settled in and come down to the lounge. When we got there she brought a huge plate of freshly made scones with homemade jam and cream to accompany the tea; it doesn't get any better than that! We chatted with her for a while then went upstairs to our room for a well-deserved sleep; although I didn't want to sleep too long as I knew I wouldn't sleep during the night.

We booked a table at a local restaurant for dinner, which was excellent; great food, great service and not over the top price wise then decided to have a wander around the town to walk dinner off. It was still light and we were able to walk in a bit of a circle and back to the car. People were very friendly and we saw numerous other people out and about but when we got back to the car we noticed that there were several police officers standing at the junction just down the road. We drove in that direction and were waved out, then noticed there were lots of police cars and officers on foot. Remembering we were in Northern Ireland I was quite unnerved about it. We were advised to pull up and wait. After a couple of minutes I thought I heard music. There was a police car coming slowly up the road with its lights flashing and by this stage we could definitely hear music. Into sight came a marching band and the penny dropped, Northern Ireland is famous for marching bands and sure enough they were excellent. We watched them go by and were then signalled to move on.

We arrived back at the guest house and went inside. The owners were in the kitchen and asked if we would like a cup of tea so we sat with them for some time. They were really interested in our travels - in Australia and the rest of our planned trip. The following morning we were on the road in good time after a lovely breakfast. It doesn't look far on a map compared with the distances we regularly travel in Australia, but in any part of Ireland you don't seem to get very far very fast. The roads are narrow, twisty and regularly occupied by tractors taking up most of the available space; but we gradually made our way north to the town of Ballymoney where our house-sit for eight days was situated. We had told the owners of the house that we would be there by lunchtime but it was looking a little doubtful so Denise gave them a call to say we might be a little late. They were not bothered and said that lunch would be ready whenever we arrived, which sounded encouraging. We eventually found the place, not really in Ballymoney at all; it was about three miles out of the town in a picturesque little village and the people were lovely. Our job for the eight days was to look after their cat, a beautiful old boy with the rather unusual name of Blacks Darling. He was absolutely spoiled to death, fed several times a day on the best food including a serve of prawns each day. There was also a visiting kitten which was a real character and always hungry so he was fed as well.

I thought the house was a strange one for a retired couple to live in - three bedrooms on three floors but it was very comfortable and homely. After lunch we were treated to a tour of the area. It's always good to be shown around by a local and we got the full treatment; they drove us up as far as the Giants Causeway and gave us a full tour of the coastline in between. We were also told about all the sights worth seeing in and around the place and the best way to get to them. We planned to have a day in Belfast and a day in Derry/Londonderry which were both within easy driving distance. We were advised to go to Belfast on the train which was a bit of a novelty as I don't often do trains. But as the traffic in Belfast was heavy and there were several toll roads it was decided that it would be the best option. The main attraction of Belfast to us was the Titanic Experience, a relatively new development at that time in the Titanic Quarter of Docklands (where the Titanic was built) and it didn't disappoint; apart from the fact that it must have been school holidays as it was packed.

We decided to go elsewhere for our lunch; there was a cafe across the square called The Dock which seemed to be the only other place to eat on the development. It looked a bit strange as we went inside but we were hungry so gave it a go. It was a sort of cafeteria and there wasn't much to choose from. But the best bit was when we got to the till and asked how much we owed, and the girl replied "Just pay what you feel represents the value for what you have chosen! It's an honesty box café". Unusual to say the least, but she explained that all the food was prepared by unemployed people, so whatever one paid was for a good cause really.

We spent the rest of the day looking at various other attractions in the city then back home on the train. The cat was still in the same place we left him; opening one eye when we went in and shortly after making it clear he was hungry and wanted his prawns; one very spoiled cat.

The following day we decided to head west to Derry. The only thing I knew about the place was what I had seen on the television during The Troubles in the seventies and eighties. It is situated right on the border of Northern and Southern Ireland. The drive there was very picturesque, as most of the driving is in Ireland, and we were struck by the pride which was obviously taken in how well the place is kept. This continued when we arrived in Derry; the town was spotlessly clean. Derry is a walled city and the walls themselves have been made into a tourist attraction with lots of plaques telling various stories about things that have happened there; and different displays and attractions along the way. Eventually we got to the area which overlooks the Bogside with its row of houses adorned with murals showing scenes from the troubled times; it was very sobering to see them and remember the history of the place. Of all the places we visited while in Ireland, Derry was one of my favourites.

When our house-sit finished we headed south to spend some time in Southern Ireland in the town of Dungarvan where we had booked an Airbnb property for the week. From Dungarvan, there are so many places to visit and we crammed in as many as we could. I love Ireland; the people are very friendly and the pace of life seems so much slower than England. The roads can be frustrating as there is no getting anywhere quickly. But there are lots of examples of grants that have been given by the European Economic Community for all sorts of projects, from new roads to tourist attractions; grants that they have put to such very good use. All too soon our time on the Emerald Isle was over and we were heading back to England to stay with my brother Greg for a week and then back down to Wales to see Denise's mum again.

Chapter 39

Censored health records

Before we left Australia, my GP, suggested that while I was in the UK it might be helpful if I was to obtain my health records from the National Health Service (NHS). I think at the time she thought that they may give some sort of clue as to what was causing my oestrogen problem, but didn't say it in so many words. I still had my National Insurance number so went armed with it, expecting just to present it at the GP Practice I attended when I lived there, along with some identifying documents. They would then be able to provide me with a computer printout of all my records. I was sadly wrong! Firstly the Practice was no longer there; it had moved to bigger premises which were reasonably easy to find. Secondly, we were told it wasn't as easy as pushing a button and getting my records. I would first have to have an interview at the main records department to ascertain why I wanted them.

We made an appointment for the interview and travelled to the office in Hull. On arrival we spoke to the receptionist who confirmed we had an appointment and asked us to wait in the designated area for the person conducting the interview.

A lady eventually came to us and took us into an office. She started by confirming who I was and who Denise was, then asked why I wanted my records. I explained about my hormone issues and reassured her I wasn't intending suing anyone for anything that had happened to me while I was in the UK. She explained that they were obliged to give me any records created after the enactment of the 2000 Freedom of Information Act (FOI), but as for records created before the FOI act became law, it was at the discretion of the NHS as to which ones I could have. I understand that the world is a different place now from when I was born and that the NHS is scared that any records they give you could be used in litigation but I wasn't expecting to have to negotiate getting access to my own information. I was probably not very understanding to say the least, but in the end she agreed to submit the application for my records. I paid the 50 Pounds required and requested that the documents be sent to me care of my brother's address. To say I felt that there was something suspicious was an understatement. We were both unhappy in the way the whole thing was handled, but felt at least that we had made progress and that my records, hopefully in full, would be sent to me in due course.

We left Yorkshire and headed down to Wales where we were staying with Doreen for a couple of days before driving east with her, to stay in Guildford for a week, looking after Denise's friend's house. The weather was beautiful and it was a perfect time for me to get into their pool - it was still such a novelty for me to be able to swim in a pool - so I really enjoyed the time we had there. Then it was back to Wales to drop Doreen off, and up to Scotland for a house-sit 25 miles south of Glasgow but via Yorkshire, as my records had arrived at my brother's house. They were in a plastic envelope all sealed up and were just photocopies of mostly hand-written notes. It wasn't what I expected at all. I just thought in this day and age everything would be kept as an electronic record; but I guess the time it would have taken to put all of them into electronic form would be massive, so they were just as the doctor had written them all those years ago.

We sat down at the table with a cup of coffee to read what had been sent. They seemed very haphazard in how they had been prepared. Many of them were out of order and several of the sheets looked as though they had been folded over in particular places to hide what was underneath. The more we looked the more it seemed that they had only given me a certain amount of the information and kept some hidden. What mainly attracted my attention was that the records from the first ten weeks of my life were completely missing. I knew from conversations with my parents that I had spent most of the first three months in hospital so was rather confused as to why those records were omitted. The earliest record provided was written when I was a little over ten weeks old.

This played on my mind for the next few days. We had been busy driving up to Scotland, meeting the owners of our next house-sit who were a lovely couple. They were heading down to Essex to spend some time with one of their parents. The house was very comfortable and our job was to look after a dog and a kitten, both of which were a little odd. The dog had three legs but managed okay and we had lots of walks; the kitten was only about three months old and was completely wild one minute then very loving the next. It was a cross between a Siamese and a Ragdoll and was gorgeous to look at, but definitely had its moments when it was tearing around the house, up and down the stairs and into everything possible. We were both pleased when it was tired as it then became very placid and cuddly.

After a few days there I decided to call the lady whose name was on the covering letter that came with the health records to enquire as to how I could access the rest of my records. My first attempt was cut short as she was not working that day but

I was told the best time to call the next day. I tried the following day but she was doing an interview so I left my number in the hopes she would call me back. She didn't, so I tried again later and finally got through to her. I explained my problem and asked if it was possible to see the rest of my records only to be told in no uncertain terms "You have been given what the department considered to be in the patients best interests and if you wish to obtain the rest of your records you will need to get a court order; a process which is currently taking around two years". As you can imagine, I was a little taken aback at her attitude and asked the reason why. She just repeated what she had told us in the interview that before The Freedom of Information Act came into force it was the at the discretion of the NHS as to what records were given out. She also said that many hand-written notes were not kept for any length of time so my records could have been lost anyway.

I was very unsettled about the way the whole thing had been handled but didn't really know what to do about it. We were on a busy schedule as we were now in the latter stages of our time in the UK before heading off to Canada to stay with my estranged wife Jayne and her partner Bill.

Chapter 40

Last few weeks in the UK

We really enjoyed our stay in Scotland. We had a day in Glasgow visiting some of the many tourist attractions and a day in New Lanark visiting the beautifully restored Woollen Mill. It had been fully renovated and offered tours around its working textile machine rooms and the workers cottages, some of which have been lovingly recreated as they would have been in the late 1800s when the Mill was fully operational.

Our next house-sit was on the south coast of England in the village Northiam just outside the town of Rye in East Sussex. I had not seen much of the south coast, even though I lived in the UK for the first 45 years of my life, so I was looking forward to visiting lots of new places. The house was full of quirky character; it was built in the mid-1600s and had lots of low ceilings and small doorways. The owners had set up a guest room for us but after the first night we had to move into the main bedroom as I got up in the night to go to the bathroom and felt very disoriented as the floor had a huge slope on it. In fact, it sloped so much that the bed had been chocked up at one side to make it level. The owners had left all sorts of things for us; fresh fruit, lots of food and snacks in the fridge, a big box of chocolates and a lovely children's book which the lady of the house had written. The occupant of the house was a cat called Victoria; she was very spoiled but lovely and very friendly. She spent most of her day sleeping in the dressing room off the main bedroom and was no trouble at all.

Rye is an historic town, being one of the Confederation of Cinque Ports which are along the coast of Sussex and Kent. There were lots of attractions in the area including Hastings, although I didn't know until then that the battle of Hastings wasn't actually fought at Hastings; the battle was actually fought a few miles up the coast which is now the site of another small town, aptly named Battle. We were able to walk around the actual field where the Battle of Hastings took place and listen to an audio recording which told us what happened; where and how William, Duke of Normandy, won the day over King Harold after being in a losing position for most of the time.

The other highlight of our stay in East Sussex was a visit to Bodiam Castle which was built in the 14th Century. It is one of very few castles I have visited which are almost intact. Standing inside a deep moat it is very imposing. We spent an enjoyable day looking around it admiring all the various features which had been restored.

As our time in the UK was coming to an end we decided to have a few days up in Yorkshire to stay with an old schoolfriend near the town of Malton. We could then say our goodbyes to family and friends of mine then a few days down in Wales so that Denise could do the same. We also took Denise's mum across to the farthest point of west Wales to a lovely town called St Davids. It is one of very few cathedral towns and is very quaint. The lady we went to see in St Davids used to live in the same street as Doreen in Bridgend and they had kept in touch ever since.

The missing medical records weighed heavily on my mind. I was imagining all sorts of things, but very little made sense. I had decided not to pursue it in court, as the lady had said it could take up to two years to get them and I didn't really have the urge to set the process in motion if I wasn't going to be there. I was hoping that my GP might be able to at least explain why they could be missing and give me some relief from my thoughts and fears. But as we were heading to Canada next for two weeks it wouldn't be for some time, and I didn't want it to ruin the rest of our trip so kept my worries to myself; for the time being at least.

Our last stop was in Guildford. It's only a short drive to the airport from there and Denise's friends kindly allowed us to leave our car at their property (and kindly dropped us off at the airport). We were going to be back in the UK the following May as my goddaughter was getting married and we had been invited and planned to be there. Staying in Guildford gave us a bit of a breather in the beautiful Surrey countryside before boarding a plane to Canada. I think we were both ready to return home if truth be known, but we had arranged this part of the trip a long time ago. I was very much looking forward to seeing Canada as I hadn't been there before, but knew Denise wasn't looking forward to spending two weeks in the company of Jayne. We had originally planned to go to Hong Kong after the Canada leg of the holiday - to visit Denise's ex-husband and to attend his wedding. I know it seems strange, but we were still in regular contact with all our collective ex-partners and and hoped it would stay that way for a very long time. It's sad when marriages break down and there is fighting and animosity. Thankfully, we both seem to have avoided that, even though things were not the happiest when the breakups happened. Anyway, that stop-over didn't end up happening as I think Denise thought it might be a little strange for all concerned if she were there - despite us having an invitation and both her adult children being there and despite having bought a lovely outfit in the UK. So we were heading straight home after Canada. We would not actually be home for long as we had also made plans to go to Canberra and Melbourne before our holiday properly ended.

The day came when we were to leave the UK. I cleaned the car inside and out and parked it in the place where we found it four months earlier. We did mention to our friends that we were happy for them to use it if needed; it was still licensed and insured and would benefit from a drive every so often.

We were taken to the airport and said our goodbyes. We had five suitcases between us which I thought might be a problem, but thankfully it wasn't. I hadn't flown with Cathay Pacific before but had heard good reports so was looking forward to the flight. Hopefully there would be some good films to watch and the food would be acceptable. Whichever way you look at it, twelve hours is a long time to sit in a chair with very little personal space around you, but I was looking forward to experiencing Canada, so it was a necessary evil, so to speak.

Chapter 41

Canada, Canberra, Melbourne then home

By the time we arrived in Vancouver we were both pretty well over travelling, but we still had to spend two days in a car before we got to the town of Creston where Jayne and Bill lived. They had moved there only a few months earlier so Bill could be nearer his sister, who also lived there. Creston is a very picturesque little town situated at the foot of the Rocky Mountains - but it is nine hours' drive from Vancouver. We would have been happy doing the whole nine hours in one go but Jayne had booked a motel about half-way there. I think she had forgotten how big the distances in Australia are and that we were well used to long journeys; especially after driving the three thousand kilometres home from Fitzroy Crossing when Denise damaged her knee. Anyway, it made it a more relaxed journey and there was a lot to see along the way, so we were kept amused.

When we arrived at Creston, Jayne had put a printed banner on the deck saying "Welcome to Canada Robin and Denise". I thought it a little strange going to such lengths, but we very much appreciated it and they both did much to make us feel very welcome. After a couple of days recovering from the jet-lag, we went on a road trip up to Banff and Jasper, stopping at a couple of other places on the way. As I am not a good passenger, I was given the job of driving which, even though it was on the wrong side of the road, I found very enjoyable. Bill's car was a V8 Toyota SUV which drove very nicely although it was a bit thirsty on the fuel. The further north we got, the colder it became and it wasn't long before we were seeing snow on the mountains.

We really enjoyed Banff; the hotel was good; not too expensive, and had excellent beds. On the other hand, we both thought Jasper was pretty ordinary. We had booked a chalet in one of the holiday complexes which was looking tired but was very expensive. Also as it was quite a way from the town the in-house restaurant was the only real option for dinner. Then there was the thing about tipping; I guess it's something you get used to, but I am quite uncomfortable with the whole concept. I much prefer to pay a reasonable amount for whatever service I want and that's it - instead of paying at the till and then tipping an expected amount on top of that.

Anyway, we were away for just over a week and then had only a couple of days before we had to head back to Vancouver for our return flight to Australia. Things had been very tense at times between Denise and me, probably due to the fact that we were with Jayne. We were both so looking forward to getting on the plane and heading back home. It had also grown pretty cold in Creston and when we arrived in Australia it would be late spring so the weather would be heating up nicely. Unfortunately when we presented ourselves at the airport check-in desk, we discovered that one of our cases was over-weight; even though we were under for the overall weight, we had to take some things out of the suitcase and put them in a cardboard box which the lady at the desk supplied (along with sticky tape and a Marker pen). She was really nice about it, but to be honest I didn't think I would ever see those things again. The box not only made it back to Australia at the same time as we did, it was still in one piece!

We were both very pleased to be home at last. If it hadn't been for the fact that we were going to see one of my favourite bands of all time (10cc) in Canberra, I could quite easily have not bothered getting back on an aeroplane a few days later. However I really wanted to see them and then go on to Melbourne to stay with Rachel for a couple of days before attending an Isagenix conference (which I was also in two minds about, but felt it could help get our Isagenix business up and running) so we went.

I really enjoyed Canberra. We visited the Anzac memorial museum which was excellent, and of course the 10cc concert was amazing. Three of the band members were the same as when I saw them in 1978 in Bridlington – thirty-seven years on and the music was still wonderful. There was, however, something that had bothered me since arriving there. On the flight I had watched a documentary, made by Louis Theroux, called "A question of gender". Firstly, I don't know why I watched it as I had a feeling it might unsettle me, and secondly, I don't really know why it bothered me quite so much. I've watched it again since and, although it still affects me, it doesn't make me feel as upset as that first time. I asked Denise to watch it with me while in the hotel room and we had a long talk afterwards as to how and why it affected me; but it has stuck with me ever since.

Then during the conference in Melbourne there was a story being told by the main speaker which also really affected me. It was based around the fact that he had lost touch with his brother over a trivial matter. Then something had happened to him which was very unexpected and thankfully they were able to make things up. I had lost touch with Nigel and then he died before we were able make things right, so I became very upset and walked out of the conference. It was a beautiful day so I just went for a stroll to try and clear my head.

Eventually, Denise tracked me down and we arranged to meet at a nearby McDonalds so we could talk it through. It's obvious now, looking back, that my mental state was fragile at this time, but I hadn't realised quite how down I was. I know that the missing medical records were having an effect on me as well. They were always in the back of my mind, taking up a certain amount of my thoughts, day in and day out; I just couldn't help but wonder what they weren't telling me.

When we finally arrived home again in early November 2015, we both breathed a huge sigh of relief. I needed to get my business back on track and start working again. Denise wanted to expand her bookkeeping business and we both were eager to get things moving on our newly bought block of land in Nannup. We had talked quite a lot about what we wanted to build on it (a steel/Colorbond kit home) and had a reasonable idea of how it was going to work; but there was lots of paperwork to organise before we obtained permission to build and as I planned to construct most of the thing myself, I had to get my Owner-Builder's licence.

I also needed to make some decisions about what I was going to do about the missing medical records. I decided the first step would be to make an appointment to see my GP and show her what records I had managed to get, and to talk about the ones that were missing. When she initially asked me to get the records, I wasn't really sure what she hoped to find but now it was more a case of somehow figuring out what was missing and why. My first appointment with her was more a case of catching up on how the holiday had gone and how I had been whilst away. She ordered a suite of blood tests and asked if she could keep the records to look through when not under a time constraint. I was happy to do that as I had read them so many times that I almost knew them off by heart. We agreed to meet again the following week by which time she would have my blood test results back and could see how my thyroid was going and check on the hormone situation.

The week quickly passed, and I was there again. She talked about my blood test results first. My thyroid seemed to be going along okay but my hormones were somewhat outside the correct zone. We talked for some time about the NHS health records from the UK and what might be missing and why. I had always been very well looked after by everyone at the Practice and frequently seemed to be the one who was in with the doctor for longer than scheduled, but this time I seemed to be in for ever. We talked and talked about the records and eventually came to the question of what were we going to do about it. She paused for a few seconds, then said she would like me to see a specialist GP in Perth. She didn't go into detail, just wrote his name and telephone number on a piece of paper and presented it to me.

Chapter 42

The bombshell

I had things to do after seeing the doctor, so didn't get around to making an appointment with the specialist until the following day. I'm always mindful of the fact that medical practices are busy places and try to avoid calling first thing in the morning when they could be busy with people needing immediate appointments; especially when mine wasn't that urgent. I was surprised, however, at the telephone manner of the girl who answered my call. I gave my name and asked if it was possible to make an appointment to see the specialist. Without any introduction she asked, "Is it for an STD check?" I was very taken aback and after a moment said "Well, no". She then said, "So you've got issues then?" She then went on to explain the reason for the question and tell me that an STD check was a short appointment whereas "Issues" obviously took longer. I asked how long I got for "Issues" and thought it might make her laugh, but she just said "30 minutes"; so I decided she wasn't someone with much of a sense of humour. I booked an appointment but after a few minutes thinking about how weird the call had been, I started to think that I had a huge amount to explain in 30 minutes and it probably wouldn't be long enough. So I plucked up my courage and phoned her back.

It was the same girl so I didn't have much to explain, only that I didn't think that 30 minutes was going to be long enough to go through the last 40 years of my life. Her response was that he didn't do appointments any longer than that, and if it wasn't enough then I would have to come back. I thought of pleading the case that I lived 250 kilometres away but decided I would be wasting my time and said "Okay".

The appointment was for the following week which was quite close to Christmas, so I thought Denise and I could do some last-minute Christmas shopping while in Perth. I had deliberately made the appointment for late morning, so the rush-hour traffic had eased and we were there in good time and went for a coffee first. I was quite nervous as I didn't seem to have the same good fortune with male doctors and specialists that I had enjoyed with females. While this may sound naïve, I didn't know what field he actually specialised in either. I had not thought to ask my GP or check on the Internet. In the surgery the same girl with whom I had made the appointment checked us in and we took a seat. After about twenty minutes a man came out of an office and called my name. He looked really familiar, like someone famous, and after a couple of minutes I realised who he reminded me of. He looked just like Hugh Laurie in his role as "Doctor House"; how fitting, I thought.

He asked me to sit at his desk and told me he had read the referral that my GP had sent. I then interrupted him and told him I had written a sort of "story so far" letter and gave it to him. He stopped talking and read it, nodding occasionally then looked at me and asked what I thought was a very strange question. He asked, "Do you always present as male?" and I answered, "Always male in public". He then asked if he could examine me. I asked, "Just the top half?" He said, "No" and asked me to fully undress and lie on the bed. I did as he asked and waited for him to come over from his desk; I was petrified. He came over and asked if he could touch me. I agreed and he pressed here and there, had a good look at my genitals and then told me to get dressed. It had all taken only a few seconds but had felt longer. I put my clothes back on and returned to his desk. He turned his computer monitor to face me and asked if the scars on the photos looked familiar. On his screen were about thirty photos of penises all with the same scars on them in various stages of healing. I said "Yes, I have scars similar to those".

What he said next will stay with me for the rest of my life. He said, "The problem with you being born intersex is that fifty plus years later there is no way I can tell you accurately to what degree of intersex you were born?" I paused then asked him to run it by me again. He started to say it again then stopped and said, "My god, you didn't know!" He apologised for his bluntness and asked me if I understood what intersex means and how it happens. I said I had heard of it but didn't really know much about it. He picked up his phone and spoke to the receptionist, requesting that she delay his next patient as he was going to be some time with me. I was absolutely shell-shocked; I could hardly speak and was in tears. He went on to explain how intersex babies happen and what had been done with me. He estimated that I had probably been born 60/40 boy girl and that was why they had "normalised me" when I was born and why the records are missing as there is huge controversy over whether or not it should be done when the child is born, or later, or at all. He then went on to talk about my hormone irregularities. His view was that no amount of scans would have identified where the problem was, as, in his opinion, the oestrogen was being controlled by my brain and was closely related to the amount of stress I was under. He asked me about my job and whether there had been any patterns in comparing my oestrogen level with my stress level. I explained about my brother's death and my marriage break up, both of which he said could have caused a spike in my hormone levels.

He asked how I had got on with the testosterone supplement given to me by one of the endocrinologists I had seen. I told him I didn't enjoy being on it as it hadn't done anything for my personality and made me very irritable. He said he wasn't surprised and asked me if it bothered me if I didn't have the right level of testosterone in terms of my energy levels. I explained that I had recently had the thyroid problem which had caused all sorts of issues but mainly too much energy rather than too little. He also suggested that I see the endocrinologist again now that the picture was a little clearer so that they could try to keep the oestrogen level under control. He said he would write to the lady I first saw in 2012 and fill her in with the details.

We spoke at length about me being taken to see the specialists when I first developed gynecomastia. The memory was, and is, still very clear in my mind so it wasn't difficult to tell him about it. After I had finished relating the story he asked me if I would like to know what the specialist would have said to my father on that day. I asked him how he could possibly know what was discussed. He told me that the specialist would have been sent copies of my records and would have known about my intersex beginnings, so would have asked my father why he had brought his child to see him when he knew the reason for the gynecomastia and that he should explain it to me as soon as possible. He concluded, "Obviously it never was discussed and that is why you are here today". He said he wanted to see me again in one month and I thanked him sincerely for the considerable time he had spent with me. He said he was sorry to be the bearer of bad news, if indeed I looked upon it as such. We shook hands and I left.

I walked out of his office not really knowing how to feel. I don't think it had fully sunk in and I was in quite a daze. I stood at the waiting room door and Denise got up and said, "Wow, you've been a long time. Are you okay?" I asked if we could talk about it over lunch and that I just needed to get some fresh air. I paid the considerable bill and we left. Denise said she knew a good place to eat so I just agreed, as my mind was still somewhere else. I can't actually remember much more about that day. I don't remember driving home, which I should have done as it was our first real drive in our new Hyundai Santa Fe which we had picked up only a couple of weeks earlier. My head was spinning; I just couldn't figure out why my parents would have let me go through all the abuse and bullying when I was at school without telling me what they knew. I don't know how well I would have dealt with it back then, but there were many times after that when they could have shared it with me and shed some light on my misery and confusion. It didn't make any sense at all. It didn't then, and it doesn't now.

Chapter Summary - Part III

Finding Stephanie - 2015 onwards

Chapter 43

A wilderness

I have no recollection of Christmas 2015, apart from the fact that I spent most of the week before, and two weeks after, with either a paint brush or roller in my hand. I had been employed to paint the house of one of my best friends while he was away for Christmas. It was a good thing in terms of taking my mind off what the specialist had told me as it would be a tough job to complete before he arrived home in mid-January. It was my first big painting job since our trip and only my second since starting my own business. It felt good to be doing it and I started to consider that this would most likely become my main source of income in the future. I find painting very therapeutic and the job suits my OCD nature; the problem is that, wherever I go, I find myself inspecting the paint job and thinking I would have done a better and neater job.

I did have one amusing incident during that time though. My credit card was due to expire and I hadn't received my new one so I called the company to ask why. It was a call centre in some far away land that I believed to be the Philippines; the man I spoke to was very helpful and apologetic and assured me he would send another one out promptly. I asked him how long it would take and he replied I should have it in five working days. I must say I wasn't optimistic, but thanked him for his help and ended the call. Ten days later I still hadn't received it, so I called again. By this time my card was just about to expire and, although I have another credit card, the deal is not as good with that; so it was now getting urgent. This time it was a lady who answered the call and again she was very helpful and apologetic and offered to send one out "express post" to me. I thanked her but said having had two sent already which have gone missing I thought we should be finding out where they had gone. She asked me if I would like to escalate the call to her supervisor. I thought for a couple of seconds then said I would. After a couple of minutes a man came on the 'phone and introduced himself. He went over what had happened and I said to him that I was concerned that they had sent me two cards which I hadn't received. He agreed, then suddenly asked if he could call me back in five minutes. I thought "I've heard that one before" and told him that he could, but not to be any longer than five minutes. He assured me that he wouldn't be any longer and that he thought he had seen the where the problem was. I said I would be waiting and ended the call. A couple of minutes later he called me back and explained what the problem had been. Before the second card could be sent out the first one had to be cancelled which hadn't happened, hence the second one was never sent out. I mentioned that the lady I had spoken to earlier that day had offered to send a third one out which would have probably had the same result. He agreed and assured me that one would be sent out that day after he had cancelled the first one. He checked the address was right and said to me "That just leaves one more thing to sort out". I asked him what it was, to which he replied "What would you like me to do with the two people who have let you down with this issue?". I was a little confused so he said, and I quote "We can no longer take them out the back and shoot them". He sounded deadly serious; I was shocked. I said I wouldn't want that so he asked if I would be happy if he organised some further training for them before they came back to taking calls in the centre. I said that sounded fine and he wished me a good day. It just goes to show how humour can diffuse an otherwise difficult situation.

As we had been absent from our home for much of 2015 and not really met many of the neighbours, we decided it would be a good idea to hold a street Christmas party at our place. The house really lends itself to events like this, as we had found with my citizenship party back in 2014. We designed an invitation and put one in each of our neighbours' letter boxes. We asked everyone to bring a "plate" (of food) and whatever they wanted to drink and set the alfresco area up to accommodate the thirty or so people who had indicated they would like to join us. The event went really well; we got to know lots of the neighbours and talked late into the night. One real high point was getting to talk to Andrew and Linda, the couple who lived (and still do live) two doors away from us. I had met Andrew some years previously through work but had not met Linda, apart from just to say "hello" if we passed in the street. That evening's get-together led to a lovely relationship with both them and their family.

The specialist in Perth said he wanted to see me again after a month so, as soon as I had finished painting the house we went up to Perth again. He requested that I have some blood tests done before the appointment so he could see exactly where my hormone levels were and would be able to discuss the results when he saw me. At the appointment he asked me how I was, and how I was coping with what he had told me previously. I replied that I had been very busy but in reality I didn't feel it had fully sunk in. We then talked for some time about my hormone levels which were almost off the scale. My oestrogen level was nearly 3000 ppm which is almost ten times that of a female, which he said was most likely due to the stress of what he had told me a month earlier. He asked when I was seeing the endocrinologist and told me to keep him informed as to progress.

Seeing the specialist again brought the intersex conversation back to the forefront of my thoughts and the more I thought about it the more it upset me. Interestingly, the specialist also gave me some literature about the various recognised gender classifications. I asked him where he thought I fitted; he considered for a moment and then said "somewhere in the middle". I asked him why he thought that, to which he replied "Well, you identify as male but there is much about you which is female, like having no Adam's apple, the gynecomastia, the fact that your voice is quite ambiguous and above all the fact that you cross dress, even if it is only in private; so I guess you could say you are "gender neutral'".

This was a whole new thing to me; I didn't know there was such a thing as gender-neutral, but I must say I liked the idea of it and it seemed to fit exactly where I was at. It also made me feel as though I wasn't alone; I wasn't a one-off type of person and there were probably lots of people in my situation. I made it my business to find out as much about the whole intersex and gender-neutral thing as possible. I joined forums, looked at lots of internet sites and read as much as I could find about the two conditions.

My appointment with the endocrinologist was interesting. Firstly, it was good to see the lady again; I liked the way she got things done and didn't let anything get in her way. As I half expected, she asked me to take off my shirt so she could check my breasts. She said she thought they had grown since she last saw them to which I agreed but she also remarked that I was a little heavier than before which could account for it. She asked me to have a number of tests, one of which was an ultrasound of my breasts. I went to the hospital in Busselton to book it and asked if it was possible to have a female sonographer to do it for me; the girl at the reception said she couldn't guarantee it but she would try. The appointment was a few days later, but when I arrived I was told that there was only a male sonographer on duty that day. I thought about leaving it for another day but then decided to let it go and hopefully the man would be sensitive with me. I knew as soon as the man called me in that it had been a bad decision. He never once looked at me and hardly spoke while he did it; he didn't spend half as much time or take anywhere near enough care for my liking and I was pleased when it was over.

As soon as I arrived home I told Denise how unhappy I was with the Ultrasound and made an appointment to see my GP to talk about it. It just so happened that, before I saw the GP, Denise had to have an ultrasound done on her leg; she had gone to a place in town rather than the hospital and had a lovely lady sonographer. So when I saw the GP, I asked for another referral and booked an appointment with that same lady. I asked if it was okay if Denise came in with me, which the sonographer was happy to accommodate. What a difference; she was kind, took her time and made conversation with us both while doing it. She explained everything on the screen and told us there wasn't anything wrong just swollen glands and severe gynecomastia.

In one respect that was a good thing, but in another it meant that there would be no progress as nothing was found to be amiss. I didn't really know what I had hoped for but in my head I could see this going on for a long time and me getting nowhere. In my head I was becoming more and more confused, and more depressed about where my life was heading. I had been in this state before; it's like a downward spiral that you just can't seem to pull yourself out of. More and more things happen to bring you down and unfortunately, I could see myself ending up in the same dark place as I found myself in December 2012 when all I could think about was ending my life. The other sad thing was that I found myself arguing with Denise regularly and generally being very short tempered. The strange thing is that I had not usually been irritable with people, only irritable with things. For instance, if I couldn't get something to work as it should I would end up breaking it and sit there crying. It's not a healthy state to be in and as we now owned three acres of woodland I found myself going there to be on my own to try and think things through. We had purchased a very cheap caravan so that we had somewhere to sit down and make a cup of tea while we were on the block; so at least we had somewhere out of the sun.

The previous owners of the block had cleared trees from several small areas for some reason but left all the debris in big piles, which we decided to dismantle. I cut up what would make good firewood and we took the rest to the Waste Disposal Facility. I have always been very adept with a chainsaw; I guess it comes into the same category as the gas axe which I became great friends with when I was in college back in 1982. They can both cause a great deal of damage in a very short time and I enjoyed the destructive nature of it; we also needed firewood, so it helped with that as well. Overall, I could feel my mental state deteriorating as time went on and I know I became very difficult to live with.

Chapter 44

More drugs, more tests and a wedding

As 2016 progressed, we gradually cleared most of the piles of debris from the block and started to think about how we were going to develop it. I liked the idea of building a kit home and originally thought of just something small which we could use as a weekender to get away from it all. I also saw it as a place where I could go and be myself; it was private enough that I could probably get away with wearing just about anything I wanted. While Denise was very understanding about what I wore at home, she wasn't comfortable with me wearing women's clothes in public.

After some serious thought we decided that we should probably make it a bigger place so we could live there full-time if we loved it. We also needed a shed for storage whilst we were doing the build; so that needed to be factored into the plans as well. We decided to erect the shed first and put a shower and toilet in it so we could stay there while we built the main house. We thought it would be good "practice" for the main house-build event. When we started to look into the rules and regulations involved in owner-building we were soon aware that there is more to it than just ordering the house and getting on with it. There were things to take into consideration - like the septic tank and the water tank - as there is no mains water on the block. Thankfully, Denise is excellent at getting things like this sorted but we soon realised that getting building permission was not as straightforward as we first thought especially as the block is in a bushfire prone area. There comes a time when it's best to get advice even when you know that advice is going to cost money. Fortunately, we had a couple of really good breaks in finding people who we could trust to do the plumbing and septic tank systems for us and an excellent electrician. But best of all, we discovered a local man who brought all the elements of the build together, advised who to approach for the different statutory elements (Bushfire rating, Energy efficiency), and most importantly of all "signed off" on the planning application (so that the local Shire Planning Department "rubber stamps" it through their system). His charges weren't excessive either, so he was an excellent find.

I spent a great deal of time at the block; making it as tidy as possible and removing the remaining debris. It was time I would spend both thinking about how my parents could possibly have omitted to tell me about my beginnings and how they must have found some justification in doing so; a fact which I found very depressing. It also gave me time to dream about the person I desperately wanted to be. Sadly, the depression side of it more often than not got the better of me and I would find myself thinking about how I wouldn't ever be that person and therefore what was the point in living. Some years ago, when Denise was emotionally very low (she had separated from her husband and had been diagnosed with bi-lateral breast cancer), she saw a counsellor and suggested I go along to see her. She had certainly helped Denise and thankfully, after surgery and radiology, Denise had come through her difficult times. I thought that seeing this lady couldn't do any harm, so I went. She was a lovely lady who certainly tried to make me see things in a different way but sadly I don't think I was ready to be helped. I had several appointments with her and am sure I did get some benefit from them, but deep down I was well and truly on the downward spiral, albeit fairly slowly.

In May 2016 we had been invited to my goddaughter's wedding in England. We had always planned to go back at some stage during the year to see Denise's mum, so this was the perfect opportunity. The wedding was a lovely event split into three parts. The first was the actual ceremony held in a tiny village church which only held about 50 people. The second was the main reception held at York racecourse and the third being the night "do" which was also in the same place. All three were very enjoyable and I caught up with lots of people I hadn't seen for years. We stayed at a hotel within walking distance of the venue so neither of us needed to drive and, as much as I'm not a big drinker, and never have been, it's better to be on the safe side. As usual, we spent time with as many friends and relatives as we could which made for a very hectic trip but I loved seeing them. Even though my life is in Australia, I still missed lots of my friends, many of whom go back to my school days.

Going back to the UK was good for me; it took my mind off my parents and how I believed they had done the wrong thing by me. I decided not to tell anyone about my beginnings at this stage; I would only end up being upset and wasn't strong enough to deal with that. It also gave me a break from the seemingly endless stream of visits to either the doctor or specialist or endocrinologist and the ever-lengthening list of drugs I was being asked to try in order to normalise my hormones. In fact, when I look back on it now, there was absolutely no wonder my oestrogen levels were all over the place as all of these things I found stressful and as my specialist in Perth told me, it was stress that he thought caused most of the hormonal problems in the first place.

All too soon we were back on the 'plane to Australia. Although we were both excited about getting on with developing the block, I was concerned about the ongoing saga of my hormones and mental state. Not long after we arrived home I hit a real low. I couldn't see a way forward at all and my thoughts returned to contemplating how I could end my life and end the torment which I was going through. I saw the counsellor again but didn't gain any comfort so decided I wouldn't go again. Deep down I just couldn't ever see how I was going to lift myself back into a happy frame of mind. I knew that I really wanted to be Stephanie but also knew I didn't have the courage to do anything about it.

My relationship with Denise was deteriorating and I know I was very difficult to live with. Denise asked me numerous times if I wanted to transition but I gave her the same negative answer every time. I knew I didn't have the courage and told her that. I said there was no way I could ever "pass" as a female in public and where would it leave us? Denise is definitely heterosexual and although we weren't getting on very well, I couldn't bear the thought of not being with her.

My next appointment with the endocrinologist offered a glimmer of hope. She asked me if I would be happy for my case to be presented at the Australian Endocrinologist convention which was being held on the Gold Coast at the beginning of August 2016. She mentioned that there would be attendees from around the world there. I felt sure that, if that were so, then surely someone would have come across my problems at some time and be able to offer an answer; so I agreed. She also wanted me to try a different type of drug to control my oestrogen. As much as I was totally over taking different drugs in order to get my levels right, and didn't really want to try it, I felt that I probably owed it to her for all the work she had put into me and she was offering to present my case in August, so I gave my consent. She asked if I was also willing to see a Registrar who would be jointly presenting my case; but it would mean another trip to Perth in the near future. I agreed to do that and she said she would give her my contact details and get her to call me. She gave me the script for the drug called Anastrozole which is a post breast cancer drug used in the treatment of women who have had an oestrogen fed cancer. It also carried lots of side effects which didn't sound very pleasant but I agreed to take it for a short time to see if it had any positive effects on my oestrogen level.

My first problem with it came when I presented the prescription at the pharmacy. I gave the assistant the script and said I would wait for it. A few minutes later the pharmacist appeared at the counter and said to me "Are you collecting a script for Robin?" and he attempted to pronounce my surname but failed dismally. I replied "I am Robin". He looked at me in disbelief and repeated what he had said, and so did I. He looked confused and by this time my patience was running low so I took out my wallet and showed him my driving licence. He just didn't comprehend that a man was being prescribed the drug so in the end he thrust a leaflet into my hand and said, "Before Robin takes this drug make sure she reads this" and then walked off. I just shook my head in disbelief at what had just happened, paid the assistant and left. As soon as I got home I made myself a cup of coffee and sat down to read the leaflet. It was scary to say the least and the more I read, the less I fancied taking the tablets; but I had agreed so didn't really think I could not go through with it at this stage.

The following day the Registrar called to arrange a meeting. She asked if I would be traveling alone; I told her my partner would be with me to which she said "That's good, as I won't have a nurse available". I was immediately worried about what she was planning to do to me but thought at least Denise would be there if things became unpleasant.

I started taking the drug and the first couple of days I seemed okay, but then things really deteriorated. I felt sick all the time, my joints ached and I just had a feeling of being unwell all the time. I took them for a week, had a blood test and stopped taking them and soon after we drove to Perth to meet the Registrar. She was lovely and we chatted about my past and my current issues while she took lots of notes. I was beginning to wonder why I had needed to have someone with me when she removed these weird looking beads from her case. She asked me if I could measure the size of my testicles against the beads and tell her which one matched in size. It was bizarre to say the least. I did as asked, but she wasn't convinced and asked if she could do it. Then I realised why Denise had to be there. Anyway, she agreed with the one I had chosen, wiped the beads and her hands and the meeting ended.

A couple of days later the endocrinologist called me to give me the blood test results; my oestrogen level hadn't changed, but my testosterone level had dropped. This was totally the opposite of what should have happened, but was typical of my system. She asked me if I would continue taking the Anastrozole and have another blood test after a week. I hesitated and eventually agreed but I made it clear that this was to be the end of it as I would certainly not consider taking the drug on a long-term basis. We then had a very bizarre conversation about my breasts. She suggested I consult a surgeon about having them removed. I asked her why I would do that and she said it would remove the discomfort I was constantly in and make it easier for me to wear normal clothes. I said I would consider it, but I knew it was never going to happen.

Chapter 45

All time low

I took the Anastrozole for a further week before the next blood test. Later that day the endocrinologist called me and asked if I would consider taking it for a little longer to see if it took some time to work. After thinking about it I agreed to take it for a few more days. The second week hadn't been quite as bad as the first, but I didn't tell her that. You may well be wondering why I would agree to do this, but she had been very good to me; she didn't ever charge me for seeing her, unlike some of her other patients who I had witnessed coming out of her office and been asked to pay $200 for the privilege. She said it was because she found my case very interesting and was hopeful that she would eventually get some answers.

I took the Anastrozole for ten days, then threw the rest away. I waited for the blood test results to come through and it did at least show a very slight reduction in the oestrogen level but no improvement in the testosterone level. She called me and thanked me for at least giving it a go and said if I changed my mind she would send me another script. I said I wouldn't, and left it at that.

The Convention was held during the first week of August and I was hopeful of something positive coming from it. I was rapidly running out of anything on which to hang my hopes, but sadly it wasn't to be. The endocrinologist called me after the event and said that their presentation had gone really well but it hadn't created any new ideas in terms of regulating my hormones. In fact, no one at the convention had ever come across anyone like me which I found really surprising and disappointing. I thanked her for what she had done, and she said she would keep looking for an answer and would be in touch. I was devastated. I had pinned so much hope on the Convention that it felt as though there was just nothing left and that I really had nothing to live for. I just couldn't see how things were going to improve; it was like heading down a one-way street with the monsters in my head in front of me blocking the road ahead. I was so miserable that I just sat in the chair and stared into space, not knowing what to do.

I thought about all the different ways I could end my life. Tablets took too long, and the effect was too easily reversed if someone found me. I researched how to hang myself; after all we had plenty of trees at the block. I figured I could stand on the top of the canopy of the Navara and just slip off and that would be the end of it; no more blood tests, no more sore breasts but most of all there would be no more monsters in my head. I felt sorry for Denise as she obviously loved and cared for me; why else would she have been there for me, supporting me through every test and disappointment over the last few years; but I just couldn't see a way past it. I researched the best type of rope to use; one which doesn't stretch but is easily tied. It's all available on the net - it quite amazed me really that people would post things like that; but sadly it's all there.

I just didn't know how to get through each day and I must have been dreadful to live with. Denise was amazing with me; we talked for hours and hours about what to do and how to move forward. She suggested I went back to the counsellor to see if that might help, but I wasn't convinced, so didn't go. I think for something like that to really work you would have to like the person you are talking to as you are going to be completely baring your heart and soul to them. I, for one, couldn't have done that with this lady, as pleasant as she was with me.

I tried to immerse myself in plans for the block; it worked in the short term but then when I got to bed I couldn't get my mind off my situation and couldn't get to sleep. I started taking more and more sleeping tablets of one sort and another, but nothing much helped. Once more I could feel myself sinking lower and lower and often wondered why Denise didn't ask me to leave. I must have been hell to live with, but she stuck by me day after day. I couldn't get motivated to find work for my business and spent most of the day around the house. At least I got a few things done there, but was so unhappy and couldn't see how I was going to get through. My GP was supportive; she increased the dose of antidepressants which I think helped a little, but left me feeling very lethargic; a sort of numbness which made me even less inclined to do much with my time.

We had encountered some problems with the building permit as there had been some changes to both the bushfire regulations and also the proposed building had to achieve a six-star energy rating. So we employed a company to sort out the energy rating but one of the options they presented was for us to remove the front veranda, in order to get some winter sun into the house. This to me was defeating the object, as I felt that keeping it cool in an Australian summer would be more difficult than keeping it warm in winter. After all, there were trees all around so there would never be a shortage of firewood and, as I have already said, I have a love affair with my chainsaw so it wouldn't be a chore collecting wood. Eventually, we got the energy rating to where it needed to be by agreeing to fit double glazing throughout the house. It has always amazed me that Australian houses aren't double glazed like English ones. It makes such a difference in terms of heat transfer which will work equally as well at keeping heat out in summer as keeping it in during winter. Unfortunately this solution had an expensive effect on the budget we had put in place for the build. But in the long run I knew that we would appreciate that it was all worth it. Thankfully, the house build was a small distraction and it worked for a short time, but I was eventually back on the block planning how to end it all and free myself from the pain; both physically and, more-so, mentally. I just couldn't imagine what my parents were thinking in not telling me about my beginnings; then taking me to specialists and lying to me afterwards about what had been said to them. It just didn't make any sense to me how you could watch your child go through hell at school when you knew the reason and then do nothing about it. It all built up inside my head and made me feel as though it was going to explode. The worst thing about it all was the fact that the only person it was hurting was me, and I didn't know how to make it stop. The only thing I could think of was ending my life, but I knew how much it would hurt Denise and that was the last thing I wanted. Day after day we talked about the hurt and she held me when I cried. She was simply amazing.

One pleasant thing which happened at that time was my first visit to Linda (our neighbour two houses away in Busselton). She runs a beauty therapy business from home and, after really enjoying my first pedicure in Eco Beach while we were traveling the previous year, Denise kindly bought me a voucher for a Pedicure from Linda for my birthday, but I hadn't got around to using it. Linda is very easy to get on with and we talked the whole time I was there. At one stage we were talking about how much she was looking forward to the summer and going to the beach. She asked me if I enjoyed going to the beach and having a swim. I told her that I did enjoy it but didn't get much chance as I didn't like going in the water when anyone else was around. She asked me why. I don't know why I had let myself get into a conversation like that, but I felt she was a really nice person and if I told her about the gynecomastia she would understand, so I told her. She had no idea what gynecomastia was, so I just unbuttoned my shirt and showed her my bra. She was surprised but very understanding. We talked for some time about how hard things had been when I was growing up; she even commented on how pretty my bra was and was totally unfazed about the whole thing. Somehow, I felt better for having told someone and it was the start of a lovely friendship between us.

Chapter 46

The walk that changed my life

August is often the coldest and wettest month of our year, but come rain or shine I somehow managed to have my walk after dinner each night with Bella our lovely Kelpie cross. She wasn't bothered whether it rained or not, she just loved being taken for a walk at any time of day or night. Most nights Denise would join me unless it was raining really hard, when I would just take Bella to the end of the road and back.

This particular evening it was quite cold but dry, and the sky was clear, so I was confident I would get a good long walk in. Denise was happy to join me, so we put our coats on and ventured out. We left the house, walked to the end of the cul-de-sac and crossed onto a large grassed area on the other side of the road which was a great area for Bella to have a run off-lead. Denise and I walked up to the junction with the next road and stopped to put Bella back on her lead and this was the moment which quite literally changed my life forever. While we were waiting for Bella to come to us Denise looked at me and said "Robin, if you want to change gender and become a lady I will support you. You are my best friend and I don't

239

want to lose you. I don't know what it will mean for our relationship, but I don't want you to move out and I want to be there for you throughout your journey". I was lost for words; I couldn't actually believe what I had heard. My head was spinning out of control and I just stood there and looked at her. When I finally found some words I said, "You would do that for me?" I was still in shock but by this time my brain was in overdrive trying to imagine what the first step would be and if I would be allowed to transition. I had read a number of times that there are very strict World Health Organisation conditions which must be met before anyone can surgically transition; and as I'm scared of a needle how was I ever going to cope with going into hospital for surgery? Not only that, but surgery to have my male genitals removed and female genitals constructed! I knew I wasn't going to sleep at all that coming night!

At this point I should point out that regardless of being scared of hospitals and needles etc, transitioning to female without having the gender reassignment surgery would never have worked for me. I know lots of people transition and present as the opposite sex without the surgery; however for me, there was never any question that having surgery was the only way I would consider transitioning. Anything else would just have created a void inside and left me even more confused.

We talked about nothing else for the rest of our walk and my head was still spinning when we arrived home. I was very frightened about getting my hopes up of at last becoming Stephanie before making enquiries to see if it was possible. We were flying over to South Australia a couple of days later for Denise's 60th birthday, so there was not much I could do before then. I decided that before we went away I would make an appointment to see the specialist in Perth who had told me about my beginnings. I felt sure he would be able to tell me if it was possible or not, and point me in the right direction. I made the appointment for the week after we arrived back. It was the same girl who booked me in for the first appointment and thankfully she didn't ask me what it was for!

I couldn't think of anything else for the next couple of days before we left, but I really wanted this trip to be special. I had spent a great deal of time choosing a pearl necklace to give to Denise at this special time but was uncertain about taking it away with us so I decided to present it to her before we left. Thankfully she loved it and agreed that it was best left in the safe, rather than risk losing it while we were away. The trip was everything I hoped it would be. I had booked accommodation for us on a vineyard right in the middle of the Barossa valley and it was a really lovely old house. It was quite cold over there, so we kept the wood fire burning most of the time. It was very comfortable and spacious with floor to ceiling windows looking out on to the vines. We had a special meal in a local restaurant on the evening of Denise's birthday and the following day we had to be up at about three a.m. to go up in a hot air balloon. This was something I'd not done before so was excited about it. We got airborne just as the sun was coming up. The views were sensational as the pilot carefully took us down the North Para river. There was a very embarrassing moment though - when we were just drifting over the river. At one point I literally nodded off - standing up! I must have begun to crumple and woke myself up leaning over the (thankfully high) edge of the basket; I had been awake very early that day! The whole trip had been wonderful and even the hire car was perfect; it was a brand new Kia Cerato which I really enjoyed driving. We had a day in Hahndorf, a small town originally settled by Lutheran Germans in 1839 and still with a distinctly German feel to it. We had a lovely day looking round all the shops and museums before returning home for dinner.

On the flight home I allowed my attention to turn towards the possibility of me transitioning. I couldn't really believe that it was on the verge of possibly happening. I had never felt I had the courage to do it before, as I always believed it would mean the end of my relationship with Denise; but with her support it was, all of a sudden, a possibility. The week we got back we collected our new Volkswagen Amarok - we had bought it before we left but didn't want to collect it until we got back as we had no garage space to park it in while we were away, and so it would have been outside on the driveway.

The day came for my appointment with the specialist in Perth. In some ways it was a good day but it also had several horror moments. I have always been a very confident driver and to go up and back in a day (a five hundred kilometre round trip) has never bothered me. As I was waiting in the waiting room I was very nervous, as I didn't really know how I was going to say what I wanted to say. Eventually I was called into the Doctor's office and he greeted me warmly and asked how I was. He said he hadn't seen any blood test results recently and I told him I hadn't come about the oestrogen problem. He sat back in his chair with his hands across his lap and said, "Go on".

I said, "I don't really know where to start, or what to say, but I want to swap sides". He looked at me, paused and then said, "I'm not surprised". He paused again and said, "I can help you do that". It was all I wanted to hear. I burst into tears so he passed me a tissue and asked what had brought me to the decision. I told him how, in reality, it was what I had wanted for forty years but had never had the courage to do anything about it, but now it was a case of having to do so as I couldn't see any other way of finding some peace and happiness. He asked me how much I knew about the process. I said that I had spent some time searching the internet but there were lots of conflicting stories so I had decided to come and see him.

He told me the first thing to do was to be referred to a psychiatrist which he could do, but it wasn't just a case of choosing a psychiatrist and going to see them. I would have to have my case reviewed by the psychiatrist before they would agree to see me. He then went on to tell me that the lady he thought would best be able to help me was of Indian descent and wasn't the easiest person to get along with, but was very thorough and he thought would be the one most likely to get me fast tracked through the system. He said you have probably read that the rules state that you have lived in your preferred gender for a minimum of two years before any surgery can take place. I said I had read that, but he said it wasn't written in stone and, between them, he thought they could get me through the system fairly quickly, given my age and history. I was very happy to hear that and he said he would write to her later that day.

He asked me who I had told and I said "no one" so he offered to write to my GP and explain my decision. I agreed and thanked him; I also asked him if he would contact the endocrinologist as she had called me, presumably to get me to try a different drug. I was happy when he agreed to do so, as I had never discussed transitioning with her and was concerned how she would react given that she had just gone to all the trouble of presenting my case at the Conference only to hear that I was now going down a different route.

Having gone into his office not knowing what to say and certainly not knowing how he was going to react I felt very happy about how it had gone. So far, so good, as they say. He told me to give the psychiatrist a week to review the "Letter of Referral" he was going to send her, then I was to call her office and organise an appointment. If she had decided not to handle my case I should contact him and he would recommend someone else. He wished me luck and I left his office feeling a measure of hope I hadn't experienced in many years.

Chapter 47

My GP, the psychologist and the psychiatrist

I waited a few days then made an appointment to see my GP. The specialist had offered to let her know what was going on so at least I didn't have to worry about that. I made the appointment for one week after I had seen him, anticipating that he would have had plenty of time to write to her. When my turn came, I was invited into her office. I didn't quite know what reaction I would get but I sat down and looked at her and she asked me how I'd been. I hesitated a moment and asked her if the specialist had written to her. She said he hadn't, to which I replied, "Oh shit". She put her hand on mine and gently squeezed it and asked if I was sick. I didn't know what to say, so just explained that I had seen the specialist the previous week and he said he would write to her. There was a very concerned look on her face so I couldn't hold it back anymore and blurted out that I was going to "swap sides". She held my hand again and said she wasn't surprised and that she was very happy for me.

We talked at length about the process, who I was seeing and who else knew about it. I told her that Denise had told her best friend - we felt that she needed some support. At this point she asked me "and who is supporting you?". I told her we planned to tell one of my very good friends, so that I also had someone to talk to, apart from Denise. She thought that was a good idea, but said she thought I should also have some local professional support as well. She suggested I see a psychologist in town who she held in very high regard and wrote her name and number on a card for me; a day later I gave the psychologist a call. My call went to her message bank so I just explained that my GP had recommended that I see her and she would be sending a referral in due course. A little while later my phone rang and it was the psychologist; she sounded very friendly on the phone and said she had a cancellation a couple of days away and would I like to take it. I said I would, but before I met her, I needed to email something to her which explained why I needed to see her. She told me that it was not the way she worked normally, but if I felt it would work then I could send it.

I sat in the waiting room in a corner trying to hide the terror I felt inside. For some reason, it was harder than going to the specialist, and more difficult than telling my GP. Eventually a lady came out of a room to the left and looked around at everyone waiting to see the various practitioners. She turned to me and confirmed I was Robin before inviting me into her room, which was just as I imagined it would be; a big leather sofa and a comfortable chair facing it, perfect for my first grilling. However, she had a warm smile and asked me how I was feeling. I told her I was petrified, and she asked me why. I said it was a fear of the unknown, as I had no idea what to expect from her. She talked about my letter and how well it had brought her up to speed; she thanked me for that and asked how I was feeling about the journey ahead. She was actually really nice, and before very long I stopped being scared and relaxed a little. She said how lucky I was to have Denise by my side; I agreed, and we talked for a while about our relationship.

I dropped into the conversation that although Denise was from Wales I didn't hold it against her (it's been a standing joke between Denise and myself for many years). Then the psychologist (her name is Hayley) told me that she also was from Wales; a bit of a conversation stopper to say the least but she took it with good humour! The time passed really quickly and before I knew it she was saying that she would have to stop there, and asked me when I would like to see her again. Despite my initial fear, I had actually enjoyed my time with her and arranged to see her again a few days before my appointment with the psychiatrist.

I went home reflecting on what a good suggestion it had been by my GP; I felt it had really helped and we were only touching the tip of the iceberg in the first session. Hayley told me, before I left, that in my next appointment she wanted to talk to me about my parents and my feelings towards them, so I knew our next meeting would be more difficult but was hopeful that she would be able to help with what had become the biggest monster in my head. It was something I knew we would have to discuss at some point, so it might as well be sooner than later. All in all, I felt it had been very worthwhile and I was half looking forward to the next appointment even though it would most likely be tougher than the first one.

When Denise returned home from work we talked for a good while about the session and whether I thought it would help in the long run throughout my journey. I felt sure it would, but the most positive outcome from the day was that I liked the lady a lot and could see myself being a long term patient of hers. I had been dreading going and not liking the person but that was certainly not the case.

My second appointment with Hayley went every bit as well as the first; we were able to discuss lots of things, talk about my parents, which at times made me cry but there was such an easy atmosphere with her that it didn't hurt me as much as usual when I talked about them. Looking back, it probably took me most of the first appointment to lower my guard, but the second time I felt at ease from the start and therefore we talked in a much more open way, and again I could feel the benefit of talking to her. Before I left, she said what I thought at the time was a strange thing, but it proved to be very accurate. She told me not to expect to have the same ease of relationship with the psychiatrist as she and I had built in a very short time. She was so right!

The psychiatrist's office was in a complex close to Cockburn shopping centre. We arrived early and found a place to have coffee before the appointment. I wanted to dress as ambiguously as possible for my first encounter with her and so wore a ladies' blouse, ladies' jeans (which I always wore anyway) and some trainers which had pink on them and could have been for either gender. We arrived just before the allotted time and were told that she would be with us soon. Thirty minutes passed before a lady finally emerged from an office to the right of us. She looked over to us and said she would be just a minute and then I could go in. She soon returned and invited me into her office; I sat down with a similar feeling of terror as I had first felt in Hayley's room.

She introduced herself and went on to say that her job with me would seem, to me, to be tough at times as she had a particular format for asking questions and some of them would be difficult for me to answer, but it was important that I was as open as possible with her. Then it started. It was as though she knew all the questions which would upset me and, once upset, she just wouldn't let them go; especially when it came to my parents and my late brother. She made me cry time and time again and just passed me a tissue and went again. I thought the ninety minutes would never end; it was just relentless. She went over things repeatedly and wouldn't let any small thing drop until she felt she had done her best to break me (or that's how it felt to me). I felt completely drained and longed for it to end. Then she just looked at me and said she was satisfied with what she had heard and would see me again in ten days. The relief must have been very evident on my face because she apologised for how tough she had been with me, but explained it was the way she worked, and that I had come through it. I asked what happened after the next appointment and she told me if she was happy after that, I would receive a letter of diagnosis. She then told me that in the next appointment she wanted to see me for twenty minutes then talk to Denise for twenty minutes before getting me back in again. I couldn't wait to tell Denise that it was her turn next time!

Chapter 48

How and when to tell friends and family

On the way home, after discussing my session with the psychiatrist, Denise and I turned our thoughts to how, when and in what order we were going to tell friends and family. Denise had already told her best friend Maggie (who had been instrumental in getting us together in 2012), which had gone quite well she thought; so now it was my turn. I had two close male friends and wanted to tell them both. However, one of them, Craig, spent most of his life working abroad and was only around for about fourteen weeks of the year. As he was away at that time I decided to firstly tell David, whom I had known for about eight years. I first met him through his business - he is a piano teacher. Piano was an instrument I had always wanted to learn and Jayne bought me a keyboard one Christmas just to see if I could learn on my own. It wasn't going to happen, so she found someone who taught and bought me a block of lessons for my birthday one year. I went to him for several years but felt I had reached a stage where I could play quite a lot of things, just using chords, and at the time didn't really want to learn to read music, so left it at that. Playing the piano is one of the most therapeutic things I know; I am not particularly good at it but know the basics and can get by; so even now I still play regularly.

We invited David around for dinner explaining that we had something to tell him regarding me, and that we wanted him to be the first to know. It was probably not the smartest reason to give him because that made him worry that I was unwell. We ate dinner and sat around the table having coffee, putting the world to rights for a while, then I told him it was time to tell him a story. I explained my issues, right from my early days up to the present and he listened carefully. He knew I had been to see numerous specialists over the last few years, but I hadn't ever really elaborated as to why. I explained that I was going to have some surgery and came to the part that I had rehearsed a hundred times. I was finally going to be able to go to sleep as Robin and wake up, some four or five hours later, as Stephanie; something I had longed for virtually all my life. That was how I finished my story. His reaction will stay with me for the rest of my days; he stood up and came to me to give me a hug. He said it was the best news ever, and that he had been so worried that I was ill. He said it was a win-win situation; I would still be the same person inside, who he and his family all loved, but I would now be happy. I had a long hug with him and there were tears in my eyes. He asked when he could start calling me Stephanie and who else knew. We told him he was only the second person we had told. He said how honoured he felt and we told him how we planned to reveal the news gradually to everyone. He said he would not tell anyone until it was common knowledge, but assured me that all his family would be thrilled for me and support my decision.

We decided not to tell any family at this point, with the exception of Denise's mum, Doreen. I had a lovely relationship with Doreen and, when my mother died in 2014, she made a point of telling me that she would happily be my mum now. It really touched me at the time and, even though I had only known her for a short time, our relationship was such that it certainly wasn't going to be difficult calling her Mum. When Denise and her husband separated she didn't tell Doreen for two years. He was out of the country most of the time and Denise and her mum were in different continents so it was simpler not to enlighten her as she would have worried for Denise. However, when she eventually found out she was very cross and disappointed and told Denise to never keep important things from her again; so we decided to tell her, as we felt this news fell into the "important" category.

While Skype is not the ideal way of telling anyone something of this magnitude, it's better than the 'phone. It's the next best thing to being there and at least you can judge the person's reaction more easily. She listened very carefully to what I had to tell her. We had regularly mentioned that I had been to see one specialist or another so she knew there were issues, but she was still quite surprised. I tried to keep the conversation going after I had told her my story and said that one of the most difficult things would be telling people locally before they saw me around town. She thought about it for a few seconds, then said to me, "Do you think people will notice?". I was a bit shocked at that remark and said I thought that high heels and a dress might give it away. She thought about it for a while and agreed that it would, and she called me Steph almost every time after that. Understanding something like changing gender is not the easiest thing to get your head around at any age, but at 86 years old to be able to get it and be supportive I found quite remarkable and it was a measure of the wonderful person that she was.

My next appointment with the psychiatrist was much easier than the first. Denise was really worried about talking to her after my description of the first encounter but she needn't have been. I went in first as directed and spent about half an hour talking about my progress and a few things which she had highlighted from the first appointment. She seemed a much more gentle person the second time around. Then it was Denise's turn; I sat outside her office hoping that she would be pleasant with her and not upset her like she did me in the first appointment. She was in for about twenty minutes and came out smiling, which I thought was a good sign. She told me to go in, that everything was fine and we could talk about it on the way home. I went in for my second stint and she was very friendly and talkative and said how lucky I was to have someone like Denise supporting me. I agreed and told her that without Denise I just wouldn't have had the courage to transition and that she had been amazing with me since December when I discovered my birth story. We talked for a short time about that and she then told me that given my understanding of the process and being seemingly well on top of things, she would see me after six weeks instead of the normal three month waiting period and, after that appointment she would give me my letter of recommendation. I was elated; there was no longer the question of "if" I transitioned; it was now just "when" I transitioned.

It was time for my monthly pedicure; a small bit of heaven in a difficult time. Linda was her usual bubbly self and she soon had me sitting comfortably with my feet in the foot spa. The last time I was there we had joked about me having my toenails painted and, knowing what I knew was happening, I had decided that I was going to have them painted pink and Linda was happy to oblige. She didn't ask any questions, just gave me the selection of different pinks to choose from. There is not a moment of my pedicure that I don't thoroughly enjoy; I love having my feet touched, especially when she is exfoliating them. I love how they feel afterwards; all soft and smooth. As a great deal had happened since my last pedicure, I wanted to thank Linda for her understanding about the gynecomastia, so when there was a suitable break in the conversation I brought it up. She went on to tell me that people tell her all sorts of things when in her room, but whatever is said during her treatments stays in that room.

She then told me that a client of hers (there was no mention of name or any identifying information) had been very worried because her teenage son had just announced that he wanted to be a girl and she didn't know what to do about it. I must have shown a lot of interest and she asked me why; I just couldn't stop myself and I told her what I was doing. She was thrilled for me, gave me a big hug, was almost in tears and said she was so happy for me. It was such a lovely experience and I just knew Linda would be there to support me if I needed to talk.

Chapter 49

A challenging appointment & the final approval

Not too long after my second visit to the psychiatrist she sent me a letter, as per our conversation, confirming my diagnosis of gender incongruence. She had sent it addressed to Robin Stephanie Ullyott which I thought was quite a nice touch. It simply stated that, after two visits, her diagnosis was that my physical gender didn't match my mental gender and it went on to say that we had a further meeting booked next month. As the appointment meant a trip to Perth, we decided to organise a medical appointment for Denise and an appointment with my gender specialist for the same day. The final appointment with the psychiatrist was to be a huge milestone for me as the next letter I would receive from her would be my "letter of recommendation" which would mean that I could organise my surgery. I really wanted my surgery to be on my birthday at the end of March (it was now November 2016) but if it was sooner than that then I would be even happier.

At this stage I hadn't dared to even look for a surgeon as I didn't want it to jinx me getting the letter. A few days before our trip I received a call from the psychiatrist's secretary to say that the psychiatrist was ill and wouldn't be able to see me on that day. I was devastated; I had built myself up for the appointment so much that the call really knocked me for six. Having made the two other appointments, we still went to Perth but would need to make another trip the following week when the psychiatrist was feeling better. Denise's appointment was first, then we headed to see my specialist.

I had decided that I was going to ask him to write his letter of support; he would have received a copy of the letter of diagnosis so I knew he would have no problem in recommending me for surgery. When my turn came, I went into his office and he congratulated me for getting so far so quickly. He wrote the letter there and then and asked whether I had done any research into which surgeon I was going to use. I told him I hadn't and would happily be guided by him; but he wasn't able to recommend anyone as he hadn't had personal contact with any of them. After he had written the letter he suggested that I should have an "activated partial thromboplastin time" test - a blood test which measures how quickly your blood clots, or not, as the case may be. He said that whichever surgeon I chose would need this test done and as it takes a while for the results to come back it would be a good idea to get the test done now. He also wanted the usual hormone checks done and said he would then put me on some testosterone blocking drugs and possibly some oestrogen if required, but he doubted that I would need any more. He gave me the letter and the referral for the blood tests. I thanked him for his time and all his help in getting me to this place and left his office.

I walked back into the waiting room and told Denise that I was just going to have some bloods taken and wouldn't be long. I knew there was a pathology room at the back of the building, as it was next to the toilets which I had used on several occasions, so I went and knocked on the door. As I walked in, I saw a lady with her back to me sitting at a desk; it was a very small room and the door only just opened without hitting her chair. I don't like small confined spaces at the best of times so, coupled with giving blood, that wasn't a good start. Looking to the right I saw a young lad standing, looking at me as much as to say, "excellent, a victim!". Then the second bit of bad news struck me; he had a badge on his shirt which said "Trainee". I could feel myself getting hot and bothered thinking about it, but I wasn't really in a position to back out, so I took a seat as directed. He put the strap around my arm and opened a drawer at the side of me. He sorted through a few packets which I could see contained needles so I thought that, to try and make conversation, I would suggest he picked a sharp one; he didn't even smile. I thought to myself, "even better - small room, trainee nurse and one without a sense of humour; great news all round". Anyway, I knew it would soon be all over and awaited the sting of the needle going in. He cleaned a patch of my arm and muttered "small sting" and it was; I hardly felt it and was impressed. He started filling vials of blood and giving them to the lady, one, two, three, four, five, six, seven, eight... Now at that point I really thought I should protest and I actually said, "You will leave me some won't you". He said, "Don't worry, you have plenty left". I then foolishly looked at the blood filling the ninth vial and that was it. I remember saying "I'm going to faint", and I did. Thankfully, he must have filled the last vial and pulled the needle out as I was going out. The next thing I remember was a lady standing in front of me, not the lady at the desk; this was an older lady with short grey hair and the frightening thing was that looking over her shoulder, with a very concerned look on his face, was my father who had been dead for fifteen years! I was really confused and must have thrown my head back into the wall as it brought me round very quickly. By this stage both my father and the older lady had vanished and the woman from the desk was holding my head to stop me hitting the wall again. She spoke to me, I'm not sure what she said as all I could think about was that I was going to vomit and I told her that. Somehow, out of nowhere, she picked up a waste bin and held it in front of me just in time to catch my projectile vomit which was heading her way. The thing is, I've been here before; this happens every time I faint. Generally I overheat, I faint and then I'm sick so I wasn't surprised; but she most definitely was, and how she managed to get out of its way I will never know. Then I was sick again and there was controlled panic in the room! She said she needed me to lie down so as to get some blood to my head and between them they managed to get me onto a bed. I was sick again and this time she didn't catch it all; it really didn't smell too good. Eventually, I got settled on the bed and I asked if they could bring Denise in from the waiting room which they did. Ironically, she had been sitting there and heard someone vomiting and thought how unfortunate for that person; it hadn't crossed her mind it might be me.

Eventually I stopped throwing up and the nurse asked Denise to bring our car round to the back entrance of the clinic so that I didn't have to go through the waiting room; I'm sure it was for my benefit; but afterwards I thought it might have been bad for business if other patients were to see me in this state. Denise went for the car while the two of them tried to clean me up a bit. Now the other problem is that after I have fainted it's as though someone has turned the power off. I can't walk, can't lift my arms; I am just a dead weight. Between them they managed to carry me out to the car park and, after telling Denise that she would need to pay the bill, bundled me into the passenger seat. Now the real horror of the whole episode became clear; I was going to have to be driven home! No matter who the driver is, I am the worst passenger ever. I just don't do "passenger"; I always drive. I thought the day couldn't possibly get any worse but I was wrong.

I don't remember much about the first half of the journey home until Denise announced that she was feeling tired and needed coffee and something to eat. She pulled off into a little cafe on the side of the highway. It was a temporary place and was in a field so the drive into it was bumpy which didn't help my situation, but she parked the car and went to the kiosk. She came back shortly afterwards with water for me, a cup of coffee and a biscuit and proceeded to eat the biscuit in the car while the coffee cooled. Suddenly, I felt sick again, probably from the smell of the coffee. I opened the door and leant out with my shoulder against the "B" pillar and my knee outside. After a short while I decided I wasn't going to be sick but Denise threw the rest of her coffee away so that it didn't upset me. She asked if it was okay to carry on and I nodded and she shut the door before I had chance to get my leg in; it really hurt! She was mortified.

We got back onto the highway and after a while I started to feel a little better. By the time we were just a few kilometres from Busselton I was almost back to normal and watching cars coming the other way. There was a Toyota Hilux towing a trailer coming towards us and just before it passed us a wheelbarrow fell off the trailer. It was so close to us that a shower of stones hit our car, one of which cracked the windscreen. The next thing was even more scary; there was a small SUV following the Hilux which was facing a bouncing wheelbarrow in the middle of the road. The driver swerved into our lane right in front of us. Thankfully Denise was able to move to the left to avoid the car. I couldn't believe what had just happened and how lucky we were. If the SUV had hit the wheelbarrow it could have flipped over right in front of us and would definitely have hit us. We just looked at each other in total disbelief.

When we finally arrived home I went straight to bed, absolutely shattered, and Denise followed shortly afterwards. I had made a new appointment with the psychiatrist for the following week and was hopeful of a less eventful trip.

The day arrived and we got there in good time and so took advantage of the shopping centre and found a shoe shop as I wanted to try on some ladies' shoes. It was spring so the shop had lots of sandals to choose from. I had not worn sandals since I was very young so it was going to be a whole new experience. I found a few pairs which I thought might fit and proceeded to take off my shoes and socks to try them on. Denise was completely out of her comfort zone with me walking up and down the aisles in sandals, showing off my bright pink toes but she stuck with me and we selected several pairs which were comfortable. I paid and then went to the car to make myself look as feminine as possible, without going the whole way; the new shoes certainly helped the look though.

My appointment with the psychiatrist went really well and we talked about all sorts of things before she said, "Right, let's get the bones of this letter written". With my assistance, she put together a letter which she said she would tidy up and send to me in the next few days. I was elated to say the least.

Chapter 50

Finding a surgeon

I wasted no time at all in researching who to choose to help make me into the person I had dreamed of becoming for so many years. The problem was where to start; which continent, which country and which surgeon. Australia is very poorly served for transgender surgeons; there were none at all in Western Australia so who ever I chose would mean I would have to travel. There were literally hundreds of reviews online, so Denise and I began the task of sifting through them. Sadly there were lots of bad reviews as well as good ones. Sentences like "this man ruined my life" and "I woke up to a world of pain" didn't do my confidence any favours but there were some good ones from surgeons in the US which looked promising. It was a place I hadn't considered going to as it is a long way from Australia; however, on the plus side, and this was a very big plus for me, English is the first language. If I had decided to go to Thailand there would have been a language barrier to some extent. I also had no idea of the costs involved at this stage, but to be honest, finding the right surgeon was much more important to me than the cost.

I asked both my gender specialist and my endocrinologist for their thoughts on the subject but neither were keen to recommend anyone; I guess it would be too high a risk that I would come back to them if there was a problem. For some reason they both presumed that I would be looking in Asia. I also made enquiries in the UK as it would make things easier in terms of accommodation and we both know how the system works over there. I kept returning to the US reviews though. One lady in particular (I really wanted it to be a lady surgeon) seemed to stand out. There were no bad reviews; in fact there weren't many reviews at all, but at least no bad ones. One thing that she offered which really appealed to me, was that after the surgery, she had some recovery suites which were offered to people who were not local. I thought we would definitely qualify for that! Having nursing cover for the first week after the operation I thought was very important, as we would be in a strange country and I had not had surgery since I had my tonsils out when I was ten years old so had no idea as to how I would feel after it.

I decided to make an email enquiry and see what the response was. I was so excited. I would have been very happy to leave the next day, but knew it wouldn't be as simple as that. I really wanted my surgery to be on my birthday as it would indeed be the "birth" of my new life but would have been happy if it were before then, as that date was fourteen weeks away. To my surprise I received a response the same evening as it was morning with them. It was short and sweet and simply gave me a number to call the following day, as the person I needed to speak to was not there at the time my email arrived. I was even more excited now that I had made contact with someone and looked forward to calling them the next day.

I was almost shaking as I dialled the number. I had been asked to call at 9am, which was 10pm our time. The phone rang for several seconds then went to a voicemail; I didn't leave a message but tried a few minutes later and the same thing happened. This time I left a message. I knew that I wouldn't get a call back so just asked them to send me an email when they were available, and I would call again. A few minutes later I received the email and called again; this time I got through to a friendly lady who apologised for not being available earlier and promptly put me through to another lady who would be able to answer any questions I had. She asked if I would like to book a Skype consultation with the surgeon. I thought this was a brilliant idea and said I would. She advised me that the consultation would cost $100 but it would be refunded if I booked my surgery with them. I thought this was fair enough and we arranged a date and time later that week.

At last the time came for the Skype consultation; 11pm our time on Friday evening. It was mid-summer for us so I wore a lady's sleeveless top and as I thought she wouldn't see below my waist I just wore some shorts. Right on the hour of 11pm my iPad started ringing with an incoming call; I was so nervous. The surgeon was dressed in what looked like hospital scrubs, which I thought was very business-like. She was very friendly and told me that she hadn't had a patient from Australia before. Denise and I had compiled a list of questions to ask her, thinking that this would just be a first step before fully deciding to book my surgery. I actually thought we would talk to several surgeons and make our decision from there but, before we could start with our list of questions, she began telling me how it all would work if we chose her. She explained how her surgical method was different from others and how it made the surgery shorter and more successful. She also told us how many male-to-female surgeries she had performed and that she had a very strict set of guidelines for patients to follow prior to having the surgery. She then asked me how long I had been living in my preferred gender, as it is part of the World Health Organisation's Transgender health guidelines that candidates have lived in their preferred gender for a minimum of two years before transitioning. I answered "on and off for 40 years"; she must have misheard me and said "4 years well done"; I considered correcting her, then changed my mind.

Before we knew it, she had answered most of our questions without me having to ask any of them. The only thing she hadn't mentioned was the cost so, when she asked if I had any questions, I asked her if she could give me a breakdown of the costs involved. She told us the cost for her services, which included eight days in one of her recovery suites, and what the separate hospital charges would be (these would be paid directly to the hospital). They seemed very reasonable to me, especially as it included a stay in the recovery suite. My next question for her was how soon she would be able to perform the surgery if I was to commit that day. She called through to a colleague and asked what dates they were currently booking new surgeries for, and she told me it would be the end of May 2017. I was surprised and a little disappointed that it couldn't be on or near my birthday in March, but decided to book it there and then. I don't know who was the most surprised, her or me, but I felt completely happy with all she had told me and I really liked her as a person. It might seem strange, but if anyone was going to make me into the person I so desperately wanted to be, then I wanted it to be someone I liked.

She thanked me and said that there would be another consultation one month before the surgery, so if I had any questions they could either be answered then or I could email her at any time. She then handed me over to another lady who took the rest of my details and a $500 deposit to fix the date and it was done; my surgery was booked!

When the call ended, I really couldn't believe what I had done. I was ecstatic and immediately counted up the days I had left as Robin - 174 to be exact. Denise and I had a drink to celebrate.

Chapter 51

The countdown begins

When I woke up the next morning I was still excited; it hadn't really sunk in, but now the pressure was really on to tell all our friends and families. We drew up a list of people to tell locally and a list of people in the UK. The ones in the UK were always going to be the difficult ones (as we had no plans to return there before the surgery) so we decided that we were only going to tell them by Skype unless there was no option but to contact them by phone. It wasn't something that I wanted to tell people over the phone, though, as I needed to gauge their reaction.

As we had already had success with inviting David over for dinner and telling him in a relaxed environment then this was the way we chose to tell people. We decided to start with some of Denise's friends who were actually my first painting customers back in 2015. A date was agreed, and dinner was prepared. I was very nervous to say the least and, midway through the meal, started by saying that as well as wanting to catch up with them there was a serious part to the evening which involved me telling them a story. They listened carefully as I bared my heart and soul to them and as I got to part where I am told of my beginnings the lady of the couple started crying. I was a mess but finally came to the part where I said that on the 30th of May 2017 I would finally go to sleep as Robin and wake as Stephanie, the person I knew I should always have been. The lady got up and came around to where I was sitting and gave me a long hug. I was now a real mess and tears were streaming down my face. Then the man came around the table and gave me a hug; the emotion of it all was immense to say the least.

The next person I told came out of the blue; I wasn't planning on telling him but he came to visit me while I was doing a painting job and brought me a cup of coffee. We sat in the sun talking mainly about cars as it was a common interest and we had very similar views on what was good and what wasn't. He is a big Volkswagen fan like me and has had several really nice VW vehicles. Somehow, the conversation came around to what we each had planned for the next year and I started by saying it was going to be a very big year for me and I was probably going to need some moral support. He was puzzled so I gave a few hints as to what I had planned and ended up telling him the whole story. He was very surprised but very supportive and said if I needed to talk at any point, he would be there for me.

Next on the list were David's two daughters, Rosemary and Jazzie, both of whom I am very close to. At the time I think they were 26 and 24 and somehow it felt easier telling younger people; both gave me a massive hug and offered help in any way possible. David had told me they would be fine, but it was still heavy going emotionally.

One enormous thing which had happened in the few days leading up to that night was that Denise said to me that, after some serious thought, she still wanted us to be partners. It was a massive thing for me and something I hadn't allowed myself to hope for. She went on to say that she still felt I would be her best friend and soulmate and it wasn't as though we were 25 years old and that at our age companionship was much more important than the sexual side of things. The elder of David's daughters, Rosemary, made a wonderful observation; she said that one falls in love with the person, not the gender. When I thought about this statement it rang very true; however I had also always known that if I ever did transition then I would be a lesbian as I had never had any interest in dating men.

Christmas soon arrived; my last as Robin. On Christmas Eve we had been asked to go around to some very good friends for a pre-Christmas dinner and I thought it a perfect opportunity to tell them my plans. They have a fourteen year-old daughter, so I thought it best to warn them that I had something to tell them before arriving so they could ask her whether she wanted to be involved or not. I went to her mum's work to talk about it and after a very short conversation in which I didn't divulge any details I think she got the gist of what was coming. After all, they knew about all my visits to one specialist or another, so I guess she put two and two together. Anyway, when the evening came, I explained the whole story to them and they were very happy for me.

We had arranged for Denise's best friend and her husband to come to our house on Christmas Day for a late lunch and a drink or two. Denise had told her best friend the week after I had been to see the specialist, but her husband didn't know so we planned to tell him during lunch. He was lovely about it; couldn't believe what I had been through and like everyone to date was very supportive and understanding.

We had decided to spend the New Year holiday in one of my favourite places in the world, Esperance. My second cousin, who lives there, had offered us their house in return for us watering their garden while they were visiting relatives in Perth, which we had happily agreed to. We drove the 700 kilometres down to Esperance a couple of days before New Year so they could show us what needed doing and spend a night with us before they left. They built their house themselves; even made all the bricks. It is a beautiful, unique property, sitting on forty acres about ten kilometres out of the town on the way to Cape Le Grande. All the best beaches in the area are located in Cape Le Grande and Cape Arid, so it was perfectly placed for our time there. I asked Denise if I could have my first outing as Stephanie while we were away from home and no one would know us. To my surprise she agreed, and we booked the Chinese restaurant in town. We had eaten there several times; the food is always good and the service excellent. I was very nervous to say the least. Denise did my makeup and helped me get dressed. I had bought a few items of clothing before we left home; nothing fancy, just some shoes and a couple of tops and pairs of pants. I think I looked okay for a first attempt and we headed out to the restaurant. I was almost shaking with nerves, but I had resolved that it had to start somewhere so it was good that we were a long way from home. We were shown to our table and given menus. Once we had had some interactions with the staff I started to feel much more relaxed and began to enjoy my first date as Stephanie. The meal was excellent, as usual, and we went to pay the bill. My credit card has "Mr" on it, so we used Denise's and even asked the lady at the till to take a photo, which I still have. When we left the restaurant I was on top of the world; I had done it! I was so proud of myself and thankful to Denise for getting me this far and I loved it. We went home to open a bottle of champagne to celebrate.

The next day was New Year's Eve and my cousin had asked us to drop off some plums at a friend's shop on the other side of town. Her friend runs a glass factory and makes all sorts of things, but mostly jewellery. After the success of the previous evening I was still elated and thought I might buy some jewellery to celebrate. It was always my intention to have my ears pierced so I bought a pendant with matching earrings and asked Denise when I should get them pierced. She said why not have them done that day. There was no time to waste and we headed back into town to a pharmacy which offered ear piercing (I had noticed it when we were last in town). I hate anything which involves pain but thought having my ears pierced was a necessary part of my journey, so I would just have to be brave. I went to the counter and asked if they did ear piercing; I'm not sure why I did that as it clearly stated on the door that they did. The girl replied that they did, so I asked to have mine done. She looked at me and asked whether I wanted one or both pierced. I said both and she then asked me if I could come back in half an hour as there were only two of them working at that point, as the other two girls were at lunch. I was a bit surprised but said that we would go and have a coffee and come back. It wasn't what I had hoped would happen, as it could possibly have given me the chance to back out but I didn't. We returned after half an hour and the same girl asked me to choose some studs from the rack and invited me to sit in a chair. She then went on to tell me that when they pierced children's ears they did both ears at exactly the same time so there was no chance of them refusing to have the second ear done. I said, "but I'm 55" and she said with a wry smile, "we do it for children *and* men". It didn't do much for my confidence but I took a seat as instructed. Another girl came over and they measured my ears to make sure they got them in the same place on each ear. It was over in a flash and I hardly felt a thing. One more step closer to being the person I so wanted to be.

Chapter 52

First daylight outing & mixed experiences

With my confidence sky-high I decided it was time to hit the town, in daylight, as Stephanie. A trip to the supermarket and a clothes shop was planned and it went really well. I didn't get a second look in the supermarket, even though I had been there the previous day as Robin. We then went into a clothing boutique called Rockmans. I had been there several times with Denise, both in Esperance and at home in Busselton. But this time I would be able to try things on. I was in my element; the shop assistant came up to us and said, "Hello ladies, would you like some help?" It was such a small thing but meant the world to me, to be referred to as a lady. We said we would like to browse for a while and would call for help if needed.

I found several things I liked and, as the assistant was on the phone, I went into the changing area, found a cubicle and put the first blouse on. It was lovely so I came out to show Denise. She approved, so I went to try the second one (another success) and the same with the third one. When I came out the assistant seemed a little uneasy with me. Denise (from the small part of the conversation she had overheard) thought she might have called her boss to tell her there was a transgender person in the shop and was asking how should she deal with the situation; but all was fine so I paid and we left. Walking around Esperance as Stephanie felt truly amazing. It's not something that anyone who is not transgender or similar can ever understand; it just felt so right and my confidence was soaring.

One of the things I hadn't attended to was my spectacles. While they were not glaringly male spectacles they were also not female so in the short term I decided to buy some ladies reading glasses from the Pharmacy. There wasn't a huge choice, but I found several candidates, showed them to Denise and took the chosen pair to the till. As I planned to wear them, I gave Denise my current pair to hold. I paid the cashier and was putting my purse back in my handbag when I noticed she was looking at the glasses in Denise's hand. Without thinking Denise just said "Oh, these are HIS old ones". I couldn't believe what she had said but the cashier just smiled at us and we left. Denise was very apologetic but I wasn't desperately bothered, and if that was the worst experience I would have to deal with, it wouldn't be too bad.

This is probably a good place to mention the problems of misgendering for Transgender people. For people who had only ever known me as the male Robin it was not an easy thing to start consistently using the words she/her/hers instead of he/him/his and in the early days everyone would get the odd one wrong and apologise, but it never worried me as I knew it wasn't intentional; in fact it was understandable (especially if they had known me for a long time). With one notable exception no-one has ever deliberately misgendered me and I am grateful for this; so if someone, even now, gets a pronoun wrong so be it.

We had booked to go to the Chinese again that evening after having such a good experience the first time, but it wasn't so pleasant the second time around. I put a lot of effort into looking the part – I wore one of the tops I had bought that day. I really needed to grow my hair a bit to make it look more feminine, but it wasn't going to happen overnight, so I had to make do with it as it was. I was certainly getting better with the makeup and felt less nervous than the first time. This evening we were taken to a table in a room which was deserted. It was used as an overflow room for when they were really busy but the main restaurant area on this night was fairly quiet. Anyway, we ordered our food and enjoyed a glass of wine while we were waiting. Every few minutes a member of the staff would walk to the entrance to the room, take a good look at me then turn around and leave. It didn't bother me to start with. Our food came and I was more interested in enjoying the meal than watching the door, but out of the corner of my eye I did see a couple of people come and go. We finished our meal and the waitress, who I believe was the owner of the restaurant, came to take our plates away. She asked us if we would like dessert, but we decided to just order coffee. Denise ordered a Long Black but for some reason I fancied something with a little milk in it, but not a cappuccino or latte, so I ordered a Long Macchiato topped up with milk. The waitress didn't understand so I repeated it. Again she just looked at me blankly, so the third time I repeated it I was getting frustrated and raised my voice slightly. She seemed to understand this time and disappeared. Half an hour went by and still no coffee appeared; there was, however, a steady stream of people coming to look at me. We did eventually get our coffees after the intervention of a lady who came to the table to ask if we were "Okay". But I was by now completely over the whole evening and wanted to go home so we drank the coffee and went to pay. The owner was at the till and she gave me a very strange look as I paid the bill. It wasn't the worst experience I've had in my life, but it certainly brought me back down to earth with a bump.

In the big scheme of things my experience in the Chinese restaurant was a reminder that being accepted as a female was not going to be easy and would have to be a "work in progress" situation. What I needed was lots of practice but in my mind I wasn't ready to go out in public in Busselton yet. I felt I needed to be much more polished and have a bigger range of clothes. I knew my wardrobe was going to have to change completely and that would mean some serious expense, but it was hopefully going to be a nice experience getting fitted out for my future life. One of the things I had always wanted to do was to go into a ladies' clothing shop and try things on and get advice on what looked good and what to avoid. Denise was excellent in choosing clothing and accessories for me but up to now we had only been in shops like Rivers, Target and Rockmans. What I really wanted was to go to a better quality boutique which sold unique things. Also, I had not found the courage to go out in a dress yet, not that I had many to choose from. This was all about to change. One of David's daughters had a friend in Dunsborough who owned a ladies clothes shop and, whilst there one day, had mentioned me. The owner of the shop had a reputation for being a little bit quirky and very outspoken. One of the services she offered was an appointment where she would close the shop to the public in order to give the customer her full attention for a given time, in order for the said customer to renew their wardrobe, or so she hoped. She asked Jazzie if she thought I would be interested in booking an appointment so that I could try on as many outfits as I desired, in complete privacy. It sounded like a fairy-tale to me and I couldn't wait for my appointment.

The shop owner was certainly different, but in a nice way. She locked the door and pushed some hanging rails in front of it so that no one could see what was going on inside. I must say it was a bizarre feeling standing in the middle of her shop in my underwear, while the three ladies (the owner, Denise and

Jazzie) brought outfits for me to try on. The owner had designed some of the clothes herself and others were bought in, but none of them would have been found in the high street retail shops I had visited up to this point, and all seemed reasonably priced. I really liked the idea of wearing dresses and she certainly had plenty. There was every colour and style you could imagine, and I soon learned how to get the zips right up to the top, which had always been a problem for me. It's just a technique thing!

My appointment was for 1.30pm and I expected to be there for a couple of hours but it didn't quite turn out that way. We had been there about an hour when the shop owner cracked open a bottle of champagne and we all had a glass I was presented with dress after dress, tops and pants, accessories, underwear and just about everything I could think of. Some of the dresses made me feel so special; many were heavily discounted as well which was a help. I did end up spending a lot of money but I didn't really care as I was having the time of my life. After I had settled the bill the owner started giving me more things to take home - jewellery, dresses, sunglasses. She even gave me dozens of wooden coat hangers which she was replacing; they were good quality ones but I think they took up too much space on her hanging rails. They came in very useful to me as I didn't have half enough for my new wardrobe. The whole four hour experience had been wonderful; something I had dreamed about doing but had never visualised it actually happening.

Chapter 53

Time to start telling people in the UK

Not long after we returned from Esperance we had a Face-Time conversation with my brother and his wife. I wasn't ready to tell them yet but knew the studs in my ears were going to take some explaining. As soon as the conversation started, it was obvious that his wife was preoccupied by something, so I decided to just tell them that it had been something on my bucket list for a long time and I had finally had them done. It was clear from the start that my brother didn't approve. I'd had a similar reaction when I showed them my painted toenails some months earlier. It didn't bode well for me telling him he was going to have a sister instead of a brother, but I was going to have to tell them sooner or later.

In the meantime, we needed to make some progress with the people at home and the first on the list was Denise's employer. On the grounds that we were going to be in America for six weeks and the UK for five weeks in 2017 Denise thought it only fair to resign from her main job at Arbor Guy (a local Arborist). She absolutely loved the job, but we had no idea how much help I would need after my surgery so it would not have been fair to the owner of the business - a gorgeous man called Guy. It was agreed that we would invite Guy around to our house during the Christmas shut down so that Denise could tell him that she would be resigning as soon as he could find a replacement for her. The first thing he said to me when he arrived was "I didn't know you had your ears pierced". Now, Guy is 6'4" tall, has a mullet hairstyle, is covered with tattoos and has multiple ear-piercings; so I felt flattered that he had noticed my studs. I told him I had been thinking about it for some time and he complimented me on them. We had no intention of telling him the main reason for Denise leaving, so after we had enjoyed coffee and Christmas cake I left Denise and Guy to talk about the details. I went into the bedroom for a lie down but after a few minutes decided it would be much easier to tell him the real reason she was resigning rather than just telling him it was for "personal reasons". I went back to where they were sitting and just said to Denise, "We should tell Guy the whole story", so out it came. He was pretty surprised at first but was very supportive and gave me a big hug. I showed him some photos of me in a dress and his comment was classic Guy - "Quite tidy!" - I took this as a big compliment! Guy then said he couldn't wait to tell Kate, his wife, but after a few minutes decided that he wouldn't tell her; he would leave that to me. We arranged a date in the next few days for them to come round for lunch. I had only met Kate a couple of times but she was wonderful with me and gave me a huge hug after I had told her my story. She then revealed that she had actually had a premonition regarding my news after Guy had told her Denise was leaving - she is one very intuitive lady!

The next on the list were Ray and Jan from the dealership. I had dropped a couple of hints but wanted to tell them the whole story, so we invited them for dinner. They are both excellent company and the evening got off to a lovely start having nibbles in the alfresco area. I decided not to wait until half-way through dinner, as with other people, because I had a hunch that Ray knew what I was going to tell him. But I started at the beginning anyway. They knew much of the history, which had unfolded while I was employed at the dealership, but the details of before and after were new to them.

Over the period of my employment with them Ray and I had some very in-depth conversations about all sorts of things and I would consider them both very good friends. As I related the story I could see that Ray was putting things together and probably knew what was coming next, but he kept quiet and let me reach the end before standing up and giving me a huge hug. He then told me that he had indeed guessed what was coming and said he wouldn't have been surprised if I'd come to the door in a dress. Jan also gave me a big hug and said how courageous I was. It's funny really because I have never felt that I was being courageous as, by September the previous year, I saw transitioning as the only option that would keep me in this world.

While Denise was serving up dinner I went to the bedroom and morphed into Stephanie. When I reappeared in a dress I joked to Ray that I didn't want to disappoint him. We went on to discuss how we planned to tell people who we wouldn't normally entertain for dinner and it was agreed that Ray and Jan would host a dinner party for two other couples from the Dealership with whom I had worked closely, and had kept in touch with since leaving. I was growing more comfortable with telling my story, but it always became difficult when I tried to explain that my parents hadn't shared my beginnings with me. I think it will always be hard, as it still hurts to this day. Ray and Jan agreed to keep it a secret but with more people knowing, it was going to be common knowledge pretty soon. I decided I should try to personally tell the whole story to as many friends and acquaintances as possible, before they heard a "Chinese Whispers" version from someone else.

The next major hurdle was going to be telling my brother and his wife. I've never been particularly close to him, but his wife and I go back a long time, so I had felt that we had become closer in the last few years. After the conversation about my ear piercings and my painted toenails I thought that they may well have had an idea about what was coming, but it turned out not. I arranged a FaceTime call with them the day before my brother's birthday on the grounds of wishing him a happy birthday, but did add that I had something very important to tell them. We made ourselves comfortable and initiated the call. It was clear from the outset that it wasn't going to be a long call because they were getting ready to go away for Greg's Birthday, so I got straight into it. They already knew that I had been visiting a number of specialists and I had told them that I had also seen a psychiatrist but didn't tell them why. They knew about the gynecomastia, as I had made a point of talking about it on my trip over in 2013; but neither Denise nor I anticipated their reaction. It was like they couldn't wait to end the conversation, saying they were on a tight schedule and that they would talk to us again in a couple of days when they were back home. After the call Denise said to me that she didn't think it had been at all well received and to be prepared for the worst. But I thought it had just been a shock to them both.

A few days later I received an email from them saying that they would like to FaceTime when it was convenient. I still didn't expect there to be an issue; I thought that by this time they would be over the shock and, with a little bit of luck, would be happy for me. However it wasn't to be. From the beginning of the call it was obvious that they were really not happy about the whole thing and asked me if I had thought it through sufficiently before booking my surgery. I told them that I had thought about it constantly for the best part of forty years, but it didn't stop there. Greg had a full scale go at Denise which upset both of us, and I came close to ending the call but

I persevered. It was very clear that Greg didn't share my views about the fact that our parents had done the wrong thing, and he vehemently defended them, even though the facts are there to see and the letter of recommendation from the gender specialist actually states that I was born with some degree of intersex. We could see that it wasn't going to be resolved so I decided to end the call. There then followed a number of emails back and forth, arguing about one fact or another, so I resolved that it was best to restrict communication for a while and just didn't reply to their emails.

I always knew there would be some difficult people to tell and that my brother would be one of them, but hadn't expected it to be as bad as it was. It really upset me then and does to this day. One of the things which came up in the second FaceTime was whether I had told Fiona my first wife, as she was coming out to visit us later that month. We had planned to tell her when she arrived, but due to the reaction from Greg (who knew Fiona as he was in the same class as her through school, and through us being married) we felt it best to tell her before she left the UK. Greg actually said that he thought she might choose not to make the trip after we had told her. This said so much about how he perceived my transition – as something to be ashamed of or embarrassed about. I couldn't see that Fiona would react in that way but we decided to tell her anyway.

Communication with Fiona is usually via FaceTime so we agreed a time and I began to tell my story. She understood a fair bit of it as she knew my parents and obviously she was aware of the gynecomastia, although didn't know what the condition was called. Somehow, after telling Greg and his wife, it hurt more when I got the part about my parents and I became very upset but battled on and got through it. Fiona said she was surprised but not shocked and that she was even more excited about her holiday and being able to talk more about it face to face. I really appreciated her understanding - it made my brother's reaction even more incomprehensible.

Telling the two couples at Ray and Jan's dinner party was a very heavy affair; Ray and Jan were busy in the kitchen whilst the six of us went into a little reception room where I could tell them my story. The two men, who I worked with, are true Aussies with a hard exterior but hearts of gold. Their wives were both lovely - one of them had tears rolling down her cheeks long before I had got to the difficult part, which just started me off as well. At the end there were lots of hugs, and a great deal of concern for Denise as well, which was lovely. I had pre-arranged with Jan to go into their bedroom and change into Stephanie clothes after I had told my story. Over dinner we all chatted very freely about my upcoming surgery. I showed them an animated clip I had found on YouTube describing a very similar technique to the one which I was having, only it was all colour coded and there was no blood about; making for much easier viewing!

Chapter 54

Settling into being Stephanie

With each new person that I told, my confidence was growing; it was much easier speaking to people face to face, but there were still lots of friends and family back in the UK to tell; and lots of them didn't have Skype or FaceTime to make it easier. I also had a house to paint before Fiona arrived. I was offered the job as they were friends of friends, and because I could do it straight away. It was a large house but thankfully there were no ceilings to paint - just a feature wall in every room to cover up. Some of the walls were easy but others were dark colours and needed lots of coats before the colour stopped bleeding through. In reality, there was no way I was going to get it finished before Fiona arrived, but they were happy for me to do as much as possible, then finish off after we had been away for a few days.

Painting houses that are furnished is never as easy as painting empty houses, but the owners were brilliant - they helped me to move furniture and even filled in some chips and holes to save time. If they were around mid-morning or afternoon I was always invited to join them at the table for coffee or tea. They were retired farmers, so my having some knowledge of farming, having grown up on one, definitely helped and we chatted away very easily. They had talked about their two grown up children a little and it became clear that their relationship with one of them was complicated. Then one morning when the lady was there on her own, and we were having coffee, she told me a little about the situation. I said in reply that families were funny things and I was currently having some issues with my only sibling. She asked me why, and I just replied that he didn't agree with something I was doing in a few months' time. Now at no point had I mentioned anything about transitioning and the only clue that she may have had was the studs in my ears but without any hesitation she asked "Why? What are you doing? Are you having a sex change?". I was completely floored but just played it down and asked why she should think such a thing. She apologised and said she had listened to something on the radio which was a story about a guy who had recently transitioned. I quickly changed the subject and got back to work. The strange thing is, that even though I hardly knew the lady, I really wanted to tell her.

My last full day painting was a Friday. I didn't think I would quite get finished but there would only be a couple of hours checking each room for anything that wasn't perfect and doing the last couple of doors. When it came to coffee time on the Friday the lady was in the house on her own again and we sat at the table and chatted for a while. I then said to her "Do you remember the other day, when we were talking, and you mentioned the guy who had recently transitioned? What would you say if I told you that you had guessed right?" At first she didn't believe me, so I showed her photos of me wearing a dress. She was so happy for me and I wanted to hug her - it was the perfect reaction. I told her quite a lot of the story and at the end when she asked why my brother wasn't happy for me, I couldn't answer her. And, to this day, I still don't have the answer.

It was becoming easier to tell people and I really wanted it to be out in the open. David's younger daughter Jazzie had mentioned to me that the father of one of her best friends at school was also transitioning and gave me her name. I finally plucked up the courage to send the girl's father a Facebook message introducing myself, and suggested we should catch up sometime. To my surprise she was really keen and we set up a time for her and her wife to come around to us for lunch. I was quite nervous, as I hadn't actually met anyone who was on the same journey as me, but I was excited to hear her story and to get to know her. The day of the lunch arrived - beautifully warm - and I had put on a dress for the occasion. I felt really good in it; it was as though I had worn dresses forever and I just felt comfortable in myself.

The first thing I noticed when they pulled up in the drive was the car; a Toyota 86 which I really like, and thought that was going to be a good conversation starter. The next thing I noticed was her accent, which definitely had some Yorkshire in it, albeit the south of the county; so we certainly had things in common. Sadly, she too had not had much acceptance and support from her immediate family back in the UK and we spoke for some time about our experiences. After lunch she mentioned that it was her birthday in a couple of days and asked us if we would like to join them at a local restaurant to celebrate. We accepted, but after they had left I realised that she would expect me to go as Stephanie as she had only met Stephanie, not Robin. The pressure was on; I hadn't planned to go public in Busselton for some time, but felt I could do it with some help from Denise in getting me ready. As much as I was nervous, I was also very excited, and as it was going to happen sooner or later, it might as well be sooner.

When the time came, I was still jittery but as soon as I put on a dress I felt much better. I just felt at ease and thought that if I was to see someone I knew I was just going to have to tell them. It would be a shock, but hopefully they would be understanding. They picked us up and we were able to park almost right outside the restaurant. There was no going back now. We walked into the restaurant and I carefully scanned around the room to see if there was anyone I knew but it was fairly quiet and I didn't see anyone familiar. We sat down for dinner and had a really lovely evening. They were obviously regulars there as most of the staff knew her and they had made a special birthday dessert for her, which was a nice touch. The restaurant filled up as the night went on, but I still didn't see anyone I recognised and was hopeful that it would stay that way, and it did. At the end of the evening we paid the bill and left. I'D DONE IT! First outing in Busselton as Stephanie and it had gone without a hitch; I was very pleased with myself and it did wonders for my confidence. The next hurdle was going out in daylight, but there were lots of people to tell before that.

Next on the list was Betty, the lady who had house sat for us while we were away in 2015. We had become quite close friends and she invited us to dinner at her house, so I thought it the perfect opportunity. When we arrived it turned out that she had a work colleague staying with her. She seemed really nice so I decided that, even though I had only just met her, I would tell my story. They both listened carefully and when I got to the end her colleague asked if it was a joke. I assured her I wasn't joking and she commended me for having the courage to do it and follow my dreams, and also for telling a complete stranger my story.

Apart from my brother, my closest relative is my father's sister. As mentioned in previous chapters, she and her husband have been wonderful with me over the years; especially my aunt who was more like a mother to me than my own mother. I knew that telling them would be difficult as they don't use any form of electronic communication. So it was going to have to be by 'phone. Thankfully, Fiona came up with a plan to help me. She and my brother's ex-wife Lynne, who was also wonderfully supportive when I had told her over Face-Time, would both go to visit Aunt and Uncle and make out that it was by accident that they were both there at the same time (they both actually visited them from time to time, so it wouldn't be too much of a surprise). Then each of them would produce a letter which told my story and ask them to read it at the same time. After that, Fiona and Lynne would both be there to answer questions and see how it was all received. They would then talk to me and I would call Aunt and Uncle later.

It all went perfectly; they were understandably surprised but very supportive from the outset. I don't think either of them had much regard for my mother and in fact Aunt said it explained a few things, such as why I was never allowed to stay with them when I was little as they might have questioned the scars if they had had to change my nappy. Telling them was a difficult job made easier with the help of two wonderful friends; ironically both ex-wives of the Ullyott boys!

The following week I was at the supermarket doing the weekly shopping and on the way back to my car I saw a lady I used to work with at the dealership. Mia and I had always got along really well; in fact I don't really know anyone who she didn't get along with. Right from my first day in the dealership back in 2006, she had been very kind and helpful and after I left, whenever I called in, she was always pleased to see me. Anyway, I went across to speak to her and we chatted for a while before the conversation turned to holidays. She told me what she was doing and asked if we had anything planned, so I told her we were going to Philadelphia. She asked why Philadelphia in particular; I hesitated and said it was a long story. Being the lovely person she is, she said not to feel I had to tell her any more but I really wanted to. So I started to say about all the specialists I had been seeing, much of which she knew about, and said that it was going to come to a conclusion in Philadelphia. I hesitated and I could feel my eyes filling up with tears and I just blurted out "When I come back from Philadelphia I will be ....Stephanie!" She was, of course, thrilled for me, wished me a safe journey, and we parted with a tear-filled hug.

Chapter 55

First daylight outing
in Busselton

Since booking my surgery I had spent a considerable amount of time getting myself familiar with the procedure, what to expect and how best to prepare myself for the life changing event. One thing that came up time and time again was the importance of being as fit as possible; being the correct weight and as healthy as I could be. In general, I am absolutely petrified of hospitals and anything remotely connected to them but for some reason, even with the magnitude of the upcoming event, I was cool with it. A couple of people actually asked me how I could be so excited about having such invasive surgery and how was I not scared to death about it. Regardless of the fact that I knew I was going to have to go into hospital, have a major operation and be in considerable pain for some time afterwards, I guess it was something I had wanted for such a large part of my life and I was able to accept all that had to take place to make it happen.

The nearer the date of the surgery came, the more I hated my male bits. They became a nuisance as I was now enjoying the novelty of wearing tighter clothes as in the past I had always worn clothes which were baggy. I was still seeing Ana, my GP, on a regular basis as she was keen to see that everything was progressing in the right direction and I think deep down she wanted to see how I developed and morphed into Stephanie. One particular appointment in March was an early afternoon one, and I had decided that the time was right to go as Stephanie. My plan was to call the surgery about an hour before my appointment and let the receptionist know what I was doing. Having been a regular visitor for almost five years, I was well known by all the ladies on the Reception desk, but I was very happy that it was Miki who answered the phone. I had rehearsed what I was going to say, and it went perfectly. I simply said that for my appointment today it wouldn't be Robin coming along, it would be Stephanie. She was understandably confused so I told her that Ana would fill her in on the details. She said that she would speak to Ana and would get back to me if there was a problem. I didn't hear from her so guessed that Ana had enlightened her.

I put on a casual summer dress, some sandals, a little makeup, made my hair as presentable as possible and headed to the surgery. It was always busy and the car park was almost full. I was very nervous to say the least, but I walked up the ramp and in through the door. Miki was taking payment from a lady, but she looked up, smiled and said "Hi Stephanie, take a seat. Ana won't be long". I couldn't believe how easy it had been, and took a seat as instructed. Fifteen minutes passed and I was doing my best to look relaxed and as feminine as possible. A patient came out of Ana's room and went to reception to pay, so I knew I was next. Ana came into the waiting room and called my name. It was such a huge thing for me to be referred to by my new name. I stood up and headed for Ana's room and she stood at the door watching me as I walked towards her. Normally I would go into the room before giving her a hug, but this time I couldn't wait. I just went up to her and gave her a big hug and she said, "You made it, and how lovely you look. People wouldn't even give you a second glance, well done!" Once in the room I took a seat and she asked how things were going. I was still coming down from the euphoria of being out in public, as Stephanie, in the daylight and in Busselton that I momentarily actually forgot why I had made the appointment.

After the appointment I had planned to return home, change back into Robin clothes and head back into town to do some supermarket shopping; but I felt so "at home" in the outfit I was wearing I decided that the time was right to be out in public. I parked the car in the supermarket car park and went into the store. It just felt so right, being there as Stephanie. I finished shopping without seeing anyone I knew, and actually felt quite disappointed, but on the way back to the car, while I was walking across the pedestrian crossing I looked at a vehicle which had stopped to let me cross and immediately recognised the number. It was Denise's best friend; the first person we told about my plans back in October 2016. She recognised me, pulled up alongside me and put her window down and said I looked fabulous and so feminine that no one would ever doubt that I was the real thing; another confidence-booster. I couldn't really believe it was happening - I was finally becoming the person I should always have been and the reality of it was quite overwhelming. The time was coming when I would no longer have to think about who I was going to be on any particular occasion, as I would very soon be full-time Stephanie. Although I had a great deal of work to do as far as making myself feminine enough to be happy and confident, every day was a step closer to that, and a step closer to my surgery.

We had been having a problem with the air conditioning in the car; a technician's worst nightmare as it didn't happen until the car had been running for quite some time. I booked it in for its 30,000 kms service and mentioned the problem to the receptionist. She said they would need it most of the day and so would organise a loan car for me. When the time came I went into the dealership as Robin and went up to the service desk; it was the same person I had spoken to on the phone and we chatted about the issue with the air conditioner while she was preparing the paperwork for the loan car. I happened to notice her name on her business card which was on the counter and commented that her surname looked even more unpronounceable than mine. She explained that she was a New Zealander and it was a native surname. She looked at mine and asked where it originated from. I told her it was French, but I didn't admit that to many people. She laughed and I told her that I was actually changing mine soon and left it at that.

Unfortunately, the car couldn't be fixed on that day and was re booked for the following week, so we organised a loan car once again. When we returned, she had everything ready for us and I noticed that she had put a line through my surname on the work order. She apologised and said she would get the name changed on her computer system as soon as possible. I asked her what she was going to change it to and she replied, "oh, I presumed you were changing it to Davies like Denise". I assured her that I wasn't changing it to Davies, so she handed me the form and asked me to write my new name on it, which I did - Stephanie Vaughan! She looked at it and the penny must have dropped and she said "that's a nice name". I smiled and said that it was a very long story. Once in the loan car we drove to one of the shopping centres and I changed into Stephanie in the car. Around mid-afternoon the same service advisor called me to say the car was ready for us to collect and that they had identified what the problem was but would need to order parts to complete it. I thanked her and said we would be in shortly, but before ending the call I said to her, on the grounds that I wouldn't want anyone to feel uncomfortable, that she needed to know it would be Stephanie who would be collecting the car. She said that was fine and that she had amended the paperwork to reflect my new name.

We parked the car outside the service department just as she was showing someone to their car. Her reaction was classic; she looked at us, then realised that it was me in a beautiful blue dress, and the look on her face made my day. She said how wonderful I looked and that she hadn't recognised me at first. She just kept shaking her head in disbelief and told us that when I had said it would be Stephanie collecting the car she didn't realise that I would have transformed into her physically. It was yet another feel-good moment and I was beginning to feel an immense gratitude for people's reactions to my transition so far.

Chapter 56

Final Skype consult and pre-admission instructions

About a month before we were due to leave for Philadelphia I received an email requesting a Skype consultation with the surgeon's Physician's Assistant (PA) to discuss what things I needed to do in preparation for my surgery. She was a bit abrupt but pleasant enough, and it soon became apparent that there was much to do. Firstly there was a huge list of things I couldn't eat or drink in the final month and an even bigger list of drugs I couldn't use. I had to stop taking the testosterone blocker, which I had been on for a number of months, and wasn't allowed to take anything which might thin my blood, for obvious reasons. Then we got onto the list of tests I was going to need before the hospital would accept me for the surgery. Thankfully, I had done the thrombophilia screen within the past six months so that was one less to do - giving blood for this test was what had caused the fainting episode in the gender specialist's surgery in Perth. There were many more blood tests to be done and an ECG to make sure I had a heart-beat and a lengthy form for Ana my GP to complete.

All of this made the whole thing very real and raised my excitement level even more. I was surprised how unfazed I was about the thought of going into hospital in a country very far from home and having life changing surgery. I can honestly say I had never wanted something so much in all my life; it was all I could think about and as the time came closer and closer I actually worked out how many hours it was to the day of the surgery. It was quite hard to work out accurately as I didn't know for sure what time of day my surgery would be but I knew the date so just went for somewhere in the middle of that day. Ana was wonderful as usual, filled in all of the forms, organised the ECG and the blood tests and at the end of it all signed in the box to say I was fit for the surgery. She knew how much it all meant to me and made it as easy as she could.

We had chosen to fly with Qatar Airways, partly because we had flown with them several times before and knew the lay-out of Hamad Airport; but also the flight times fitted in with us even though there was to be a twenty hour stop-over in Doha. They were also the cheapest by some way and although I wanted to minimise the flying time as much as possible the whole exercise was going to be an expensive one. The idea of spending twenty hours in an airport was quite daunting so we looked into the possibility of taking a hotel room for the duration of our stay. Thankfully Qatar Airways owns a lovely hotel in the city and did a deal for us to stay there for a very reasonable amount, so we booked it. The thought of being able to have a good sleep and a shower or two was very attractive.

I was still doing all I could to get as fit as possible and was pedalling 25kms every day on the static bike, managing to get the time for the 25kms down to what equated to an average speed of of 40 kms per hour. I was absolutely spent after each session but it gradually became easier and I managed to improve even more, the nearer it came to our departure date. As I was pedalling I would watch a Music Video channel on the television to help the time pass, but most of the time I was thinking about what lay ahead for me in finally becoming Stephanie. There were often tears as I remembered the worst times throughout my journey since discovering about my secret birth history, but also recalled the tough years at school and other times throughout my life when having the gynecomastia and mixed up feelings about my gender had made things very difficult.

The next hurdle was organising a visa to enter America. Denise had made enquiries on the internet and come to the conclusion that the visa which we needed was going to mean a trip to the American embassy in Perth. Here we would be interviewed to see if one was to be granted. The visa we needed was a B2 which covered entry to America for medical treatment. The problem was that since Mr Trump's election as President, lots of visas had been cancelled or changed, so it was important that we did everything right; crossed every "t" and dotted every "i" so as not to have any delays when we arrived in Philadelphia. We had made an appointment at the Embassy and were both taken aback by the level of security; it was immense! We weren't allowed to take anything up to the Embassy (all belongings had to be placed into a locker) and went through airport style security before being escorted to the interview room. Once there it was a two-stage system and I was surprised to see that all visa processing was done in the open, not in a closed room. The first stage was to make sure all the forms were in order and all seemed to be going well when the man behind the counter noticed our UK passports amongst the paperwork. He asked us why we were applying for a visa for our Australian passports when the US's reciprocal deal with the UK made it much more straightforward to apply with our UK passports; it also meant we would end up with a multiple entry visa. We asked him to explain, which he did, and offered to change our application to our UK Passports – we appreciated his advice and took him up on his offer. The second stage of the process was a different experience altogether; it was an interview with another official who asked us about our reasons for wanting to visit the US. It was going fine right up to the point when he asked me what medical reason I was going for. As soon as I said "transgender surgery" he became brusque (we assumed he didn't approve of it) but in the end we were granted our visas so it didn't matter.

While we were in Perth we took the opportunity to visit the offices of the Gender Reassignment Board and lodged my application to change my Gender marker from Male to Female. The Board which considered these applications only met every two months so it was important that we did it before we left for Philadelphia as we wanted to lodge my Name Change application as soon as we arrived home and felt it was better to have my gender marker changed first and then my name. A further complication was that to be able to officially change my gender marker I had to be single and so needed a divorce from Jayne – something I had never got around to doing. The reason for this requirement was that at that time, early 2017, same-sex marriage was illegal in Australia. Thankfully, later that year, on 9th December, after a Referendum, same-sex marriage became legal. So, my divorce was another matter that I finalised in the months leading up to our departure. The lady at the Gender Reassignment Board was lovely; she checked the application thoroughly and said it all looked in order, took the $40 fee from me and said the next meeting was on the 22nd of May. Ironically, this was the day we were flying out to Philadelphia. My application was approved at that meeting and I left Australia as Ms Robin Ullyott, although my passports still said "Mr".

I had to pay the surgeon's fee before leaving and experienced considerable difficulty doing so. As we have a very good "points" deal with our credit cards, I decided to make the payment in two parts to keep it within my credit limit (and earn a considerable number of bonus points in the process). While I can understand that credit card security is very, very important and fraud is common, we did everything possible to get the payments through. We advised the credit card provider in advance to expect a large payment to an American business, but still had some issues. Little did I know that we were going to have to go through the whole process again in Philadelphia when trying to pay the hospital account.

The day of our departure was creeping ever closer and I just couldn't wait. We made arrangements to meet up with all of our closest friends before we went, and the diary was very full. Not what I really needed when I was trying to keep my weight down to the very minimum, eat all the right things and abide by the total ban on alcohol. I was completely focused on being as healthy as possible and thought if I did everything right then the surgery would be a breeze and recovery would be swift. The reality wasn't quite like that, but it still felt right to make every effort to be in the best possible health. I had regular contact with the surgeon's office and became good friends with the office manager. She was very "Philadelphia"; quite loud but absolutely gorgeous with me and I couldn't wait to meet her and the rest of the team, especially the surgeon who was going to change my life for ever.

We decided that we wanted a party when we returned to introduce the new Stephanie to all our friends. We called it "Stephanie's Stepping Out Soirée", chose the date (two weeks after we were to return from Philadelphia), had special invitations made and sent them out before we left to give people plenty of notice. All that was required was an outfit for the occasion and this was resolved during a stopover in Manjimup on our way to Albany one day. There is a lovely ladies' dress shop there. It wasn't one that I'd been into before, so we decided to have a look. I wanted to wear black with some bling on it and found exactly what I was looking for. Thankfully they had a sale on, and I managed to buy it for half its original price of $400. Perfect!

Chapter 57

Departure day finally arrives

The last few days before we left were manic and I was so excited I could hardly contain myself. We had arranged to leave our car with my cousin in Perth who was driving us to the airport. Before we left their house, I received an email from the Gender Reassignment Board telling me that my application to change my gender marker from "Male" to "Female" had been approved and that technically I was now Ms Robin Ullyott. It was a huge thing for me and felt like the first official step in becoming Stephanie. I took it is as a good omen for the whole trip and the adventure which was in front of me. We had dinner on the way to the airport and I have no idea what I ate as I could only focus on the next and most important stage of my Transition "journey".

The difficult thing for me was that I had to travel as Robin, as that was the name on my passport. The original plan was to change before arriving at the airport but for some reason it didn't happen and I decided to just be as ambiguous as possible, stay dressed as Stephanie but answer to Robin. We checked in and going through into the departure lounge was a big step for me; there was no going back now, even if I had wanted to. Of course that was the last thing on my mind; in reality I couldn't get onto the plane quick enough.

The flight to Doha is eleven hours long which, by any standards, is a long one. I didn't sleep at all, watched several movies and listened to some music; but it felt like an eternity. Unfortunately, the worst was still to come as the flight from Doha to Philadelphia is even longer at almost fourteen hours. It would seem like an age and I imagined I would get so bored. First though was our stopover in Doha; a chance to have a shower, have dinner and a good sleep in a very comfortable bed. It was all very civilised; we were given a voucher for the various restaurants and shown to our room. I really wanted to have a walk but it was forty degrees outside and very humid so we had something to eat, a shower and went to bed. I slept so well with the help of my usual sleeping tablet. I was now in the final few days as a man, although I had been presenting as Stephanie for some time. All the bookings had to be made in the name of Robin which was sometimes difficult to remember but until I returned from Philadelphia and lodged my name change application there was not much I could do about it.

Lots of transgender people don't ever have the surgery for whatever reason, and it is certainly a personal choice; but for me having the surgery was absolutely everything. Presenting as Stephanie when I still had the genitalia of a man didn't, for me, feel authentic; I would never have been satisfied with that situation. I was so thankful that between my gender specialist in Perth and the psychiatrist I was able to fast track through the system and organise my surgery without spending the mandatory two years in my preferred gender. Waiting those two years would have been very tough indeed and looking back, my deal with the psychiatrist - that I agree to have counselling with a clinical psychologist for a minimum of two years after she had given me my letter of recommendation - was, in comparison, much easier for me.

We headed back to the airport for the long flight to Philadelphia. All I could think about was waking up after the surgery knowing I now had the body of a woman; something I had wanted for so many years. The flight was very long indeed. I did manage to sleep but woke up with a dreadful back ache. It was late spring in Philadelphia so we were looking forward to some nice weather, and at the same time would get to miss part of the winter in Australia.

One thing we were both dreading was going through customs and immigration at the airport. We both knew there would be lots of questions about why we were there and why we had chosen to go in on a special visa when, as British Citizens we could have applied for the most common online visa. Obtaining the visa had been troublesome in the first place so we were quite sure it wouldn't be straight forward when we got there. Eventually the plane landed at Philadelphia airport. It was quite early in the morning and the whole place looked a bit tired compared to Hamad airport in Doha, which was all brand new. We were ushered to the immigration gates. The first thing I noticed was that there were forty-four gates and only eight were manned; six of these were for American passport holders and two were for visitors. That in itself seemed strange as obviously it would take the officers longer to process visitors than it would non-visitors but we waited in line as directed. Eventually we were called forward and I let Denise do most of the talking as she has more patience than I have but the officer was, in fact, very polite. He did ask why we had applied for the specific visa in our passports and I simply told him that I was here to have some surgery. He seemed happy with that and stamped our passports and waved us through.

We found the car rental depot - we had booked a Ford Focus but as I scanned the car park I couldn't see one, so guessed straight away that we would be fobbed off with some inferior model and was right. The car they wanted us to have was a Nissan Versa, definitely a class down from the Focus, but to be fair it was brand new and on the face of it would do all we wanted of it. The paperwork was completed pretty quickly, and we were given the key to our vehicle. Denise decided to sort the 'phones out before we drove off to find the accommodation we had booked; in fact it was a necessity to get them working as we needed them for navigation. We had both bought American SIM cards before leaving Australia so that we could get internet coverage wherever we went. She tried to get hers activated but was having some difficulty. This actually turned out to be a blessing in disguise, as the longer I sat in the Versa, the less I liked it, and so I decided to complain. I left Denise in the car and returned to the office. The lady we had dealt with was busy with another customer, so I spoke to someone else. I explained that I found the Versa very uncomfortable and noted that it wasn't in the same class as a Focus. She begged to differ on that point, but to my surprise started listing alternatives. She tried a Hyundai Accent, Kia Rio, both of which I declined. Then she asked "What about a Kia Soul?" Without hesitation I said that would be perfect - it's a bit higher off the ground, very comfortable and easy to manoeuvre.

By the time the paperwork had been changed, Denise had sorted out the phone and we were done. Our accommodation was about 20 miles away, and it was about the same distance from there to the clinic. I am not a good passenger at the best of times but the cost of putting two drivers on the hire car agreement was considerable and knowing that, after my surgery I wouldn't be able to drive, we decided that Denise would do all the driving from the day we arrived. She gave me her 'phone, already tuned into google maps and we were on our way.

Chapter 58

Conshohocken and the first few days in Philadelphia.

The drive to our first Airbnb was pretty eventful to say the least. Firstly, as mentioned before, I'm the worst passenger in a car that you can imagine. Being uncomfortable in the passenger seat is one thing, but being uncomfortable in the passenger seat on the wrong side of the road is a different thing all together. There were times on that first drive that I was absolutely petrified; so many lanes of traffic, different road rules, strange signs and symbols and all this in a car which Denise was not familiar with. Anyway, we arrived safely and things improved after that. We both settled into our roles in the car; Denise driving, and me navigating with the help of google maps.

Our first accommodation was a converted garage. It had been done tastefully and had most things that we needed but the bed was not very comfortable. The following day was going to be huge for me; I was going to meet the surgeon and I was very excited to say the least; I just wanted to get on with it now. It was over 170 days since I had booked my surgery and I still wasn't nervous at all. This even surprised me, to be honest, and I knew deep down that the nerves would come at some point but was happy that it wasn't today.

The twenty minute drive to the clinic the next day was fairly uneventful; we travelled through some pretty areas on the outskirts of Philadelphia. I had seen photos of the clinic online so had a fair idea what the place would look like. It was an old house which I believe was where the surgeon had previously lived. Three stories high with a basement, it was a house full of character. Ardmore looked like quite an affluent area; most of the houses were on big blocks and all were kept very neat and tidy. As much as I didn't expect it to be in a rough area, I was surprised at how well presented everything was.

We parked in the clients' car park at the front and went inside. I walked up to the reception desk where the young lady was on the 'phone so I waited until she had finished and then told her my name. Her reaction took me a little by surprise - she jumped up off her chair and ran round the front and gave me a massive hug. She asked how the journey had been then proceeded to go into the other offices to tell the rest of the team their Australian "celebrity" was here. I was very touched, but made it quite clear that I was no celebrity. It was lovely all the same. It was Friday the 26th of May 2017 and my surgery was booked for Tuesday the 30th.

The receptionist apologised and told me that unfortunately the surgeon had gone home early as she was not feeling well. Monday the 29th May was a public holiday, so in theory the first time I would see her would be in the operating theatre on Tuesday morning. It was a worry to me as I expected she would want to examine me thoroughly before then, just in case she found there was a problem. I mentioned this to the receptionist who said she would contact the surgeon and see what could be arranged. We were immediately given the key to the

Recovery Suites (on the floors above the clinic). We weren't moving in there until the Monday but given the public holiday no-one would be at the clinic that day to let us in. Monday was the day I would start my preparations for the surgery. This was something I was definitely not looking forward to, as it involved a very thorough bowel preparation, which I was dreading, but it had to be done and Denise was definitely going to make sure I complied.

We left to do some shopping for supplies, including the bowel preparation medication. We were given the names of the best places to buy everything, including adult nappies for post-surgery requirements. Everything was different from what I expected, although in reality I didn't really know what to expect. We found the pharmacy from which we could buy most of the supplies, and then a supermarket to buy some food for the weekend.

The next job was to find the hospital and touch base with the person who was in charge of admissions and payments. She took my credit card details, but unfortunately it was declined for some reason. I was pretty upset about it as we had gone to great lengths to make sure the credit card issuers knew exactly what was going on; I had given them the name of the hospital and roughly how much I would need to pay. We had experienced similar problems when trying to pay for my surgery when we were back in Australia and thought we had covered all bases this time. We called the card issuer and eventually got through to someone who understood the problem. The lady at the hospital had by this time gone for lunch so we decided to pay over the phone when we got back to Conshohocken and eventually the payment was approved.

Just after we had arrived back in Conshohocken I received a phone call from the surgeon herself. She apologised for not being at the clinic when we called in, and asked why I wanted to see her before my surgery. I explained about my beginnings and told her that I didn't want to go through all the preparations, then get to the hospital and find there was a problem. She agreed and suggested we meet her at the clinic on the Monday morning even though it was a public holiday. I was very happy and thankful. I don't think many surgeons would turn up on a public holiday to see a patient when she was confident that there wouldn't be a problem; but it was comforting that she wanted me to be completely at ease.

We spent the weekend getting to know the area, did some more shopping, bought pillows and towels for ourselves as we were going to be in Philadelphia for the next four weeks or so. Pillows are very personal things I think, and I am very particular as to how hard or soft they are. We also purchased a frying pan and a kettle as we both like tea first thing in the morning and the last drink before bed, but it seems that Americans don't generally have kettles. The frying pan was only a cheap one, but I need a particular type to cook my favourite scrambled eggs. The ironic thing is that we ended up bringing it home to Australia and we use it every morning to this day.

That night we were both very tired but strangely I felt the need to be intimate with Denise one more time before I had my surgery, as of course I wouldn't be able to in the same way again afterwards. It felt strange and wonderful at the same time and I spent part of the time thinking about how it would feel on Tuesday night when I would be minus that part of my body that I had resented in some way or another for such a large part of my life. I still had no fear of the surgery and just wanted it to happen; for so long I had wanted it and now, as it was so close, it felt unreal in some way.

We spent the weekend exploring the area and checking out the shops. It wasn't as I expected as they seemed to be scattered around instead of being in large shopping centres. We found one store which seemed to sell just about everything; it had rows and rows of clothes, almost as far as the eye could see. There was one dress which I really liked the look of, a size 10, and I almost walked past it. Then we realised that American sizing is completely different to Australian sizing so I decided to try it on. Now I must point out that I really didn't need any more dresses but when I put it on I just fell in love with it. The best part about it was that it was only US$25 so it was a bargain as well and is still one of my favourite dresses.

Sunday was our last night in Conshohocken. The tension inside me was just about at breaking point; I was so excited. We went to bed early as we had to be up and away in time to reach Ardmore by 9 am to see the surgeon. I think I was actually too excited and had a dreadful night's sleep, but we were up in time to get the place tidied up, pack our things and get on the road by 8.30. My mind was racing as we drove the twenty minute journey to Ardmore. I was going to meet the surgeon for the first time and I had rehearsed everything I wanted to say. We both had a number of questions, including how we would be getting to the hospital and for what time. At that point I didn't know what time my surgery was but I was hoping I would be first on the list even though it would mean another very early start. All would soon be revealed when we arrived at the clinic. This was it. This was the actual start of my surgical transition.

Chapter 59

First meeting with the surgeon and preparation time

We arrived at the clinic a little early, but there was a car in the carpark so we decided it must be the surgeon's and went inside. There was an entry alarm on the door so she knew we had arrived and met us in the reception. As this was the first time we were to physically meet the lady who was, the following day, going to change my life it was such a big moment for me. She came straight up to us and gave us both a hug and asked how our mammoth journey had been; it was a greeting I hadn't expected and I very much appreciated it. We were invited into one of her treatment rooms where she asked me to take off the bottom half of my clothes and put on a robe and she would be back in a minute. I was very nervous to say the least. What if there was a problem and she couldn't operate after all? I would be so devastated. She had a quick look and I explained about being born intersex and modified. She had a good look at the scars and said that, just in case there was an obstruction, she would insert the catheter while I was in the final preparation area to make sure she didn't have a problem later on. Apart from that she was happy that all would be good. I was so relieved that I gave her another hug. We all went through the preparation procedure so that she was sure we knew what we had to do. She told us that I was first on the list so would need to be outside the front door of the clinic at 5.15 am ready for the taxi to collect us. That was less than twenty hours away; my heart was racing. I just wanted it so very much, and now it was only a matter of hours away!

We took our suitcases upstairs to our recovery suite. It was fairly basic, but spacious and clean. There was a large fridge in the bedroom and the communal kitchen was across the hall, next to the communal bathroom. There were two other suites on the same floor, but neither was occupied, so at least I would be able to use the bathroom without having to worry that someone else needed it. I had never done a bowel preparation before, but imagined it would not be a very pleasant experience. Having said that, I could see why it was very necessary and was determined to follow the instructions to the letter. I knew if I tried to cut any corners Denise would be straight on my case, so there was no getting away with it.

I drank the first bottle of liquid and it didn't taste too bad; it was a sort of thick citrus flavoured drink. I had definitely tasted worse so thought that if that was the worst thing I had to endure it wouldn't be too bad. The preparation also involved taking Arnica tablets under the tongue for the some days before the surgery so I had already been taking them for a couple of days - they are supposed to help the healing process. Denise went out to the supermarket to get some food in, although we weren't sure what would be open, being a public holiday. But it seemed as though most shops were. As each hour passed I counted down to the time to when we were being picked up. The bowel preparation involved carefully timed tablets and drinks so I couldn't imagine getting much sleep over the next eighteen hours or so. I tried watching the television, which would have helped pass the time, but didn't have much luck in finding anything that interested me. There was a film on one channel which I had seen before and it was already part of the way through so I watched the last hour or so of it then got on to the next part of my preparation.

The worst thing was that I couldn't eat anything, apart from clear liquids or broth, so I was very hungry. Denise returned from the shops and was very considerate in not eating her lunch in front of me. The cooking facilities were fairly basic; if you couldn't microwave it or toast it then it wasn't going to be cooked! The comforting thing was that after my surgery, during business hours at least, there were nurses just a floor below; so if I had a problem then someone was close at hand to help. I would also receive a visit each day, post-surgery, from either a nurse or the surgeon herself to check on my recovery, which was good to know. My last drink of the bowel preparation was at 10pm so after that I decided to try and get some sleep. I had to set the alarm for 1am for the final part of the preparation (an enema) but hopefully I would get a few hours sleep after that. I couldn't take a sleeping tablet so it took me a while to get to sleep but I did manage a few hours either side of the final preparation. When the alarm went off to get up for the taxi I felt weak with hunger, but just wanted to get on with what the day had in store for me. I had a ten minute shower using special anti-bacterial soap, washed my hair and made myself look as presentable as possible. I felt really churned up inside; I didn't know whether that was due to the fact that I was very hungry or I was at last feeling some nervousness. In reality, it was probably a bit of both. I walked up and down the corridor trying to fill in the time. My suitcase was packed ready; not that I was going to need many clothes in the next couple of days. The room I would be in for my stay in hospital had an extra bed for Denise, so thankfully she would be with me at all times except for when I was actually in the operating theatre or the post anaesthetic care unit.

The staircase was at the front of the building so I could look out for the taxi arriving. To fill in the time I even walked up and down the stairs several times. I kept wondering what would happen if the taxi didn't turn up and we had to drive to the hospital. That scenario would have been so stressful. I need not have worried; the taxi arrived two minutes early. Even though it was late spring there was a chill in the air at that time of the day; we put our suitcase in the boot and got in. The driver checked he had the right destination address and we were on our way.

Once we got moving I think the enormity of what was happening hit me like a freight train. This was it; this was what I'd wanted for most of my life. This was why I'd counted down the last 174 days. For the first time I was absolutely petrified! I held on to Denise's hand so tightly; I didn't know whether to burst into tears or smile. The roads in Philadelphia are very badly maintained and the car didn't appear to have very good suspension. We bounced about on the back seat, so much that I thought I was going to be sick; not that I had anything to bring up, but it was a horror ride! I was surprised at how much traffic there was, even at 5.30am, but we seemed to be making good progress. The driver talked on his 'phone for most of the way and I just kept hold of Denise's hand while we looked at each other. I couldn't believe it was finally happening after all these years.

Chapter 60

Hahnemann University Hospital

Arriving at the hospital ahead of schedule, we checked in. By this stage I was quite well focused; I knew that there would be forms to fill in and lots of questions to be answered. We were told to go and sit in a waiting area from which we would be collected in due course. There was only one other person waiting; a young girl who was on her own. I felt a bit sorry for her as she didn't have anyone to hold her hand, as I did. I never let go of Denise's hand; just kept squeezing it tightly. I think the adrenaline had kicked in by now and I just wanted to get in and be put to sleep. I kept wondering what I would feel like when I woke up in the post anaesthetic care unit. I had only ever been anaesthetised once before and that was when I was ten years old. The only other time I had been sedated was for a dental surgeon to remove a tooth, and that wasn't a good experience, but the end result this time was going to be so worth it.

After a short time we were instructed to go to the eighth floor. By this time there were probably nine or ten people waiting, so the lift was full. When we arrived at the eighth floor I heard my name called out and we were escorted to the pre-op room. Once there, I was shown to my cubicle and asked to undress and put on my operation gowns. This in itself was a complicated job as hospital gowns (and how to put them on) are one of life's mysteries. Thankfully, Denise was there to help, which was fortunate, as I was all fingers and thumbs and not getting on very well. Then it started. One after another, a nurse or administration person would come to my bed and ask the same three questions; my name, my date of birth and most importantly what I was having done today. I realise that they don't want to perform the wrong operation on the wrong person but they must have asked those questions ten times or more. Another question they asked me was what my preferred name was. My wrist band had my male name on it as that was still officially my name, even though my gender marker was now female. They were obviously very used to caring for patients who were undergoing gender reassignment surgery and knew how important it is to use the preferred name and pronoun.

The administration lady was really nice, but was having a great deal of trouble with our address until she realised that it was in Australia. Apparently there is a Broadwater in Pennsylvania, so her computer was trying to make our address fit that one but the postcode/zip code didn't fit. Eventually she figured it out and had to manually enter all our details. Then I had a visit from the surgeon just to make sure all the preparation had gone as planned and that I hadn't eaten anything since the night before. I had also not been allowed to drink anything since midnight, so was feeling pretty thirsty as well as very hungry. She squeezed my hand and said that everything would be fine. I was so close to tears; even remembering it while I am writing this, is making me tearful. I can't overstate how momentous a time this was for me. All my preparations back home, my getting fit, going through all the visits to the psychiatrist and the psychologist, even all the dramas with the payments, was to come to fruition in the next few hours.

I had a visit from the anaesthetist, who introduced himself and the two people who would be assisting him. The assistants seemed very young to me and I guess, as Hahnemann was a teaching hospital, that they were probably students. He also asked me a number of questions, as well as the three regular ones. He wanted to know about my history; if I had ever had a bad reaction to anaesthetic and if I had recently had a thrombophilia screen, which of course I had done six months ago back in Perth when I had the fainting episode. He seemed happy with what I had told him and said he would be back soon to insert the cannula for the anaesthetic. I knew this was likely to be the worst part of the day but thought it would soon be all over and I would be asleep. I was still holding Denise's hand, but I knew she would be asked to leave shortly as they probably wouldn't want her around when I went under. I was also not sure if that would happen there or in the final pre-op room which was across the room from where my bed was. I was already uncomfortable on the bed, something which worried me as I knew there would be many hours lying like this after the surgery.

At this point I was asked if I needed to go to the bathroom one last time before the cannula was put in, I said I would and an orderly came and escorted me, perhaps to make sure I returned. I did have last minute nerves but there was no way I wasn't going to have my surgery that day. I was so ready, having waited all those years. I was taken to a toilet and asked if I preferred to use a male one or a female one. I chose the female one and, I know this might seem strange as I only needed to urinate, but I sat down to do it. I thought at the time that I would need to get used to it, so might just as well start now. I washed my hands thoroughly and opened the door. The orderly was waiting outside to take me back to my bed; he accompanied me all the way, chatting as we walked; it was quite a surreal moment. When I returned to my cubicle the anaesthetic team was waiting for me. I got back on the bed and they were straight into action. The nurse on my left side took my hand and wiped it with an antiseptic wipe then placed a strap around my arm so the veins stood out better on the back of my hand. Her first attempt missed the vein all together and it really hurt. I couldn't believe she had missed it. She then went further up my arm and tried again; a second failure which hurt even more. Thankfully on the third attempt she managed to get it into a vein. There was blood running down my hand which she covered with a dressing. She then went on to tape the cannula to my arm securely and started to prepare a syringe full of yellowish liquid. There were a few final questions then she said "I'm just going to give you a light sedative so you aren't stressed when we take you across to final pre-op". At that point they asked Denise to leave. It was horrible; I was very upset and didn't want to let go of her hand, but she comforted me and said that everything would be alright and reminded me that this was what I'd wanted for all these years. I knew she was right, but I didn't want to be on my own. Eventually I let her go; she gave me a final hug and I watched her walk across the room.

The nurse then connected the syringe to the cannula and started to squeeze the plunger and I felt a weird warm sensation as it went into my bloodstream. The rest of the team then unlocked the wheels on the bed and started to push me towards the final pre-op and I knew this was it. I don't even remember going into the other room; it was certainly no mild sedative, it was the real thing. I was out and when I woke up I would have the body I had wanted for so many years. At least, if everything went to plan I would.

Chapter 61

The other side

Coming out of an anaesthetic wasn't something I had had any real experience of. I didn't remember what it was like when I had my tonsils out when I was ten, so I had no idea what to expect. The first thing I remember was a lady's voice saying very softly "Stephanie, Stephanie, are you with us". She repeated this a number of times until I realised she was calling me. As much as the name Stephanie had been an inner part of me for such a long time, having been known as Robin for 56 years it took a while to sink in. I must have opened my eyes suddenly and made her jump, as by this stage she was bent over me and quite close. She calmed me down and asked if I knew where I was. I looked around and nothing looked familiar, but then things started to sink in. She said to me "You're all done" and I remember thinking for a short while, then saying "What, I'm a girl?". She smiled at me and asked, "Has it been a long journey dear?" Again I thought for a while then replied, "Yes more than forty years". I floated in and out of full consciousness for a while and was told I would soon be taken to my room. I was hoping Denise would be there waiting for me and sure enough, after a seemingly never-ending ride along corridors and in an elevator, we arrived on the eighteenth floor and I was wheeled into my room, where Denise was waiting for me. It was a lovely reunion; quite tearful, and I was so happy to see her.

For a while there seemed to be lots of people in the room. Eventually most of the nurses left, leaving just the one who would be looking after me until 7pm, when the night shift would begin. She also told us that she would be in every hour to check on me and to take my vitals. A little after 7pm she came in and introduced us to the night nurse who was equally lovely. She asked us where we had come from and was very surprised when we said Australia. She told us it was her dream to visit our home country and would love to hear all about it when she was doing her rounds. Each nurse had just 4 patients to look after, worked a 12-hour shift and most of the nurses worked just three shifts a week. About an hour later she returned to record my vitals and as both Denise and I were wide awake she pulled up a chair and chatted to us for some time. She wanted to know all about Australia and what we did there. I suggested to her that Australia always needs nurses and that she should come over and stay with us. I don't think she really believed us but it was lovely chatting to her.

Up until then I had not been in much discomfort. I guess the anaesthetic was still wearing off but as the night went on I was in increasing pain. The next time the nurse came in I mentioned it to her and she asked if anyone had told me about the morphine drip. I told her they hadn't, so she showed me the little controller which was buried under the sheets. She explained about pressing the button to get some relief and that it was not wise to wait until the pain was unbearable – it was more effective if pressed when the pain was at 5 or 6 out of 10, so that if it was going to get worse the morphine was already getting into my system. It was a great help and I thought I might get some sleep after all.

Denise made up her bed and we eventually settled down. Unfortunately, as the first nurse had explained, she would be in every hour to check on me so I didn't think I would be getting much sleep. But when she did look in on me I must have been fast asleep so she didn't wake me. As I usually sleep on my side, lying on my back was not very comfortable; but I would have to get used to it for a few days. It usually gives me back ache but I think the morphine took care of that for the time being. I felt very fuzzy in my mind, presumably due to the anaesthetic, and also very sleepy. It was the kind of sleep which just creeps up on you and then hits you like a brick wall; I would be awake one minute and then would feel my eyes closing before dozing off for a while.

The nurses came in to do their checks every hour or so. The breathing sensor up my nose was very uncomfortable but if I took it off for more than a few seconds an alarm would sound, so I had to put up with it. The following day the surgeon's surgical assistant came in to check on my progress. She had a look at my drains and the surgery site, announced that she was happy with it and asked me how I was feeling. It was quite difficult to answer, really, as I didn't know how I was meant to feel; I wasn't in any real pain as I was keeping it down with the morphine. I knew, however, that the morphine would be removed about six hours before I was due to leave hospital just to make sure I had the pain under control. They had already given me a stock of opiate painkillers for when I returned to the recovery suite and I was certainly not going to be slow in using them if I felt it necessary. An orderly came in and asked what I would like for lunch and dinner; to be honest I wasn't really very hungry but knew I would need to eat something. I was also conscious of the fact that at some stage I would need to learn how to use the toilet while connected to the various tubes and things; thankfully this wouldn't be necessary until I got back to the clinic.

My second night in the hospital was better than the first. I think the anaesthetic was slowly getting out of my system and I felt more alert. I hadn't been in much pain and had not had to use the morphine as much as the first night, but was dreading having to get out of bed and get dressed to leave the hospital. Another concern was the taxi ride back to the clinic. The drive to the hospital had been pretty hair-raising, and that was at 5.30 in the morning. The road surfaces seemed very bumpy and the car didn't seem to have much in the way of suspension; so two days post-surgery it was not going to be very pleasant but I was looking forward to getting back to the clinic. The staff at the clinic had made such a fuss of me I was sure I would get the best of care there.

The nurse had reminded me she that she would be removing the morphine drip six hours or so before my departure, so if I was in any pain then it would be a good time to top up on morphine at that point. I pressed the button as often as it would allow for the last couple of hours before she came back and removed it. I was not in any pain but knew it would wear off pretty quickly and I would be on my own. She asked if I would like to take some painkillers just to get me back to the clinic. I accepted of course as I knew what was coming. My first steps as a girl were very tentative, but so far so good. Denise helped me get some clothes on, albeit not very glamorous clothes, and an orderly came with a wheelchair. The journey back to the clinic was upon us. I was taken down to the hospital entrance while we waited for the taxi that had been ordered. It was late afternoon, still hot, and the orderly pushed me out to the now waiting taxi and put my bag in the boot. With Denise's help I very carefully climbed out of the wheelchair, feeling very unsteady, and gingerly settled into the back seat of what seemed like an old-fashioned car. The ride certainly left lots to be desired. We felt every bump and I hung onto the grab handle to take my weight off the seat and pro-tect myself from the discomfort.

What happened next really worried me; the driver asked us which was the best way back to Ardmore. I couldn't believe what I was hearing; he didn't seem to have much idea and had no built in GPS to guide him. After a while he took his phone from his pocket and presumably consulted google maps - whilst he was driving I might add! He realised he was on the wrong road and was suitably annoyed. It did nothing for the comfort of the ride, I can assure you; it felt like he deliberately drove over every pothole just to make things worse for me. I could feel a dampness in my clothes; I knew I couldn't have wet myself as I still had a catheter in so I presumed I must be bleeding. This also did nothing to help me enjoy the ride home and the journey seemed to go on for ever, but eventually we arrived back at the clinic.

It was almost time for the clinic to close, but as soon as we arrived, several of the staff and nurses were out to help me and welcome me back. It felt like coming home.

Chapter 62

Ardmore, our home for the next week

Very carefully I was helped up the stairs to our first floor suite. The stairs were fairly steep and circular, so it was quite a challenge but eventually we made it. When I walked through the door, the first thing I noticed was a beautiful arrangement of flowers sent to me from my very good friend David and his family back in Australia. It cheered me up no end and made me feel very special. One of the nurses helped me into the bed which was huge but quite low, so it was a big effort. I was in a considerable amount of pain by then and asked Denise when I could have some more Percocet. This was the American opiate painkiller I had been prescribed and I was hoping it would work pretty quickly. It was a good four hours since I had been given the one in the hospital, so I was allowed to have another. Thankfully, we were still the only people occupying the first floor, as I would soon need to visit the communal bathroom for the first time since the surgery. It had been two and a half days since I'd had a bowel movement, but I guess I was pretty well empty before the surgery. I had been told not to strain and if I was having problems to take a laxative; but thankfully all was good on my first toilet visit. I was very unsteady on my feet, which was not made any easier by having lots of tubes and drains connected to me; thankfully, Denise was by my side to steady me.

My first night out of the hospital was good. I managed to get a reasonable amount of sleep now that there was no nurse coming in every hour to check on me, but was in considerable pain at times which needed controlling with more Percocet. When the morning came I was awake early and very hungry so Denise went to the communal kitchen to sort out some break-fast. With the very limited facilities available (a microwave, toaster and coffee percolator), Denise cooked me some scram-bled eggs and toast which is my favourite breakfast. This was day three of my new life. Life without the male bits which I had, in the last few months, really come to resent. It was a strange feeling in some ways, knowing that going forward I would be the complete person I had always dreamed of being. I remember lying in bed watching Denise as she made sure I was as comfortable as possible, ensuring that I took my medication and administering the painkillers as and when needed (as long as it was by the book). I owed so much to this lady; she was and is my hero, my rock, my best friend and my soulmate and I loved her so much as I still do now.

A little later in the day there was a knock on the door and the surgeon came in. I was really happy to see her as it would give me a chance to ask her about my surgery. I wanted to hear her say that it was a perfect job and I would indeed have the vagina I had hoped and longed for. She took a look at the wound and announced that she was happy with the results so far, which was encouraging. There was a little problem in that she didn't think the drains were working quite as they should but wasn't overly concerned at this point. She asked me if I was in much pain - at the time I wasn't as I had recently taken some painkillers, so I came clean with her and told her I was keeping topped up with them. She didn't seem concerned at that point, but told me not to take them unnecessarily as they would hide any real problems. I agreed, and she left. I was a little concerned that tomorrow was Saturday and there would be no one in the clinic; so if I had a problem it would be a case of calling the emergency number and hopefully getting some help.

Thankfully the weekend passed without problems and I was looking forward to Tuesday and getting my drains and catheter removed. When Monday came I was feeling quite a bit stronger and had been moving around pretty well considering I still had numerous tubes coming out of me, which I needed to be very careful with. I was looking forward to having a shower after Tuesday; I couldn't remember the last time I had gone a week without having one. We were settling into a sort of routine. Denise was in charge of emptying the drains and I looked after the catheter bag. We had got through most of our food stock so she made a trip to one of the local supermarkets to get more supplies. As she came in through the front door of the clinic the office manager told her that Kathy, the surgeon, would be up to see me shortly. I was pleased to have Denise back as I was in quite a bit of pain by then; she made sure I was presentable and we waited for the surgeon to arrive. When Kathy had a look at me she was concerned that the drains were not working so she told me she would take them out. I was a bit worried on two counts; firstly that they were not working and secondly that she told me she was going to inject some hydrogen peroxide into the drain holes to try and unblock them. Now I remember hydrogen peroxide from my younger days; it was used by my hairdresser when she was putting highlights in my hair; but the thought of having it injected into me filled me with horror. She told me to be ready and the office manager would call me when the treatment room was free.

Soon after she left we received the call to go down to reception. I was pretty scared of going down the stairs as they were very steep; but we made it and arrived in the reception area in one piece. We were shown into a treatment room where there were lots of machines; I didn't want to know what each one did. Kathy came in and asked me to sit in the chair and put my feet in the stirrups. She removed the drains without causing too much discomfort and proceeded to inject the hydrogen peroxide into the holes. It was a weird feeling but not as unpleasant as I expected; the sad thing was that even with a little squeeze from Kathy there was not much happening. It was, however, good to get the drains out as they certainly made getting dressed a challenge. An appointment time was made to have the catheter removed the following day. Another procedure I was definitely not looking forward to!

We were now getting into a good routine in our little residence upstairs. I had regained my appetite and was starting to enjoy the meals which Denise lovingly prepared within the limitations of only having the microwave. Tomorrow was going to be a big day as not only was the catheter being removed but all the vaginal packing as well. Then I would be shown how to dilate, something which was going to be an important part of my daily routine for a good while to come. When the time came for my appointment I must say I was very nervous. The procedure was going to be carried out by Kathy's PA who I had not taken to at first but she seemed okay the last time we met. She just didn't seem to have much warmth, unlike the rest of the staff. Anyway, it had to be done so it was just a case of it being part of my journey and I would just have to get on with it. There had been lots and lots of occasions over the last eight months which had taken me well outside of my comfort zone and this was just going to be another one. I was sure there would be many more of them over the next few months.

We made our way down the stairs once again and went into the waiting room, from which we were called into a treatment room. I was even more nervous at the sight of a large syringe on the table next to the treatment chair, but the nurse assured me it wasn't going to be used for anything painful. The PA came in and asked me how I was doing, I replied "Okay but I will know better in half an hour or so"; she didn't even smile! The catheter was the first thing to be removed and I then discovered what the syringe was for. The catheter is held in place by a balloon type arrangement which was deflated by the syringe and removed without any pain. The next thing was the packing; yards and yards of it! It was a strange feeling having it pulled out; not painful though, so it wasn't a problem. After disposing of it all, she produced a strange lilac coloured package which she unrolled on the table. It contained three dilators of varying sizes, all of which made my eyes water; even the smallest one was about 25mm in diameter. Dilation is necessary after Transgender surgery, to stop the newly created vagina from closing up. I was shown how to lubricate the new vaginal opening and the smallest dilator was selected. It wouldn't even go close to fitting, so package number two was located and a much more amenable sized item was selected. I held my breath as it was inserted. There was considerable resistance, but it went in to the required depth and I could breathe again. This was going to be my routine four times a day for the next month; then it would reduce to three times a day for the following two months and twice a day for the three months after that. From then on, three or four times a week should be sufficient. It was going to be a long hard slog, but hopefully worth it in the end.

Chapter 63

Last few days in Ardmore & my first real emergency

I cleaned myself up and dressed but before I left the room I was asked to try and urinate in the bathroom attached to the treatment room - it was a very weird first experience. First of all having to sit instead of stand, and secondly not knowing how it was all going to work or feel; however it all seemed to work well and I felt pretty happy.

I had requested another prescription for pain killers so we were told to wait in the reception area. When we walked back into the waiting room I was aware of two ladies who were sat facing us; I smiled at them and started talking to the office manager, a lovely bubbly person who had been very kind to us since we arrived. After a couple of minutes one of the ladies asked where I was from. She had a familiar accent herself and when I replied "Australia" she said "No, where from originally?". I said "Oh, Yorkshire". She asked where exactly in Yorkshire and I told her, as I do most people, "York" which is not technically correct as we lived about thirty miles east of York, but it is the nearest place most people have heard of. She told me she was from Heckmondwike which is just about as far West as you can go in West Yorkshire and still be in Yorkshire. She went on to say that she had lived in Florida for the last thirty years and that the woman next to her, who was very attractive and, I guessed, about thirty-something, was her daughter; then she added "well, she will be in a couple of days". At that point I realised that the person next to her was technically male; I couldn't believe it! She was so pretty and feminine; more so than I could ever hope to be. We chatted for some time until my prescription arrived. The younger woman was obviously very nervous about her upcoming surgery and her mum was keen for me to talk to her about my experience, which I was happy to do. We arranged to meet later over a cup of tea, so that I could do my best to put Niki's mind at rest.

Right from the start it was a very easy relationship. I guess it was always going to be so, as we had something very special in common in our decision to Transition and we both had connections to Yorkshire, although she had lived in Florida most of her life. It was decided that, as they didn't have a hire car, Denise would drive the mother, Anna, to the supermarket so that they could get stocked up with essentials. We also needed things for the next stage of our journey, so it worked in well. While Denise and Anna were out shopping, Niki and I got to know each other and compared our journeys . It was excellent for me, as she was the first transgender person I had met who was going down the surgical route and also good for her as I was able to tell her exactly how the day of her surgery would unfold, and what would happen at what stage. By the time Denise and Anna had returned from their shopping trip it was obvious that Niki and I were going to be great friends. We worked in very similar industries, had similar interests and were on the same journey.

Both fridges were filled up with essential supplies and we chatted as if we had all been friends for years over a cup of coffee and the all-important cake. By the time I was awake the following day Niki would already be at the hospital waiting for her surgery and, as we were moving on to our second Airbnb the following day, we wouldn't see them for a while. We made arrangements to call and hopefully visit them a few days later.

I had a very poor night's sleep. It was my first night without the catheter and unfortunately I was up and down every hour during the night. I felt as though I needed to pee, but when I got there it was only a dribble; it was so very frustrating. Denise thought it would just be my bladder getting used to not having the catheter in anymore and that it would settle down over the coming days. I hoped she was right! We were both awake at about 6.30am and Denise went to make some tea. While she was in the kitchen I tried to sit up in bed but couldn't; the pain in my bladder was excruciating. It just felt as though whatever urine was left in my urethra had set solid and I couldn't move; I was in so much agony that I screamed out and Denise was back in the room in a flash; I tried to explain to her what it felt like but it was difficult as the pain was incredible. Denise brought me two biscuits and instructed me to eat them so that I had something in my stomach, and then gave me a couple of Percocet.

Denise brought in the tea and I tried to sit up but the pain hit me again, causing me to scream out. I had never felt anything like it before. Denise asked me if I wanted her to take me straight to hospital (as there was no-one in the clinic below our room at this point) but we decided to call the surgeon's 24-hour help line first and it was all a bit strange. A female voice answered the call with "Dr Rumer's clinic, how can I assist you". I remember thinking at the time that it wasn't a voice I recognised, but it got even more strange. Denise explained that I was in a great deal of pain and didn't know what to do about it. She asked what our location was, and when Denise answered, "at Dr Rumer's clinic" she asked, "and whereabouts is that?" So we gave her the address. It was clear, from the conversation we had with this lady, that going to a Hospital's emergency department was absolutely not the thing to do as the staff at A&E wouldn't have experience of transgender patients and it could cause more problems. We were told that she would contact one of Dr Rumer's staff who would be in touch shortly.

After about thirty minutes the painkillers had started to take effect and I was able to very carefully move around the apartment without too much pain. I felt as though I needed to pee again but nothing came out which made me even more concerned. Eventually, I received an email from Dr Rumer's PA with some instructions. Firstly, I was to go and stand in the shower for at least twenty minutes with the warm water running down my stomach, hopefully making me want to pee. I stood in there for thirty minutes; the water went cold and I wasn't feeling any better. The next instruction was to walk around the apartment carefully until that made me want to pee. I must have made myself dizzy walking around and around but it didn't make me pee. By this time we could hear movement in the clinic below so I decided to make myself look presentable and go downstairs to see if someone could look at me and advise what to do. As I still had a considerable amount of beard growth I decided to go to the bathroom and have a shave. Now, I don't know what caused it, but about halfway through my shave I had a very warm feeling as urine ran down my leg onto the floor. It was a huge relief and there was a lot of it, all over the bathroom floor! Quite what had caused it to flow at that point I don't know but I was very happy to see it. Maybe it was the vibration from my razor, or just the position I was standing in which made it happen but at least it happened and, more importantly, the pain was gone.

A little later the PA called me to see how I was doing. She knew we were moving out later that morning and offered to check me over before we left which I thought was very kind of her. We agreed upon a time which allowed us to pack all our things up and load them into the car; not that I was permitted to lift anything at that stage, so it was all down to Denise. At the agreed time we went and waited in the reception for her to be free. She checked my wounds and decided to give me a prescription for some "anti-bladder spasm" tablets, to be on the safe side. She told me only to take them in an emergency and to be sure I was close to a toilet at the time.

We finally left the clinic late morning and headed into town. The plan was to get some lunch, do a little shopping for our next stop and go to the pharmacy and get the prescription filled. I did notice on the script that she had asked for just ten tablets, and thought at the time that it was a small number, but soon found out why only ten. When the pharmacist gave me the tiny little plastic container she said, "That will be $77 please". I thought "Bloody hell, these had better work at US$7.70 a tablet". Thankfully I only needed to take one more, as the problem seemed to sort itself out. But I brought the tablets home with me and still have them as a memory of that day.

Chapter 64

Drexel Hill

We drove to our next 'home for a week'; Denise driving and me navigating. It was the first time I'd been in the car since my surgery and it was, at times, very painful. The road conditions in Philadelphia were dreadful; lots of bumps and potholes to contend with, as well as (for us) being on the wrong side of the road. By this stage Denise was doing a great job and I'd just about got the navigation under control, with the help of google maps of course. We eventually arrived at the house in Drexel Hill and parked outside. We were a bit early and it was clear from the door being open and there being people going in and out that it was still being cleaned, so we sat in the car and waited. It was quite a strange arrangement as, when the property was let out, the lady who owned it moved into the basement and lived there. The accommodation was clean and tidy and had everything we needed.

The weather was warm, so I was pleased to see numerous air conditioners in the house. Having been used to our very effective and efficient "split system, reverse cycle" units in Australia these seemed, in comparison, a very agricultural way to cool the place down but they were much better than nothing. They had chosen a suitable window, and precariously balanced the air conditioner on the sill, then closed the window to trap it in position and filled up the gaps on the side with filler panels. While not what we were used to, we were extremely grateful for the relief they offered from the heat.

Once Denise had carried our bags inside (I was still unable to lift anything heavier than a couple of kilos for the first few weeks) my first task was to take myself off to the bedroom and attend to my dilation. This was only day two and the thought of doing it for the next year, at least, was not a pleasant one; it hurt immensely! There was blood mixed with lubricant and it was not a pleasant experience at all, but it had to be done and it was going to be a major part of my daily routine for the foreseeable future. The deal was that you kept it inside you for twenty minutes. Once it was in place the pain wasn't too bad, but actually inserting it really hurt. I comforted myself by thinking that it would get easier and the end result would be worth the discomfort. Thankfully I only needed the bladder spasm tablets once more and even then the pain was nowhere near as bad as it had been in the recovery suite. I was very careful when I first got out of bed each morning, scared that it would happen again, but thankfully I was okay.

The following day was spent getting to know our way around the house and I did manage a very gentle walk around the block after dinner. My evening walk is a very important part of my life back in Australia and I was pleased that I had been able to manage one, albeit a very short one. We soon got into a routine and the dilation got a little easier as I became more used to it. It still hurt a lot, but gradually I learned the best way to sit and the least painful way to insert the dilator. The thought of doing it for at least a year was daunting, but even in the short time since my surgery I was getting used to my new physique and, to be honest, it still hadn't sunk in that I now had the body of a female. When I looked at the surgery wound I could see that the bruising and swelling were decreasing and the new shape of my body was emerging. It made me very happy.

Sitting was still very uncomfortable and we began to think about how unpleasant the 55-hour journey back to Australia was going to be. We decided that if it hadn't improved after another week we would need to look into upgrading our flights home to Business Class. It would be a big expense, but if I didn't improve then the flight back would be horrific. Thankfully, we had the stopover in Doha, which would firstly allow me to dilate and secondly have a shower or two and a good sleep. Each night I managed to walk a little further and felt it was getting easier. We were coming to the end of our week in Drexel Hill and I was looking forward to our next stop which was about a one-hour drive north to the town of New Hope, which is on the Pennsylvania/New Jersey border. Our accommodation there was in a converted fire station which was owned by a couple who ran an antique shop in the town. The description on Airbnb was that it was filled with antiques and curiosities, so we were both looking forward to seeing it.

It was the weekend and we decided to call Anna and see how Niki was going; she was having a fairly rough time, so as I was feeling fairly bright, we decided to have a drive to the clinic and see them. It was lovely to be able to compare notes, as it were, with someone going through the same process as I was. They were very pleased to see us and we had an enjoyable afternoon. I was able to warn Niki about the bladder spasm episode and what to do if she had the same problem. As I still tired very quickly and also had to get back to do the dreaded dilation, we didn't stay too long.

It was a considerable drive to New Hope (and in the opposite direction to the clinic), so I decided to get checked over before we left the area. The staff there were happy to oblige and it was a good opportunity to talk about my progress and what they thought about our very long journey home. The nurses were happy with my progress and I collected another script for painkillers, which I had almost run out of. While I realise that I had paid for my surgery, and the service which had accompanied it, we had both been overwhelmed by the kindness of both Kathy and the staff employed at the clinic. They were all beautiful, caring people for whom nothing seemed too much trouble. It had been a real eye opener for us both.

Chapter 65

Destination New Hope, in more ways than one

We packed all our belongings into the car and set off for New Hope. The name was sort of fitting really, as the new life I had longed for was unfolding day by day. Each time I dilated I would take the mirror, supplied by the clinic, and examine my new genitalia. It looked better every day; it was still far from the pretty thing I had been promised, but I knew I would need to be patient. I had, after all, waited over forty years to get this far, so a little longer was a small price to pay. Especially when I look back and think of the years gone by when I was convinced that I would sooner or later take Stephanie to my grave as I didn't think I would ever find the courage to do anything about it.

The drive to New Hope was long and unpleasant to say the least. I was in pain for the whole time and, the longer it went on, the worse the pain became. Each and every bump in the road would unsettle the little Kia Soul and send a wave of pain through me. The hospital had given me a blow-up ring to sit on and it certainly made things better, but the pain was still considerable. We eventually arrived and found the apartment. There were two down sides to it; firstly there was no parking with the apartment and very little long-term parking available in the whole town. The second was the twenty-three very steep steps from street level to the apartment. Once up there, though, it was lovely; very different, but lovely all the same. The kitchen was extremely well equipped and spacious. The bedroom was huge and there was a large roof-top balcony overlooking the town and surrounding area which could be used when the weather was good. It did mean negotiating another flight of stairs, but taken slowly, I could manage them.

The bed was huge but was only 20cm off the floor; it was almost like just a mattress with a frame around it. It was very comfortable but being so close to the floor made getting in and out of it quite a challenge for both of us. I got on with my dilation while Denise went to check out the town to see where supplies could be obtained. She was away quite some time as she had problems finding a parking place where we could leave the car overnight. The bathroom was excellent - it had a big shower with multiple jets and a seat in it so if I needed a rest I could perch myself on it for a while. The description was certainly correct; there were all sorts of antiques in the place and some very interesting pictures on the wall. There was a full native Indian head dress which I couldn't resist putting on and having Denise take my photo.

Given my ongoing pain and discomfort, we needed to make a decision as to whether or not to upgrade our flights home, if indeed that was possible. Denise called Qatar Airways to check availability and to see what the monetary damage would be. The lady at Qatar was very helpful; she put us on hold while she went off to do some checking and returned a few minutes later with good news. There were Business Class seats available and, although the price was pretty hefty, we decided to go for it. I had only flown Business Class once before and that was a free upgrade back in 1989, so it was going to be a big experience. We had to get through the next ten days or so first though.

While we were there it was Father's Day in both America and the UK. Having lost my father some 16 years before, and never having had children of my own, it wasn't a day that I had celebrated recently but the issues I had at that time about my parents, and them not telling me about being born intersex, were still very raw for me and I knew it would be quite a tough day. Deep down, I don't blame my father as much as my mother, as Dad would just have done what he was told to do by Mother; such was his loyalty to her.

As dilating was very uncomfortable, to pass the time I took to watching YouTube music videos on my 'phone. It was tricky using just one hand on the phone, but I soon got used to it and my personal "play list" was growing every day. At home we had the basic satellite TV package to allow us to watch the "Smooth" channel which was 24/7 music videos, most of which were from our era (70s, 80s and 90s music). Some months earlier I had been sitting watching and a track called "Insatiable" by Darren Hayes came on. I really enjoyed the track (and the video) but at that time couldn't have told you who Darren Hayes was, or what his claim to fame was. It was a track often played on "Smooth" and I enjoyed it every time. So I looked it up on YouTube and discovered that he was the vocal half of the Australian band from the late nineties/early 2000's "Savage Garden". I had heard of this band and quite liked some of their music. As YouTube does, it put together a mix of Darren Hayes/Savage Garden tracks which I settled down to watch while dilating. In a strange coincidence, that particular day (Father's day) was the first time I had really listened to the words of their track "Affirmation" and the fourth line really touched a nerve. I went back to the beginning and listened to it again, and again, and again. There are lots of really profound statements in the track but the fourth line really stuck with me. It goes like this; "I believe your parents did the best job they knew how to do". I really struggled with it and, although I didn't believe it to be true, I kept on playing it every time I dilated. It was as though it had been played on purpose to make me think about those words on Father's Day.

To this day, I still believe that what was done to me when I was born was wrong, but it was how intersex was handled in the nineteen-sixties. I know my parents would probably not have had a choice in what happened to me; they would just have been told what the issue was, what was needed to "correct" it and to sign the consent form to allow it to happen. However, I believe that them not explaining to me why I then had the gynecomastia, and allowing me to suffer the mental and physical abuse at school that I did, was a very bad decision to put it mildly. Whether or not they were advised to do that I'll never know, and choosing to tell me at any time would have been difficult; but they should have tried. It is something I have resigned myself to, as I am the only person hurting over their failure to tell me, and there is nothing I can do to put it right.

Chapter 66

Last Airbnb and the long journey home begins

Our week in New Hope was coming to an end, as was our time in America. We just had three nights left in an Airbnb apartment in Plymouth Meeting. It was a strange arrangement really, as it was clear from the owner's communication that she wasn't really supposed to let it out. She asked us not to talk to anyone in the complex about who we were or on what basis we were there, but the apartment was nice so we kept ourselves to ourselves and enjoyed it.

Talk about going from the sublime to the ridiculous. The bed in New Hope had been a problem as it was so close to the ground and had a very annoying plinth around the mattress which made it even more difficult to get in and out of. The one in the new apartment came up to my waist. Denise almost needed a step ladder to get into it – she had to lever herself off the windowsill to get in. It was, however, very comfortable and huge. Provided I was not in and out of bed too often it was okay. The apartment was equipped with everything we needed so we didn't venture far. We spent three nights there and would be leaving very early on the final morning to return the hire car and arrive at the airport in good time for our flight.

The day before we flew home I had my final appointment with Kathy. I was very stressed about it as I felt I hadn't progressed much over the last 10 days or so and I was dreading her saying I was not well enough to fly home. That would be a disaster to say the least. We were up early as my appointment was at 9.30. After a slight detour due to a failure of my (and Google maps) navigation skills, we arrived on time and were met by one of the staff who said they had missed us, which was lovely. We were shown into a consulting room and I was asked to undress and prepare myself for Kathy. After a few minutes she came in with the nurse and had a good look. Thankfully, she was happy with progress and gave me the okay to fly home. She did have a small concern about the swelling of my mons pubis area and decided to make a small incision where one of the drains had been located to see if anything came out. It didn't, so she cleaned me up and basically sent us on our way. Before we left, each and every one of the staff gave us both a big hug. I was almost in tears; this was a well renowned surgeon and her team, all of whom had been amazing, caring and compassionate with us; it was very moving. Whilst there, we went into Ardmore town, had an early lunch and then headed back to Plymouth Meeting to prepare for the flight in the morning. I was still dilating four times a day, so had to do that first.

The following morning we were up at 5am. First job was dilation while Denise made breakfast. The rules say twenty minutes but as I didn't know how long it would be before I would get the chance again I kept the dilator in for thirty minutes. In reality it was going to be the only time it happened that day. By 6.15am we were on our way to the hire car depot where it was just a case of returning the car. Thankfully we had not had any issues with the vehicle so we handed in the keys and caught the courtesy bus to the Terminal. We were the only ones on the bus so the driver said he would take us straight there, which was kind of him. We arrived at the airport in plenty of time and I was swiftly put into a wheelchair and taken to check-in. That all went very smoothly and we were whisked off to the business class lounge. Qatar Airways don't have their own lounge in Philadelphia airport so we were taken to the American Airlines lounge. It wasn't particularly luxurious, but at least we were given coffee and something to eat and the seating was comfortable for Denise. I remained in my wheelchair, which made me feel very feeble indeed, but I know it was for the best in the long run. After about an hour the porter returned and escorted us to the departure gate. I was placed at the front of the line and immediately wheeled down the chute to the aircraft. At that point the man helped me up, Denise gave him a tip and he left. I felt a bit of a fraud having used the wheelchair, so I waited until he was a reasonable distance away before walking the last few steps into the aircraft. We were shown to our seats by a lovely flight attendant who explained that she would be looking after us throughout the flight and offered us some champagne to be going on with. I hadn't had any alcohol since my surgery, but decided that it would be great to have a glass to celebrate going home.

When the flight attendant returned with our drinks she went through the menu and explained that we could have anything we wanted at any time. I was very impressed indeed as you often don't want to eat when they serve meals on flights, so this would make a lovely change. We were also shown how to adjust the seat and make it into a bed, but told to just press the button and someone would come and make it up for us when we wanted to sleep. It was all very grand indeed. I made myself as comfortable as possible and began to check out the entertainment; there was so much to choose from it would take me a while to decide what I wanted to watch.

The aircraft was an Airbus 350; not one I'd been on before and after a while I realised that something was very different. The seats in the middle of the Business Class area were arranged in pairs, in a sort of herringbone layout and then there was a single line of seats along the window sides of the 'plane. Each seat was set at an angle so that it had its own little pod area. The difference between the middle seats and the window ones was that there were no compartments for hand luggage in the middle so the ceiling was much higher giving the feeling of spaciousness. This was lovely and for me felt much less claustrophobic; however the downside was that there were no overhead vents for fresh air over the centre seats. This didn't occur to me as a problem until about two hours into the flight when I started to overheat. My hormones were all over the place and from a position of having had an oversupply of oestrogen for most of my life, I felt as though I had little of anything left. Consequently, I had been experiencing regular hot flushes. I have always had the same sequence of events when overheating; I faint, then vomit! Not what I needed on a fourteen hour flight so I tapped on Denise's shoulder and told her I was overheating and was going to the bathroom where there was a vent to cool me down. I had been sitting in there for probably five minutes when Denise knocked on the door. She asked if I was okay and how much longer I would be in there. I opened the door and came out. I had cooled down considerably, but was concerned that it could possibly happen again.

I needn't have worried. Denise had spoken to the flight attendant and when I returned to my seat I was surprised to find all my things had been moved across the aisle to a window seat with air vents. I have no idea what they did with the guy who had been sitting there, as he was nowhere to be seen. But the attendant quickly made up my bed and made sure I was comfortable, while Denise looked on. In the course of the conversation the attendant asked me if I was sick and I told her I had simply overheated as there were no vents above my seat. She asked me why I had overheated so I told her I was recovering from some surgery which was why we were in America. She asked me what surgery I was recovering from and I looked at Denise who at that point intervened and said it was internal surgery, which the Attendant seemed to accept. She asked if there was anything she could get for me, so I requested a black coffee and she left. She returned a few minutes later with my coffee, plus some lovely honey coated cashews.

By this time Denise had returned to her seat so, after placing my coffee and nuts on the tray she squatted down beside my seat and asked me again what my surgery had been. This time I didn't have Denise to help me out, so I beckoned her to come close to me and I whispered in her ear, bearing in mind that I am still traveling as Robin Ullyott; "I'm not a he anymore I'm a she!". She took my hand and squeezed it and said she had thought that was the case, but didn't want to presume. She was gorgeous and told me she was in awe of my courage and was proud to be looking after me. I cried! After she left, Denise came across to ask what she had wanted, so I told her the story; she smiled, shook her head and went back to her seat. No sooner had she left but another attendant came to my seat and knelt down beside me. She had introduced herself as the Purser at the beginning of the flight and had said if she could be of any assistance then I just had to ask. She took my hand and explained that the other attendant had revealed the reason for my surgery; she told me how brave I was to follow my dream and that she was so pleased I had told them. I was blown away by their kindness; such lovely people. I settled down to watch a movie and the rest of the flight passed very enjoyably. I felt I received extra special treatment from these two ladies and received a lovely hug from the Purser when we disembarked at Doha.

Chapter 67

Welcome to Australia Stephanie

When we arrived at Doha I was collected from the plane by a young lady with a wheelchair (we had requested special assistance for me on the journey as I knew I wouldn't be able to walk far, or lift luggage). We were taken to the main area in an electric buggy and escorted through the immigration area at high speed. The lady then took us to the desk which dealt with stopover hotels and we were given a voucher for the same hotel as on the outbound flight. We were a little disappointed as we had hoped for one in the main airport complex which would have meant we didn't need a temporary visa; but at least we knew the hotel layout and restaurants etc. We were guided through the priority lane at the customs desk and taken to the airport foyer where we would be collected by a driver and transferred to the hotel. The chauffeur driven ride to the hotel was much less painful than it would have been in a minibus, but it still seemed a long drive when I was in quite considerable pain. The hotel was pretty quiet and we had a very short wait before being given our room key and the Restaurant voucher. First job was the dreaded dilation. I had no idea how it would go as it had been almost a full day since the last dilation. Thankfully, it wasn't too bad and a shower was next on the list, followed by some sleep. I decided to dilate three times while there, so set my alarm accordingly. Each time it went reasonably well, but not without pain. So it was followed by a painkiller each time, which also helped me to sleep.

We were in Doha for twenty hours, but by the time we had arrived, been processed through the airport and taken to the hotel we probably only spent about fourteen hours in the room. It was an excellent opportunity, though, to enjoy some proper sleep, good food and a couple of showers. After being driven back to the airport and taken straight to the Al Mourjan lounge, we were beautifully "fed and watered" before our next flight. The flight back to Perth was eleven hours, which normally would be a very long flight; however, in Business Class it seemed to pass pretty quickly. The aircraft for this leg was a Boeing 777 which was not as pleasant as the Airbus, but it did have the advantage of my being able to sit next to Denise rather than on the other side of an aisle. We had some dramas with my entertainment system not working, but it didn't really bother me as I wanted to sleep as much as possible.

We arrived in Perth on time and I was dreading the rigmarole of getting through customs. Perth is famous for the time it takes to get through customs and immigration and I'm not saying that is a bad thing, only that I don't quite understand why there are about forty immigration desks and only ever a handful of them are manned. However, this time, as I was in a wheelchair, I was through in no time. We collected our cases from the priority section and we were on our way. When we emerged, Louise and Josh were waiting for us with our car. We received massive hugs from them both and were soon out of the airport and on our way to my cousin's house in City Beach, where we were to spend the night. I had dosed myself up with painkillers towards the end of the flight as I thought there would be some walking to do which would cause me a great deal of pain but thankfully it was kept to a minimum and all was well. When we arrived at the house I felt very cold so I climbed into bed to try and warm up. Louise brought me a heat pad which helped, and eventually I stopped shivering. She also made us dinner, which we appreciated, and we then had an early night; after I had dilated of course. It had been a long couple of days, but we were glad to be back on home soil again.

The following morning we had an appointment with the Registry of Births, Deaths and Marriages (to lodge the application to change my name) and we also wanted to collect my Certificate (certifying that I was now Female) from the Gender Reassignment Board. The young lady at the GRB was delightful; very helpful indeed. We then walked to the Registry of Births, Deaths and Marriages office and attempted to lodge my application to change my name. This was a different case all together. My name was called out and we went and sat at the counter. The man dealing with us barely spoke to us, just took the paperwork and began to go through it. He turned to me and asked why I wanted to change my name and I replied "Transgender", at which point he rolled his eyes and went back to checking the paperwork. The list of required items included proof of living in Western Australia such as credit card statements or bank statements showing payments to utilities, for example. As all of our utilities were paid through our joint card, of which Denise is the primary card holder and I had a "Supplementary" card, my name was not actually on the Statement, so we had just included my personal Credit Card Statements which had lots of entries going back the prescribed length of time and included many payments to local Western Australian businesses, including supermarkets. Sadly, he wasn't happy with that and virtually threw the paperwork back at us saying there was not sufficient proof of living in Western Australia. I was devastated; I couldn't believe it. I was all set to have it out with him, or ask to see his supervisor, but Denise stopped me and said that she would sort it out, and we departed very quickly. It was obvious to me that he didn't approve of me being transgender, from the way he rolled his eyes when I told him. It wasn't my first experience of negativity towards me in my journey to date (the official I encountered in applying for my US Visa had been the same), however officially changing my name was an important milestone for me and the man's attitude really upset me.

At last we were on our way back to Busselton. Unfortunately, it was a very painful ride home, so much so that I moved into the back seat so I could lie down. However, that position hurt my back, so I was very happy when we eventually pulled into our driveway. It was winter in Australia and I was feeling the cold; thankfully our house sitters had left us plenty of firewood to be going on with and we soon had the wood-fire roaring. Within a few days Denise had sorted out my change of name, after speaking with a very helpful lady who advised us exactly what was needed and we speed-posted the information to them.

I soon got into a routine with my dilation; it didn't get much easier, but thankfully I was soon down to three times a day, which is more convenient to work around. I was still unable to lift much, but managed to stoke up the fire when Denise was out. I had very regular visits to Ana my GP and the first brought up quite a difficult question; do I offer to show her my surgeon's handiwork, or let her bring it up. She was upfront in telling me it would be a first for her, but I had no issues in showing her. In many ways without her none of this would have happened, and I have told her many times how much I appreciate all she has done for me. To my surprise, when she did see my new vagina she was very complimentary. I expected her to be concerned about the amount of swelling and bruising still evident but she assured me it would settle down eventually. She also went on to say that I needed to be very patient with the healing process, as there had been major work done both inside and outside. She gave me a huge list of blood tests which she wanted me to do and asked me to make an appointment for the same time the following week, when all the results would be in.

When I went back the next week she said there was little wonder I wasn't coping very well with heat and cold as I had absolutely no oestrogen, no testosterone, no iron and lots of other deficiencies. All easily fixed, although the oestrogen level was to be the source of many problems over the coming months.

Chapter 68

Stephanie's Stepping out Soirée

The day of my party (which we had organised before we left for Philadelphia) was approaching quickly. In hindsight, it would have been better to have held it later in the month to give me more time to recover; but I wanted as many people as possible to meet Stephanie for the first time at the party, so it was set for the 8th of July 2017.

I had been struggling with sleeping as I was having to go to the bathroom multiple times a night, but thankfully Ana seemed to have solved that problem with the introduction of a little blue tablet called Endep. This has many uses, but one of them is to relax the bladder to allow it to fill fully before needing to go to the bathroom. Taken along with my regular sleeping tablet it worked a treat and I was confident that my recovery would speed up now that I was sleeping more soundly.

The few days before my party were filled with lovely experiences as well. On the Thursday Denise and I went into town to do some shopping and to call at the post office to collect mail from our PO Box. As I opened the little door I could hardly believe my eyes; there was a letter addressed to Ms Stephanie

Vaughan! My first ever mail in my new name and I knew it would be my change of name certificate. I asked Denise to open it as I drove back home. I had expected a large envelope with the certificate in it but it was just a normal size envelope with the certificate folded up inside. It didn't matter, it was now official; I was now officially Stephanie and I felt elated. We had just arrived home when my best friend David's daughters came round with morning tea. They had brought a lovely chocolate cake and some rather nice sparkling wine. They are two beautiful young ladies who I feel very blessed to have in my life.

Without delay we arranged an appointment with the Post Office to sort out my new passport and driver's licence. It was a complicated process as they had to be done in the right order, as the driver's licence is needed for the new passport application (as identification) but the two ladies who looked after us were wonderful. It was quite funny really, as one of them said in passing that "obviously she hadn't done one of these before" then realised how inappropriate it had sounded. I wasn't offended and admired her honesty and the fact that she called the passport office to make sure she had done it correctly. All was in order, and my passport would be posted to me as soon as possible. I thought it best to pay for the express delivery, as I would need it for our flights to the UK which were only a month away.

Friday afternoon was spent at Linda's, our next door but one neighbour, who was responsible for making me look as feminine as possible for my party on Saturday. It was the full works! Feet and toenails, eye lash tinting and eyebrow shaping and tinting. She is a gorgeous person and we chatted non-stop throughout the treatment. She was also doing my makeup for the party and her wonderfully talented daughter was challenged with making my hair look something like acceptable, which was to be a big job.

Saturday arrived and I must confess to being a little nervous. It was my first official occasion as Stephanie and I wanted everything to go well. The first job was take delivery of some outdoor furniture which we had organised through one of Denise's bookkeeping clients, Clare, who very kindly loaned us sofas/bars/stools to transform our Al Fresco area. Then we both went over to Linda's for hair and makeup. I couldn't believe the transformation - I hardly recognised myself, so I did wonder how other people would. I felt very feminine and I hoped I looked the part. The caterers arrived and set up. I was growing very nervous by this stage. One of the caterer's assistants came up to me and said she had heard the reason for the party and was in awe of what I had achieved and how I looked. It made me feel very special and certainly calmed my nerves.

People soon started arriving. I didn't really want to answer the door but as Denise was ensuring things were running smoothly, I found myself backwards and forwards to the front door numerous times. It worked well in a way, as it made sure that I spoke to everyone and had some time with them as they came in. Everyone who had accepted the invitation arrived and I felt very honoured that my GP Ana and her husband had joined us. As I have said on a number of occasions, she has been much more than my GP and I think the world of her. The whole night went really well; my speech could have been better as I got a bit lost in the middle, but I doubt that anyone noticed. The food was amazing and I think everyone enjoyed themselves. I presented a lovely flower arrangement to Denise and one to Ana for all they had done in getting me to that point.

After this wonderful, confidence-boosting experience, it was now time to focus on our upcoming UK trip which would come round very soon and I had some healing to do beforehand, or it was going to be a very painful five weeks.

Chapter 69

Introducing Stephanie to friends & family in the UK

Before we knew it, we would be heading off to the UK. After my very difficult time over Father's Day while in America, Lynne (my ex sister-in-law) suggested I contact Stephen and Yvonne, some very good friends of my parents, to see if they had been aware of my beginnings. I was sceptical at first, as they were people who I hadn't really related to when I was young. I found Yvonne quite frightening at that time and Stephen used to make fun of me for being overweight. I hadn't had much contact with them during the last twenty years or so, and wasn't sure that they would tell me, even if they knew anything. As I only had their home address, I decided to wait until I returned to Australia and I then posted a letter to them.

We had also received an invitation to my godfather's golden wedding celebration. Thankfully, it had an email address to reply to, so I sent a long message explaining that we wouldn't be able to make the party and why, along with a letter outlining my story. I posted the letter to Stephen and Yvonne and sent the email to my godfather's wife within a few days of arriving back from the US and was surprised to receive replies from both of them quite quickly. The reply to the letter was the biggest surprise - mail usually takes weeks to get from Busselton to the UK, but within the week I had a reply, by email, from Yvonne and it was uplifting. Firstly, she and Stephen berated my parents for allowing me to be bullied at school, when Mum was a teacher and could have home schooled me; and secondly, Stephen was mortified as he remembered that he used to tease me relentlessly and he whole heartedly apologised for that. They also invited us to stay with them when we were over, which I thought was a beautiful gesture.

The second reply arrived the same day, also by email, in which my godfather's wife said she had shed a tear when she read my story and couldn't believe what I had gone through throughout my life. She also said they would love to see us when we were over. It all bode well for our visit; if everyone I met while over there was as positive, then the time would be very enjoyable.

We flew out to the UK on 16th August 2017 and again decided to travel Business Class. In all honesty I could not have coped with Economy Class seats - my recovery was progressing slowly, and I was still a long way from getting back to pre-surgery health and fitness.

After a visit to Wales to see Denise's mum we headed up to Liverpool for the Beatles festival. Personally I'm not a massive Beatles fan. I think I was a little too young and therefore didn't get into their music much. Denise on the other hand, being five years older, is a huge fan and we were meeting my best friend from Busselton there. David (who had organised the tickets) is a massive Beatles fan and it had been an ambition of his to attend the annual festival for a long time. When it was booked some eleven months earlier I hadn't made the decision to transition, so could not have envisioned being anything but fully fit. As things turned out, I was not at my best and we explained that I would not be able to do as much as I would have hoped to have done, due to the surgery. David and his partner Lynette were very understanding and we had a lovely time experiencing the excellent main attractions, including visiting Paul and John's old houses and doing the Strawberry Fields tour. We also made a pilgrimage (for me anyway!) to Anfield. I have been a supporter of Liverpool Football Club since I was seven and have long wanted to do the tour of their home ground, Anfield. It didn't disappoint; it was a really well organised tour and it felt very special to sit in the dugout and in the managers chair (from which he gives his press interviews). We also visited the merchandise shop and bought a couple of mementos to bring home.

Our next stop was Yorkshire to see my friends and family. Yvonne and Stephen had offered to have a "get together" for us to catch up with many friends and family in one place (their house), which I thought was an excellent idea. We decided to spend a couple of days with them early in our stay so that we could finalise arrangements. It was the first time I had seen them since Mother's funeral in 2014. Now, however, I was a different person and I think they were a little apprehensive as to what I would look like, as they knew another local transgender lady who struggled with her appearance. I know how lucky I am, having fairly fine features, no Adam's apple and relatively small hands and feet. "Passing" as female is something that all male-to-female transgender people'aspire to, so, having physical attributes which are more on the feminine side can make the whole journey easier. They welcomed us both with open arms. They wanted to know all about my journey and were 100% supportive. We spent two happy days with them and finalised the details for the party. I was quite surprised to hear how many people they had invited; lots of people who were my parents' friends, and some relatives, many of whom I hadn't seen for a number of years. It would also be the first time I had met a number of my friends since my transition, which I knew would be fine, as all had been supportive.

After leaving Yvonne and Stephen we spent some time in a rented property in Garton-on-the-Wolds, three miles from Driffield; we had stayed there previously and it worked particularly well. It's lovely staying with friends, but it is very restricting in terms of getting out and seeing other people while on a fairly tight timeline. It was from there that we had our first meeting with my brother and his wife. I knew this was going to be a tough one. They had been very unsupportive since the day we told them, and I therefore didn't have high expectations when we met for the first time. It's particularly sad that it is often the case that close family members are the ones most likely to disapprove of a transitioning sibling or close relative. I had hoped that once we had seen them they would soften their stance; but instead, when we arrived at their house they had invited an old school friend of mine who is also my brother's biggest customer and the brother of a very close friend in Australia. It meant that Greg could talk to him all night and not to me. The restaurant was busy and noisy so it was almost impossible to talk anyway. After the meal we went back to their house for coffee, but the atmosphere didn't improve there, so we left. It upset me a great deal, and Denise and I sat up till very late talking about it afterwards. We had made no plans to see them again, so at least it was over.

We had arranged to meet my godparents for lunch; in fact both my godfathers were going to be there as well as Aunt and Uncle, who had been so supportive. We met at a local restaurant and it all went really well. Unfortunately, my other godfather's wife couldn't be there, so we arranged to meet with them both another time, at their house.

Next came the day of the party. We were all up early as there was lots to prepare before the event at 1pm. I couldn't believe how much food Yvonne had organised. There was plate after plate of food; every type of cold meat, salads, pork pies and what seemed like dozens of desserts. It was a lovely event; I stood up and said a few words towards the end and managed to keep it together. It was lovely to see so many people and it was an excellent way of catching up with so many in one place. I had a long talk with my ex-boss from the Renault dealership; he and his wife had done a wonderful job of telling my story to all the people I had worked with. He was there with all his family with whom I had come into contact at one time or another. All in all it was a very successful and emotionally rewarding day and we were all exhausted at the end of it.

Our next stop was back to Wales to stay with Denise's mum. We took her to visit one of her old neighbours, Mary, who now lives on the west coast of Wales in the beautiful town of St Davids. It was quite a long drive but well worth it. She is a lovely lady who tells it as it is, and takes no prisoners; my sort of person completely. Later that night I had my four-month Skype consultation with the surgeon in Philadelphia. I had, as requested, sent some photos by email, and an accompanying letter to tell her about some concerns I had. Dilation had become very difficult and very painful as it looked as though the skin was joining up at the back and making access difficult. From the start of the consultation it was clear that there was a problem and after the pleasantries had concluded she just said "I'm really sorry dear but you need to have some revision surgery done". I was completely lost for words and in tears. She was lovely with me and suggested we speak again when we had returned to Australia and had had time to digest what she had told me. She also told me not to dilate anymore as it was probably doing more harm than good as I was splitting the skin every time I put the dilator inside me. We ended the call, and I just sat there in floods of tears.

Chapter 70

Down to earth with a bump but an unexpected bonus

We flew back to Australia at the end of September and were pleased to be back home. It was still quite cold, but thankfully we had missed the worst of winter. Not that winter in Busselton is bad; it's just that you get used to the lovely weather that we enjoy for most of the year and any cold weather goes down badly. We had plenty of firewood stored, so we were never cold. I arranged a Skype consultation with the surgeon and prepared for the worst. She was lovely, as always, and told me that she was very happy to do the revision work and that there would be no charge for her services. The only costs would be getting there and the hospital charges. She also said she was happy to advise/work with a surgeon in Australia if I decided not to travel to Philadelphia again. As much as I was devastated at having to go through it all again, I decided to go back to Philadelphia. She obviously knew what she was doing and she knew my body; so the date was set for the 29th of November 2017 which was just eight weeks away.

I had much to do in that time. First of all I needed to get fit again; over the last four months I had put on quite a lot of weight and needed to lose it. I wasn't sure I'd be able to sit on the exercise bike comfortably but gave it a try. It wasn't particularly comfortable, but I managed to do short sessions which were better than nothing. We also had the pleasure of having the son of a second cousin from the UK, and his friend, to stay for a week. They were having a "gap year" before going to University and wanted to see Australia. It was a good distraction as they needed to buy a car and that's one thing I could certainly help them with. They also came to Nannup with me and helped with some burning off so were very useful, as well as being ultra-polite and a real pleasure to have to stay.

Before I knew it, I was back at the GPs getting my patient forms filled in again and having the relevant blood tests done. It seemed like only yesterday that I had done it all for the first surgery. At least this time I knew how it all worked. I also had to get a new visa to get into America, as I had changed my name since the first one was granted. Denise's multi-entry US visa in her UK passport was still current so she had nothing to do. I went up to Perth on my own as Denise was working and this time it all seemed much easier; in fact I was in and out before my allotted appointment time, as I was there a little early and the place was quiet.

Once again, we had to organise house sitters, hire cars and flights etc. We knew I would need to fly business class so didn't even look at economy. This was a good deal more expensive, but in my condition, a necessity. I must confess that as much as I was keen to get the problem fixed, there was not the same level of excitement for "Round Two" as there was for my first round of surgery. Knowing the drill at Doha was definitely going to be an advantage; at least we would know where to go when we arrived for our 20-hour stopover, but first we had to get to Perth for the flight. For this we engaged our good friend Betty who had house sat for us in 2015 and who kindly offered to drive us there. Once through the priority check in we headed straight for the Qantas lounge which was shared by Qatar. There were plenty of places to sit, a good choice of refreshments, and televisions to watch if desired. But I just wanted to get on our way, head to Philadelphia and get "sorted". However, there was still a long journey ahead and when all was done there would be the familiar "pleasure" of dilation, something I was not looking forward to but would be a necessary evil. The flight to Doha was uneventful; once again we were looked after very well and it was a Boeing 777 so we were seated next to each other. We arrived at Doha around midday and, as Business Class travellers, disembarked the plane first and were subsequently first through immigration and to the desk where you collect your visa to be allowed into the country. We then caught the courtesy bus to the Rotana Hotel and, having been there twice before, we pretty much knew the drill. We decided to have a late lunch before heading to our room to have a shower and some much-needed sleep. Thankfully on this leg I didn't need to dilate, so took my usual sleeping tablets and had a good rest.

The second leg of the journey was even longer than the first but the aircraft was an Airbus 350 which, while not being as easy to communicate with Denise, had better facilities and a bigger area in which to spread your belongings. The biggest plus was being able to choose whatever I wanted from the menu whenever I wanted it; and I did! I also had a couple of glasses of champagne and, whilst I was not really supposed to be drinking alcohol, and hadn't done for the previous two months, I felt the odd glass couldn't do too much damage. I slept quite a lot on the second leg which is unusual for me as getting comfortable is always a problem, even in Business Class. But when we landed in Philadelphia I was bright and breezy; a bit like the weather.

We managed to make our way through customs and immigration without too much trouble; the man who dealt with us in immigration actually wished me luck with my surgery, which was unexpected, but nice. We located the Dollar Rent A Car depot and asked for our pre-booked hire car. When we booked the car I opted for a Ford Focus, but knew from the last time that it most likely wouldn't be one that was offered to us, and I wasn't wrong. Again, we were offered the same car as last time, a Nissan Versa, which is in no way the same class as a Focus. The lady was pretty stroppy but I wasn't giving in and when she offered several options they were all in the class below; Kia Rio, Hyundai Accent, Toyota Yaris, none of which I accepted. By this time she was getting very annoyed so I suggested a Kia Soul and told her that was what they gave us last time. But she said it was more expensive and then offered me a Nissan Juke which is in exactly the same class as the Soul, so I accepted and we were on our way at last. Destination Ardmore!

One very welcome bonus, which happened the same day we arrived in Philadelphia, was a payment I received from my Superannuation company. They have a local representative in town and after our UK visit I called in to make an appointment to process my name and gender change. I was pretty sure it would be a lengthy procedure, so thought it only polite to make an appointment, rather than just turn up unannounced and expect it to be done. The guy who runs it wasn't in but I spoke to his secretary. When the inevitable question came of her asking my name, my reply was "that's where it gets complicated". Of course she asked why, so I gave her my new name (which obviously meant nothing to her) and then gave her my old name. She looked at me and said "I thought I recognised you but obviously you look much different from the last time you were in". I said that I hoped that was a good thing, and she laughed. She complimented me on how good I looked and made the comment which is so lovely to hear, "I wouldn't have picked that you were transgender". I thanked her and she said her boss would call me to arrange a time convenient to both of us. He called me later that day, greeted me with "Hello Stephanie" which I thought was a good start and said his secretary had filled him in with some details but he looked forward to meeting me in person. We agreed upon a day and time and left it at that.

I was early for the appointment, as usual, and I waited in the Reception. The office is shared by several businesses and a number of people came in and out while I was waiting. Most were staff at the office and asked if they could help. It was a lovely feeling, as not one of them gave me a second glance. I was probably over dressed for the occasion and one actually said how lovely my dress was. When Sean came out of his office he just stood and stared at me, and said, "Wow, what a transformation!". I was almost in tears. To save time I had taken along a brief outline of my story which he read. When he had finished it, he ironically said that I should write a book about my life and that he thought it would make a great movie! We gradually made our way through the seemingly dozens of documents which needed signing. He asked another lady to come and witness them and the meeting ended with a lovely hug and a parting shot of "You'll have to bear with me on this as it's the first application of this sort that I've done; so don't be surprised if I call you in a few days to ask you to come in and sign some more". I smiled and said it wouldn't be a problem. He also gave me an up to date Statement of my account balance. Sure enough, two days later he called me to ask me to drop in and sign a couple of forms that he had missed; so I returned the following day. Having had some time to read the Statement I had a couple of questions; so it was good for both of us. One of my questions was about the various insurances connected to my account. The premiums seemed quite substantial and I questioned whether they were indeed necessary.

One of the insurances was a salary continuation plan which, while I was working in the motor trade, earning good money, was worthwhile; but since I had not really earned much since then I questioned its value to me.

We talked about it for a while then there was a light bulb moment. He looked at me and said, "I wonder if we could make a claim as you are now unfit for work". I didn't want to get my hopes up and I replied "Probably not, as it was elective surgery". He said it was worth looking into and promised he would be in touch.

A couple of days later I received a call from a lady at the insurance company attached to my Superannuation who asked if it was convenient to talk, as she had a couple of questions following a conversation she had had with Sean. I was happy to talk, and after going through the various identification questions she asked me to explain a bit about my story. I enquired as to how much she wanted to know, as it's quite a long story, to which she replied "I have plenty of time". So I told her the whole story. I still get emotional when I get to the part when whoever I'm telling asks "So, your parents didn't tell you about being born intersex?". This time it wasn't me who was in tears; she was sobbing down the phone, which then started me off. When she had gathered herself together she asked just one more question, "Do you have, or can you get, a letter from the specialist or psychiatrist who recommended you have the surgery". I told her I had three letters from three different specialists (including a Psychiatrist and Psychologist) and she said she would see that the claim was paid. I could hardly believe my ears; what an unexpected bonus!

Chapter 71

Round Two

Having collected our hire car we made our way to Ardmore. Everything seemed less complicated the second time around and, as arranged, the keys were in the mail box and we went in. The place was deserted - all of the recovery suites were empty, so we had the place to ourselves. Our room was on the top floor this time; it was a bit smaller than the last one but it was warm and cosy and the kitchen seemed nicer than the one below – although there was still only a microwave to cook with. We unpacked a few of our things and then went into town to get some supplies for the coming few days. It was Sunday and we weren't sure what would be open but remembered how to get to the supermarket and purchased what we needed.

My first appointment with the surgeon was at 10am so we were up and showered in good time and went down to Reception. We were greeted with massive hugs from all of the staff, especially the office manager. I was shown into a treatment room and told to undress in readiness for the surgeon. When she came in there were more greetings and hugs. They were all so lovely and welcoming, it really put me at ease with what I was sure was going to be an unpleasant experience. It didn't disappoint. The surgeon put on some surgical gloves before inserting her finger as far inside me as it would go. It hurt. In fact it hurt a lot and she could see it. She apologised and then went through what she was going to do. She told me that she would need some skin to basically re-line me, so would use skin from my stomach area and give me a sort of mini tummy tuck at the same time. As I had spent the first fifty plus years of my life overweight, there was plenty of loose skin to spare from that area but she said it would restrict my movement a little for some time after the surgery. We discussed some other things that she would do, including re-positioning my urethra further back, as going to the bathroom had been a challenge to say the least. She said it wasn't a big job and so wouldn't be a problem. We discussed the pre-op process and the bowel prep and we bade her good day. The next time we saw her would be in the hospital before the operation.

We went back into town with a list of things needed for my pre-op preparation, and had some lunch. It would be the last solid food I would get to eat until after my operation, so I had a good feed. We also bought some towels and pillows to make our stay more comfortable, as the ones in the room were a little tired. The bowel preparation the second time around wasn't quite as unpleasant, as I knew what to expect. The feeling of being hungry hadn't improved though, and by late evening I was famished. All in a good cause I thought! I received a phone call from the lady who organised the transport to and from the hospital to tell me that I was second on the list this time, so no getting up at 4am and being picked up at 5.15am; this time the taxi would be there to pick us up at 7am. The ride to the hospital was just as scary and uncomfortable as the last time. I don't know what it was with taxi drivers in Philadelphia but the ride was again erratic and if felt like the driver was aiming the car at every pothole in the road; and believe me, there were many.

We arrived at the hospital in good time and were sent straight up to the eighth floor, where the surgery would take place. We sat in a waiting room with just one other person until we were called through. Last time, Denise was able to stay with me until I went into the final pre-op room; but this time she had to leave virtually straight away. I was given a gown to wear and told to get changed. I was expecting what came next; a stream of people all asking me the same questions but it wasn't as bad as previously. This time it only happened a couple of times just to be sure they had the correct person on the table. The worst part about the first surgery was the anaesthetic team putting in the cannula. I have fairly easy-to-see veins and couldn't understand how it could take three attempts to get it into my arm. This time, before leaving Australia, I had talked to my psychologist who had given me strategies to work with at this very moment and for any other of what she described as my "doomsday moments". She told me to think of my favourite song and recite the words in my head, or even out loud if it helped. I was ready for them this time, only it was a completely different experience. This morning it was a man who had been given the job, and I told him it was the worst moment of the last surgery. He said he could make it much better for me and offered to give me four very, very light stings instead of one big one. I agreed and he anaesthetised the area around where he was going to insert the cannula with four very small pricks, which I hardly felt. I was so relieved; he then waited a couple of minutes before inserting the cannula which was absolutely painless. He left me for a couple of minutes then returned with the lady who was heading the anaesthetic team for the day. He began to tell me the same as the lady did in the first surgery; that he was just going to give me a light sedative, so I would not be stressed as I went into final preparation. I stopped him half way through, and told him I'd heard that one before. He smiled and said "Okay, this is the real thing"; see you on the other side!

While all this was going on Denise was sitting in the waiting room, worrying about me. The surgeon had told us that it would take approximately two to two and a half hours so when my status on the patient board hadn't changed after four hours, poor Denise was very worried indeed, imagining all sorts of dreadful things that might have happened. She finally managed to get the attention of a nurse who kindly offered to find out what was going on. She returned and said all was fine; it was just taking longer than expected and I would be out of theatre very soon. She was still believing the worst when, just to add to her worries, an email came through from her brother telling her that her mum was in hospital in Wales. Shortly afterwards, my status changed on the board to PACU which stands for "post anaesthetic care unit". The nurse came back to her and told her that I would be in PACU for thirty to forty minutes and would then be taken to my room. Two hours later and Denise was having the worst day imaginable as I was still in PACU. She was still imagining terrible things when a nurse came in and told her that I was okay, but was still in PACU because my room wasn't ready for me. Denise breathed a sigh of relief and shortly afterwards was taken up to my room on the nineteenth floor. She arrived before me and, when I saw her there, it was the best sight I had seen all day; we hugged for a long time. I was then very sick and my bedding had to be changed. I didn't have that problem after the first surgery, so it was a bit of a shock. I was given some anti-nausea tablets and they did the job.

Chapter 72

The long road to recovery begins again

I was still very drowsy and don't remember much about the first few hours after my surgery. Although I was pleased to be "on the other side" there was no euphoria this time. I remember so clearly thinking, when I had fully come round after the first operation, that I had physically become the woman I had felt myself to be for so long; whereas this time it was just some adjustments and some modifications. Quite amazingly, the nurse who took over at 7pm was the same one who had looked after me after the first surgery, so we had lots of catching up to do. It really made me feel better; I couldn't sleep so she stayed with me for much of her shift. We talked about Australia as usual and I extended an invitation for her to visit us at any time. She was also very good at keeping me pain free, which was a bonus. When 7am came I had another lovely surprise, the next nurse to be looking after me had also looked after me in May, so again there was lots to talk about. The day shift is always busier than the night shift so we didn't see as much of her, but knew she would appear every hour or so to make sure I was doing okay. I was to be discharged later that day and taken by taxi back to the recovery suite. I was dreading it! The last time, I felt so ill that I almost threw up on the back seat. The second time I wasn't as sore, but the driving was worse and I did manage to throw up; thankfully Denise produced a plastic bag in the nick of time.

Eventually, we arrived back at the clinic. It was late in the afternoon, starting to get dark, and pretty cold. I was helped from the car by one of the nurses and guided up the stairs to our second floor suite. I was in considerable pain, so dosed myself up with Percocet. Getting around for the first week was not easy as I had to carry my catheter bag with me. I was dreading them taking the catheter out after the bladder spasms I had experienced the last time (it was the most painful part of my recovery after the first surgery). The catheter had to stay in for the first week, so I didn't venture far from my bed. I was still getting over the anaesthetic and so was a bit wobbly to say the least; but the pain levels were not too bad this time, although the scar across my abdomen was pretty sore.

The first night back at the clinic went okay; on the bright side there was no nurse coming in every hour to check my vital signs, but there was also no one on hand if I did have a problem. Thankfully, I didn't and we woke the next morning to a covering of snow. Had I not seen my share of it growing up in the UK it would have been pretty, but unfortunately to me it just meant it was cold out there. We did however have a visitor on the fire escape outside the window; a little grey squirrel trying to keep out of the snow.

At about 11am I had my visit from the nurse and the office manager; the nurse checked me over and we had a nice chat. I felt I had a real connection with the staff at the clinic - I often wonder what it would have been like, if I had followed my first thoughts and gone to Thailand for my surgery as many people do; would I have had the same level of support, care and love?

As the week went on I was able to move more easily; the scar across my abdomen was probably the thing which gave me the most pain, but I was sure it would improve quickly once I got moving and maybe went outside for a walk; but first I had to have the catheter and the wadding removed which happened on the Wednesday. I was dreading it; firstly because I was pretty sure there would be pain involved and secondly because it would mark the start of dilating again. The pain wasn't too bad and I was happy when the nurse was able to insert a larger dilator than I had ever used after the first surgery. I took this as a very good sign. Dilating is definitely no fun, but this time it was certainly not as painful as it was after the previous surgery; so I was pretty happy with the progress. One of the other things which the surgeon attended to was to re-position my urethra. Going to the bathroom had been a real source of frustration as I often couldn't make the flow of urine go into the bowl; instead it sprayed onto the floor or, if my bladder was full, I could wet the toilet door, which was very embarrassing to say the least. So she moved it back about 15mm which directed the flow downwards, and it definitely worked. I was very happy about that part of the surgery, even though it did look a bit odd; sort of like a big exclamation mark. I was sure it would heal though, and not having the frustration each time I went to the bathroom was a big bonus.

We spent almost two weeks in the recovery suite and once I was more mobile we were able to walk, very carefully, into town. It was only about 200 metres, but it was made a little slower by the amount of snow and ice around. The method used by the local council to spread salt on the footpaths each day involved someone on a tricycle. It was funny to watch, but very good exercise for the person involved and, I guess, environmentally friendly. I had to be careful what I ate if we visited a cafe or restaurant as the portions are huge and I wasn't exactly getting much exercise to work it off. After my first surgery I regained all the weight I had lost before it, plus some more; so I didn't want to do the same again.

At this time Denise's mum, Doreen, was still in hospital and Denise made the decision to travel back as far as Doha with me and then divert to Heathrow where she would collect a hire car and spend Christmas, which was only a couple of weeks away, with her mum and brother. I was a little sad that my first Christmas as Stephanie would not be spent with the love of my life, but understood how important it was for her to support her mum. As it was, it was the best decision, as Doreen passed away the following April. So Denise had a lovely final Christmas with her.

I continued to improve slowly, and was confident that the journey home would be better than the first time. After saying our good-byes to the staff at the clinic, who had again been wonderful with us, we spent the last three nights at a hotel close to the airport. We also enjoyed a very special evening with the clinic's office manager and her husband; we had both really connected with her, and it was a lovely end to our time in Philadelphia.

We returned the hire car a day early so that we could simply take the shuttle bus from the hotel straight to the airport. The fact that I didn't need a wheelchair this time, made the time in the airport easier. I was looking forward to the flight, as we were traveling business class again and Qatar Airways always looked after us well and this time was no different. It was a 350 Airbus again, very comfortable in your own little cubicle and the best seat/bed I have come across on a plane. The 14-hour flight passed fairly easily; we were on our way home, albeit to different destinations.

Chapter 73

Doha and finally home

Getting through passport control and immigration in Doha was a little more complicated this time, as Denise and I were on different onward flights and the only Qatar ticket that Denise had been able to book to the UK was an economy ticket. Technically, I was the only one eligible for the hotel, but as Denise had a 9-hour wait we were both able, after some deliberation by the airline staff, to catch the courtesy bus to the hotel. I was allocated a single room, but as it had two beds in it we both enjoyed a shower and some sleep.

Saying goodbye to Denise was a very emotional time for me. Firstly, I hate being apart from her and secondly, I dislike going through airports alone. Being so far from home, on my own, after major surgery was immense for me. I did my best to hold back the tears as I didn't want to make her feel bad, but it was difficult. We parted in the hotel lobby when she boarded the courtesy bus back to the airport, and I felt very, very alone. I returned to my room and got on with the dreaded dilation for the second time since arriving. I was quietly confident that it was going well; there was little pain after the first insertion and not too much blood at the end. It still was not a pleasant procedure and I couldn't wait for it to be reduced to three times a day. Dilating four times every day was extremely restricting, but I knew it was necessary for the surgery to work as it should.

I still had about nine hours before leaving for the airport, so decided to try and get some sleep. I set my alarm in case I slept really well; however I need not have bothered because I was awake again long before I needed to leave. I ordered and ate a tasty room-service meal, dilated again and then I had a long shower. The bathroom was spacious and well equipped; I do however struggle with the concept of having a telephone next to the toilet. The thought of someone using it, while using the toilet, was unsettling so I was not at any point tempted to use that particular telephone. I wrote a short post on my blog and packed my things ready for the beginning of my onward journey.

We had visited Hamad Airport lots of times and I was slowly getting to know the layout. Knowing how well you get looked after on the flight there wasn't much point in eating too much so I made my way to the Business Class lounge, settled down with a coffee, small cake and my iPad, and caught up on news back in Australia. I'm always one to make my way to the departure gate early in case of an unexpected delay - I would be so embarrassed to be the person whose name is called on the public address system as being late for their flight. The security at the gate in Doha was higher than anywhere I had encountered. It is a good thing in the long run, but all cabin baggage was scanned again and the usual body scan taken. When the time came to board, I wondered where Denise would be at that point and I also wondered who would be sitting next to me. The aircraft was a Boeing 777-300 so the layout of the business class seats is not as private as the Airbus. They are spacious enough, but you are able to hold a conversation with the person next to you quite easily. Mine was a window seat, not my usual choice in an aircraft as I usually go for the aisle seat, but in this case it gave me a bit more space to spread out my belongings, and no one would be stepping over my legs when I had the bed made up. A guy came and sat in the seat next to me. He was in his sixties I would guess; he said "Hello" and we exchanged first names. When he heard my Yorkshire accent he asked if I was heading for Australia on holiday; I explained that I lived there and was just on my way back from a trip to Philadelphia. He didn't ask why I had been in Philadelphia, so I didn't mention it. He told me about his trip and we both started flicking through the options on the entertainment system. He told me he didn't think much of the entertainment system on Qatar Airways but thought the service from the cabin crew was excellent; I agreed with both observations.

Shortly afterwards the attendant came, armed with her iPad, and spoke to us both in turn. After my companion had told her his choices of welcome drink, the time he would like his main meal to be served and what he would like from the menu, she turned to me and said "Mr Vaughan?" I looked at her and asked her to repeat what she had said. I think she realised her mistake, but denied calling me "Mr", at which point my companion interrupted and said, "You definitely referred to her as Mr and you should apologise". She said how sorry she was and said she hadn't read my full name and thought it had said "Mr" on the screen. We moved on, I made my choices and we never saw that particular attendant again. After she had left I looked over at my companion and thanked him for his support. I felt I probably should explain why it was a raw nerve, but he had obviously already figured it out. We talked for some time about my transition; I was careful not to bore him with the details but he seemed interested enough. I gave him a very shortened version and he thanked me for sharing it with him. He also recommended a book to me which he had recently read. I wrote down the name and author in my phone so that I didn't forget it. For the next hour or so we chatted about our lives in Australia and our backgrounds. He lived in Melbourne but his elderly mother was in Perth, which is why he was spending some time with her there before going home. The eleven hour flight passed fairly quickly - I was still in some pain but felt I was in much better shape than I was on the previous flight back to Australia; the only downside was that I only managed to have short sleeps as I needed to visit the bathroom regularly.

By this time, Denise was back in Wales with Doreen, who had been discharged from hospital and was at home; although she still wasn't well enough to be left on her own for long. She was having regular visits from various divisions of Social Services and most of them looked after her well but, as in 2015, Denise being there would be the best tonic for her. It would also be good for Denise to be able to spend Christmas with her; something she hadn't done for many years.

My friend Craig was collecting me from the airport and I was really looking forward to the drive home with him. We have lots of common interests, the biggest being cars, so there would never be a lull in conversation. Some people would not entertain the idea of driving up to Perth and back on the same day but Craig, like me, wasn't worried by it and his timing was perfect. I phoned him when I landed and he was about twenty minutes away. I had just got through customs and immigration when he phoned me to tell me where he was in the parking bays outside the Arrivals building. I walked out of the terminal and saw him immediately; he helped me with my bags and we were finally on our way to Busselton.

Chapter 74

Home alone

The drive down to Busselton went smoothly, as expected; Craig is an excellent driver and as his career has involved driving all sorts of cars during their development, he certainly knows his stuff. We had chatted non-stop on the way home and it did strike me that when I arrived home it would be to a complete contrast as there would only be me and the pets for company. It didn't bother me; I was so ready for my own bed and having my things around me. However, before I could go to bed, I needed to dilate! It went as smoothly as could be expected after a break of about eighteen hours. After the first surgery I had learned how best to position myself and also what things I needed around me. Thankfully, I would be able to establish a routine now. I also had a chat to Denise on Face-Time which was lovely.

The next morning, having slept well, I was eventually was woken by a text message from our neighbour Linda, asking how I was and if I needed anything. She was not the only person wanting to know if I was ok; I felt very cared-for indeed, which was just the tonic I needed.

I decided that I should take things easy and started the day with a coffee while I opened the pile of mail which had arrived while we had been away. One notable item was the official invitation to my stepdaughter Natalie's wedding in May. We had received a "save the date" card some months earlier, but the official one was lovely to receive. It was going to be a special event and I would be seeing lots of people who I hadn't seen for many, many years and certainly not since I transitioned. The wedding was first talked about when we were in England in 2017 and Natalie's biological father, who I have known since I was four years old, said to me that he would need some help with his speech. I have never had much trouble getting up and speaking in public, so I said I would be glad to assist him or even write the speech for him; but I hadn't heard from him since, so I presumed he was okay with doing it himself.

I decided to drive into town to collect some supplies. It was Sunday and, being the middle of December, it was a beautiful warm day. The town was just starting to get busy with tourists but it was easy to get a parking space close to the supermarket, so I wasn't too concerned. The supermarket was busy and I felt sure I would bump into a friend or acquaintance, but it didn't happen and I was at the checkout before I knew it. I always chose carefully when it came to checkouts as there was one particular lady who worked there (and still does) who always gave me a hug and made me feel better if I was not on top form. She had known I was going back for more surgery, and even though she had the longest line of customers waiting I joined the end of her queue. It was worth waiting for and, as no-one had joined her line after me, we were able to chat freely about how it had all gone; and I left with a very heartfelt hug and returned to the car a very happy lady. She has the ability to share positive energy and I so appreciate it every time.

I returned home and lay on the bed so that I could dilate. I had calculated that Denise would be getting up about that time, so I messaged her, and we enjoyed a long talk on Face-Time. She told me how Doreen was doing and how, in the following week, she was going to put things in place to make life easier for her mum when Denise returned to Australia. She told me all about their plans for Christmas and asked about mine. Linda, our neighbour, had asked me to go to their house on Christmas Day, for which I was very thankful. It was only a very short walk and I could come and go as necessary, to fit in with dilation. I knew it would be a food fest as she is an excellent cook and provider; I would just have to be careful about how much I drank as I was still on various pain killers. It was certainly going to be a different kind of Christmas that year - my first as Stephanie (although part of it was as Stephanie in 2016) and the first one I had spent away from Denise in the time we had been together. I was not looking forward to that part at all.

Some time ago Andrew and Linda had told us about a place in the Porongurups called Woodlands Retreat; a beautifully furnished chalet with all the amenities you could wish for. It was set in forty acres of woodland overlooking the Porongurup mountain range in the south of Western Australia. Denise and I had since stayed there a couple of times. So in March 2017, just before my first round of surgery, we booked to stay there with them over the New Year period. It has a wonderful spa which overlooks the mountains but sadly I wouldn't be able to use it this time as I had to be careful not to get any infection. I'm sure the spa is impeccably maintained but it was not worth the risk so soon after my surgery.

Early the following week I had an appointment with Ana my GP. She was pleased to see me and was keen to have a look at the surgeon's handiwork. She was a little concerned about the 26cm long scar across my abdomen and her first comment was that it must have been a very big baby! I laughed, which was not altogether a good idea as it hurt if I laughed when in a certain position. Unfortunately, she gave me the sad news that she would be leaving the practice at the end of the month. This was an enormous blow to me as I had total faith in her, and finding a replacement GP was going to be tough. She was happy with my progress, asked me to have some blood tests to make sure all was in order and tidied up some stitches on the scar which were catching on my clothing. As her final day was not far away I made an appointment to see her again; I specifically booked her last ever appointment at the Practice. I took her in some flowers from both of us as she had been so wonderful with us, especially me, and I wanted to show her our appreciation; I got into trouble for that!

Christmas came and went; I ate far too much but managed to regulate the alcohol intake. Denise arrived home the day before we had to leave for Woodlands Retreat. She was very sad at having to say goodbye to her mother in the UK, as she felt it might be the last time she would see her. She hardly had time to catch up on sleep before we set off on the three and a half hour drive. It was only a month since my surgery, but I was comfortable doing the driving; I'm a terrible passenger and at least the steering wheel gave me something to hang on to and keep me from sliding around on the seat, which would sometimes hurt. I also had various soft Ikea cushions; I slept with one between my knees and kept another in the car. They just helped make life a little more comfortable while I was recovering. Our New Year celebration was certainly one to remember - lovely company in picturesque surroundings. What more could anyone want?

Chapter 75

Time to get life back on track

As the most invasive procedures were carried out in the first surgery, recovery from the second one was much faster. I chose a new GP at the same Practice, as I was known to the receptionists and my records were all there. Kamarin didn't have the same bedside manner as Ana; in fact I felt she could be a little brusque, but at least you knew where you stood. Before long there was a definite patch of granulation tissue growing, which concerned me. Kamarin was straight to the point and asked me if I would like her to deal with it. I hesitated as I was petrified that it would hurt a great deal. She said it might sting but needed doing. She left the room to get the dreaded silver nitrate. When she returned she asked me if I was happy for the nurse to do it as the nurse would have used it more times than she had so would be very proficient with it. She also had a waiting room full of patients and she was on duty on her own, so she should be attending to them. I agreed, and went to see the nurse; Kamarin came in and explained what she wanted done and left us to it.

I'm afraid I was very scared and let the nurse know and she was lovely with me; I had seen her a few times as she did my ECG before the first surgery. I asked her if she had ever seen a neo-vagina before to which she replied "No". She did add that being a midwife, nothing I had would surprise her as she had seen vaginas of all shapes and some pretty messed up ones amongst them. It made me feel much better. She asked me to lie on the bed, took a look at me and appeared puzzled. She asked me to point out what was what, which didn't fill me with confidence; in the end she decided that she wasn't comfortable with applying the Silver Nitrate. In a way I was very relieved, but knew I could only put it off for so long. She left the room and when she returned told me that she had spoken to Kamarin and that I was to make an appointment to see her as soon as was convenient with me.

Two days later I was back in the waiting room feeling a bit scared of what was to come. When Kamarin did eventually treat me I didn't feel a thing. She said that I would probably be sore the following day, which I was, but nothing too bad. The scariest part of it was that she encouraged me to watch the application with my hand-mirror and explained the procedure, in case I ever had to ask someone else to do it who perhaps hadn't used silver nitrate before. For several weeks she treated me once a week to try and keep on top of the granulation tissue, but it was growing at an alarming rate and, even worse, it was growing inside me as well. This was evident by the considerable amount of blood I was losing during dilation. She decided I should see a gynaecologist to check whether there was anything they could do about the problem inside. She very kindly made numerous calls to local doctors to ask if they would be willing to treat me, or even have a look at me, and eventually found one in Bunbury. It had taken some time but eventually I reached the stage of giving Kamarin a hug at the end of an appointment; I thought she was a little uncomfortable at first, but it soon became the norm at the beginning and end of my visit. It may seem a very small thing, but to me it is huge; all of the practitioners I see give me a hug and it means so much to me.

Denise and I had arranged a visit to Esperance towards the end of January with our very good friend David and his partner. They had not been to Esperance before so I was excited to show them all it had to offer. It would have to rate as one of my favourite places in the world and I never tire of its magic. The downside is the 720km journey to get there. It is a long way to drive by any standards, but we had done it lots of times before and knew the best places to stop en route. We took the Amarok as it was much more at home on the beach than the Santa Fe, but the downside was that the ride was more agricultural due to the leaf spring rear suspension. It is by far the best riding Ute on the market, but it is still a Ute at the end of the day. It was also a bit tight on space as we had replaced the rear tub with an aluminium tray which was not secure, so everything had to be put inside the cabin which was always going to be a struggle. Our visit that year was the first since I had transitioned. My cousin, who lives close to Esperance, is a friend of the owner of the apartments we had always rented. She had spoken to him and told him of my transition but it is always a bit of an unknown the first time I meet someone who knew me as Robin. There were absolutely no problems though; he got up from his desk and gave me a big hug, complemented me on how well I looked and proceeded to process the paperwork for our apartment.

We visited all the wonderful beaches and attractions and caught up with my cousin, which was exciting as it was the first time I had seen her since my transition. We had a lovely few days; the only disappointment was that it was pretty windy whilst we were there. Being on the south coastline of Australia it is often the case, but the beauty of the place more than makes up for it. I managed to dilate at least twice every day, and three times some days which I thought was a good result. Throughout the trip I had managed to maintain my evening walks without too much pain, which I was thankful for. Most times I would be on my own, but I didn't mind too much; it allowed me to walk at whatever pace I wanted to and for as long as I liked. Walking makes such a difference to my feeling of wellbeing, both physically and emotionally, and, as such, is a very important part of my day. In some ways it's a good thing that Esperance is such a long drive as I would spend far too much time there if it were closer. But it's a place I will never tire of, and being able to introduce friends to it is very special.

When we got back I felt it was time to get serious about my business. In reality I hadn't done much in the way of paid work for almost a year and it had made a serious dent in my financial position, especially having to return for the revision surgery, which I hadn't budgeted for. I did, however, have the unexpected bonus from the superannuation company to offset that. Before I left for Philadelphia I had received a call from a friend asking if I was interested in painting all their interior doors for them. I explained that I was having further surgery but he was happy to wait until I was well again; so I called him and arranged a meeting. It was a very enjoyable job, I was able to come and go as I pleased in line with my dilation and took me about two weeks to complete. I had no side effects from doing it and he told me there would be some more jobs in the future, which was pleasing to hear. I also had plenty of work to do at our Nannup property which was slowly taking shape. It was at lock-up stage now, and as I had not had any experience of doing plaster board on interior walls, I was happy to employ someone else to do that. Whilst I am all for learning new skills, I thought that in this case discretion was the better part of valour.

Chapter 76

Surely it can't be happening again?

In the weeks before my appointment with the gynaecologist things got considerably worse and dilation became very painful. I went back to using the smallest dilator in the set and still struggled to get it far enough in. There was also a great deal of blood about when I had finished which indicated that there was a lot of granulation tissue inside me. When the day of my appointment came I was extremely nervous as, apart from my gender specialist, all my health providers had been female. Kamarin said he was a very gentle person and I would be okay with him but I wasn't convinced. Denise accompanied me to the appointment and I asked if she could come in with me. He was very happy for that to happen which certainly helped. Kamarin was right, he was very gentle with me; he sat us down and asked lots of questions first and then asked if he could have a look. The dreaded speculum came out and he very gently inserted it. It hurt but not too much; he said he couldn't see much as the passage was very tight but he thought the granulation tissue was mainly on the outside. I disagreed with him and explained that when I inserted the dilator there was a great deal of blood present. He asked how big the dilator was and I reached for my bag and showed him the one I was using. I had thought the question might come up which was why I had brought it with me. I said I was happy to insert it to prove how much blood came out, to which he agreed. I put some lubricant on it and pushed it in. There was lots of blood! He asked me to remove it and enquired if I wanted him to treat the granulation tissue which he could see. I agreed, as it would save me seeing Kamarin later in the week. Sadly, he then said he couldn't treat the tissue inside as he had no experience of treating transgender patients and it wouldn't be right for him to do so. I was very disappointed and actually a little annoyed; if I'd known that he would have a problem treating a transgender patient, I probably wouldn't have attended the appointment. He was very nice about it and I understand why he felt he was unable to help me, but I thought he should have told Kamarin that before agreeing to see me.

We were back to square one again. It was now mid-March and I needed to get something sorted before my trip back to the UK for Natalie's wedding. I decided to make an appointment to see my gender specialist in Perth. It would be the first time I had seen him since my surgery so it would be an interesting meeting to say the least. He is a lovely kind person but has one fault - he has no verbal filter so, whatever he thinks, he says. A perfect example occurred during my appointment. We talked for a while about the various complications which had happened and discussed ways of alleviating them. He then asked if he could take a look. I was expecting this, so I went over to the bed and removed my dress and my underwear. I laid on the bed with a sheet covering me. When he pulled the sheet back one of his classic comments followed; "Wow, what a mess. You must be so disappointed!". I didn't know what to say and the tears rolled down my cheeks as he proceeded to examine me. Seeing how upset I was, he apologised for his bluntness. I replied that the result of the surgery was not yet what I had hoped for. We discussed several options and he spent some time feeling and pressing my mons pubis area. He said he thought it was a fat pocket and perhaps I should lose some weight, which also made me cry. I weighed about 78 kilos at the time so didn't think I was particularly overweight but this made me think that maybe I should at least try to lose a little more. One of the options we spoke about was stopping the dilation and just leaving the vaginal passage to close up. I had never intended having a relationship with a male so, actually, it wasn't the end of the world. If I ever did want it re-opened I felt sure I could find a surgeon who might be willing to replace it using the colon method (they use a section of the colon to create a vagina). He told me that it would never close up completely and would probably weep a small discharge for ever.

I decided to arrange a Skype consultation with the surgeon in Philadelphia to hear her thoughts on it before making a decision. Much of the pain I was feeling was coming from the mons pubis area, so I was keen to also get her opinion about. that. During the second surgery she had used liposuction to remove over 200 ml from the area but the swelling soon came back so she thought that there could be some inflammation present. She also said that she thought the vaginal opening would simply close up on its own over a couple of months; a completely different prognosis from that of my gender specialist. As a result of my conversation with her I arranged to have an ultrasound and a CT scan of the area to find out just what was going on.

I also had some help from an unexpected source. My brother's wife, who I have known for over twenty years - long before she met my brother - kindly did some research for me as to whether there was someone in the UK who would be willing to at least have a look at me. She found a surgeon in Brighton who said he would; so I called his surgery. It's a pretty difficult thing to explain over the telephone but I managed to get the general gist of it across. His secretary said the surgeon would indeed be happy to see me, but would need some sort of referral from a GP. Kamarin thought it was a good idea and prepared a referral which I emailed to the hospital where the surgeon worked. I explained that I was going over for a wedding some six weeks later, so they made an appointment for four days before the wedding.

It was now less than four weeks to my departure so I was busy trying to get all my work up to date. Denise had decided not to accompany me to the UK as she was basically exhausted from traveling - seven international flights in 2017 had taken it out of her; she was both emotionally and physically drained. I was tired too, but was also looking forward to Natalie's wedding. A couple of weeks before I was due to depart, Doreen went back into hospital again. She had reached the stage where it was not realistic for her to live on her own, so Denise and her brother researched Residential Aged Care homes that she could move into. She had always been very against going into a Home, but I think she realised that there was now little alternative. They managed to find a lovely "Masonic" aged care home but, before she could be moved, she deteriorated quickly and passed away on the 19th of April, just before I was due to leave. We looked at lots of different options and it was decided that Denise would fly over about a week after me and she would arrive the day before my appointment with the surgeon in Brighton; this was a huge bonus for me as I hate going to such things on my own.

In the scheme of things, my flight over was quite pleasant. I flew Business Class with Qatar and was very well looked after. I managed to sleep well and arrived in Manchester quite refreshed. I contacted the Car Hire company and was told to make my way to the train station entrance, which is a considerable walk from the Arrivals terminal, where I would be picked up by their courtesy bus. As I had been sitting for some time the walk was good for me; however I then waited at the designated meeting place for what seemed like hours before the courtesy bus arrived. There was then a thirty minute drive to the depot in the rain and a further wait at the depot before being attended to. The car I was allocated was a Peugeot 2008 which is a sort of crossover vehicle; it doesn't know whether it wants to be a small hatchback or a small SUV and consequently does nothing well. It felt comfortable but had a very asthmatic 1.2 three cylinder engine to which I took an immediate dislike; but I needed to get on my way as soon as possible, so I accepted the car and made my way to the motorway to head east. It became apparent that I wasn't going to get to Driffield in daylight (the weather was foul and traffic was heavy) so I picked up some food at a motorway Service Station. The nearer I came to Driffield the lighter the rain fell and thankfully by the time I was exiting the motorway it was dry. It always takes me a little time to adjust to the huge amount of traffic, but the roads were still very familiar to me so at least I didn't need navigation aids.

At last I arrived at Fiona's house and breathed a sigh of relief. The next day was Friday and Fiona was at work so I had some time to do a few jobs and formulate a plan for the first few days. It was only just over a week to the wedding and Natalie's father wanted to catch up so I could give him some help with his speech. His plan surprised me - he explained what he had in mind which was basically to stand up, welcome everyone to the event and hand over to me at the earliest opportunity, so that I could present the main part of the speech. While I was honoured to do it I needed to make sure that Natalie was happy with this arrangement. I shouldn't have worried; she said she was relieved that I was doing it, so I was happy to go ahead.

Lots of things were to happen before the wedding. Denise was due to land at Heathrow on Tuesday evening so I travelled down from Yorkshire to meet her and we stayed at a hotel very close to the airport. We picked up her hire car the next morning - she was only going to be in the UK for about a week and a half and, understandably, would not make the journey to Yorkshire. The drive down to Brighton was in dreadful weather but we made it in plenty of time.

The hospital was a private one built in a lovely setting overlooking the south coast. By the time of my appointment, the weather had improved; it wasn't warm like we are used to in Australia, but at least the sun was shining and it wasn't raining. We sat in the waiting room until I was invited into the surgeon's office. He introduced himself and asked me to sit at his desk so he could get the full picture of why I wanted to see him. He asked lots of questions and made some negative remarks about my surgeon not attending the meetings of the World Professional Association for Transgender Health, of which he was some sort of official. He then asked if he could take a look. He wasn't the most gentle of people and continued to criticise the job my surgeon had done, which I didn't think was very professional or helpful at all. He asked if I would like him to treat some granulation tissue. As I was in the UK for several more weeks I thought it a good idea but regretted it shortly afterwards. He must have touched an area which wasn't granulation tissue as it stung a lot. He did apologise but it was very sore. We discussed some of my options. My gender specialist had said that I should have the whole vaginal passage removed, but the surgeon said it carried some big risks of damaging other things and was really best left alone. He said he was happy to have a go, but I could see he wasn't optimistic about the outcome; so unless things became considerably worse, I decided to leave it be.

Chapter 77

A final goodbye; RIP Doreen

After leaving the hospital we headed back up towards London then west to Wales in our two hire cars. It would be a long drive, but the traffic, once away from London, was pretty light so it wasn't too bad. Unfortunately, there were several lots of roadworks and the exit at which we needed to leave the M4 motorway was closed. We were directed off the motorway two junctions early and had to find our way to Bridgend using mostly country roads. But eventually we arrived at Doreen's house. It felt very strange being there without her but Denise's brother had put the central heating on and bought some provisions for us, so at least it was warm and we could feed ourselves.

It was going to be a very busy few days, making final preparations for the funeral on Thursday - meeting the celebrant, organising the audio-visual part of the service and finalising the order of service.

As mentioned in an earlier chapter, I first met Doreen when I went up with Denise to pick her up from Perth airport in 2013. Our first encounter was her being wheeled out of the Arrivals area in a wheelchair looking very under the weather. She had dehydrated on the flight and had wandered, disoriented, into Business Class shortly after landing had commenced and was taken care of from that point on. She recovered quickly and we had a bonding day whilst I took her out to show her local areas of interest whilst Denise had a big day at golf, culminating in a celebratory meal back at Denise's house for multiple guests, which I had to take charge of when Presentations had gone on longer than planned. Over the years we had lots of good interactions – she had a wicked, infectious laugh that often came into play.

Her reaction to my Transition was incredibly supportive. One more thing that I would love to share was a call Denise received from her, asking if she was on her own. Denise walked into our bedroom, closed the door and said "Yes". Her mum proceeded to say how she had dozed off the evening before and had become disoriented and had called the Carer support service to say her carer hadn't turned up – she had thought it was morning and was totally confused, and when reminded that it was evening, not morning, she was worried that she was "losing it". After relaying this story she asked Denise "Also, did Robin tell me that he was going to become a lady?". Denise said that we had indeed told her that. Her response was "Thank goodness for that – that just shows I am not losing it!". No judgement as to what I had told her – she was just grateful that she had remembered correctly!

The funeral was a real celebration of Doreen's life; more in the style of an Australian funeral than a UK funeral, which we felt she would have approved of. The celebrant was perfect, and was able to speak in some depth about Doreen after her visit with us the previous day. The audio-visual part worked really well - Denise put together a montage of pictures of Doreen covering all stages of her life. It was projected onto a screen, accompanied by a song that Doreen had liked.

She had a wonderful sense of humour, which I could relate to. She didn't mind me making fun of her accent and certainly gave as good as she got; something which I'm sure helped our relationship. Denise read the Eulogy - it summed up Doreen's life perfectly. I read a poem which was uplifting, and which was so "Doreen". I wasn't sure how well I would cope, but managed to hold it together. The day was a beautiful send off for a very special lady.

Chapter 78

A beautiful event

On Saturday morning I said farewell to Denise, who would spend the next week in Wales sorting out her mum's house with her brother, before flying back to Australia. The day was mostly spent driving up to Yorkshire for Natalie's wedding on the Sunday. It was all very well organised and everything went according to plan, including the preparation of my speech which Denise kindly helped me with on Friday evening. I decided to start my part with a brief explanation of who I was, as I probably hadn't ever met 80% of the guests, and most of the ones that I had met wouldn't have seen me since my transition. So I would certainly have changed somewhat since.

When I first learned the date of the wedding (a Public Holiday in May) I immediately assumed that it would be a wet day as Public Holidays in England, from my memory, always seemed to be wet. The reality was completely different; it was a perfect, warm and sunny day, with very little wind. So we were able to take the photos outside on the lawn. It was my first real "event" apart from my party after the first surgery. I was a little bit nervous and I asked Jon's sister to organise someone to do my make-up and hair when I arrived at the venue. Both Jon's sister and the make-up artist were lovely with me; the latter was particularly patient with me as I didn't really know what I wanted done. She made a few alterations to my hair and did a brilliant job of making me look respectable.

It was soon time to go downstairs for a pre-wedding drink with the other guests. I knew a few of them but not many. However, I was made to feel very welcome and was introduced to lots of guests. It was quite funny listening to people trying to introduce me to their friends; most just stopped at "Stephanie" but some tried to expand on that and it ended up with me having to explain which made it a lengthier process. After a little while we were invited to go through to where the ceremony was due to take place. I took a seat at the end of a row and a young man, who I didn't immediately recognise, came and sat next to me. I had actually met him fifteen years before, when he was about six, so I told him a bit of my story and he said he had heard of my journey.

The celebrant asked for our attention and explained how the ceremony would proceed. She sat down and the music started; it was one of my favourite songs. We all turned round to see Natalie and her father walking towards us; she looked truly beautiful. After the ceremony there was an opportunity to take photos of the newly married couple while they signed the register. They looked so in love and were obviously very happy.

At the conclusion of the service we were asked to adjourn to the front lawn for champagne and to congratulate the happy couple. The photographer took lots of very natural photos and, of course, the organised ones of the family, which I was asked to join. The weather could not have been more perfect; the sun shone throughout the day and there was very little wind. It was also a chance to meet lots of Natalie's friends; I remembered many of them from her school days and all seemed to accept me without question. Then came the time for the Reception and we were called to our seats. I had looked at the seating plan briefly before the ceremony started but hadn't really taken in how the room was going to be laid out. I was on the top table with the bride and groom and the rest of the close family, which made me feel very honoured. Jon had decided that the speeches would be before the meal, which is somewhat unusual, but he was nervous about his speech and felt he would enjoy the meal more if the speeches were done first. Natalie's father stood up first and said his very few words and then it was my turn!

As all the tables were round, I was seated almost with my back to the rest of the guests. I'm no stranger to speaking in public, but it had been some time since I had done it and I was a little nervous. I needn't have been, as it went really well thanks to how Denise had laid out my notes. I began by saying how honoured I was to be there and especially to be given the chance to say a few words. What I said next caused some sharp intakes of breath. I said "There won't be many people in the world who can stand up at their stepdaughter's wedding and claim to be her stepfather turned stepmother"; a quick glance around the room saw lots of "Oh wows" and shocked faces, but it all went really well. I gave a quick recollection of my history with Natalie and made the speech pretty short and sweet. By the number of people who came to me after the reception and said my speech was amazing, I'm claiming it as a huge success. The rest of the speeches were also excellent - there were two best men who did a great job of re-living Jon's past as much as they could without embarrassing him too much. It was a memorable day, enjoyed by all involved.

Chapter 79

Catch-ups, home and sliding doors

The remainder of my time in England would be spent catching up with as many friends and family as possible. I love living in Australia but I missed my UK friends a great deal - and this time I didn't know when I would be visiting again. The best thing was that I was so much more comfortable that year (2018) than I was whilst there in 2017. I felt much more polished in both my appearance and my body language; I knew that Stephanie had matured. The downside was that I didn't have my best friend and soulmate with me to keep me right; so it was all up to me this time.

Long before I left Australia Natalie asked me if I would be interested in house sitting for them for part of my stay. House sitting rather than staying with people gives you much more freedom to come and go as you please; so I agreed. The downside of it was that they lived in Anlaby which is some way south of most of my friends and relatives. But the benefits far outweighed this small negative and I enjoyed looking after the cats for them. I woke up most mornings to find both cats asleep on my bed, which was lovely.

In the last few days of my visit I received two of the best compliments given to me over my whole transition journey. The first was from an old friend from my childhood and later at college. I hadn't seen him for over fifteen years and his comment on seeing me for the first time as Stephanie was "You make a much better-looking girl than you did a boy!". Now I realise that could be taken as a backhanded compliment but I took it as a compliment and that's all that matters. The best one however, came from the very good friend of my parents, Yvonne, who had hosted the party for me the previous year. As I arrived at their farm she was just coming out of the garage. She took one look at me and said "Oh really, look at you! Just look at you! How could you ever have been a boy?" It made my day, my week, my year and quite honestly, my life! It says it all in one short sentence and brings me very close to the end of my story.

I eventually returned and settled back into life in Australia. It was time to get my business back on track again and finish the house at Nannup. I often find myself contemplating how my whole life could have been so very different. There have been so many sliding door moments in my life:

What if my parents, after taking me to the specialist when I was thirteen, had decided to tell me the truth about my beginnings? How would my life have played out? Would I have gone off the rails there and then and been locked up or worse? Would it have answered enough questions to make me at least understand why and how I was different and to go about my life in a different way; to search for answers until I was at peace with how I felt? Would I then have tried to go down the route of transition earlier?

What if I had been caught cross-dressing? It's a well-known fact that cross-dressers push the boundaries and become more daring as time goes on and I was certainly no different. Would it have forced me to come out earlier and seek out both the information and the answers which eluded me until I was fifty-four?

What if, instead of learning of my beginnings at fifty-four, I had found out earlier (not from my parents but perhaps from an observant doctor such as the doctor who ended up being my gender specialist)? If it had been while one, or both, of my parents were alive it would have certainly led to a very difficult conversation. I would like to believe that they would have come up with a good reason for not telling me, however hard that may be to imagine. Yet, finding out whilst one or other was alive might have given me enough answers to allow me to forgive them for not telling me at thirteen, and to move on from that.

What if I had pursued the transition route back in 1998 after visiting the shop in Manchester? I certainly thought about it and did a considerable amount of research. It was all fairly hush-hush in those days but the lady who owned the shop had done it, so the medical technology to transition was certainly there. The problem was that firstly, I didn't know where to start and secondly, I didn't have the confidence or the courage to speak to anyone about it.

What if I had not come to Australia? Would Jayne and I have stayed together? Would I have even reached the stage of seriously considering the possibility of transitioning? Would my ties to my home country, family and friends have not let me move on to the mental shift that paved the way for my transition? Would my circle of friends in England have been as supportive as my Australian ones have been? I do believe all my close friends would have been understanding and supportive, however I'm not so sure that the general British public at large is as accepting of people who are different. However, I haven't lived there for fifteen years so I might be doing them an injustice. I would certainly never have met Denise, but that's not to say I wouldn't have met someone who read the signs and supported me as she has done. Would the medical profession in the UK have been as helpful and supportive as the Australian medical profession has been?

What if I had simply decided that, after Jayne and I parted, I didn't want any type of relationship and so had just kept on cross-dressing in private? Eventually, I believe it would all have become too hard, so I would have left this life early. Indeed, it came very close just twenty-seven days before my first date with Denise.

What if Denise had wanted nothing to do with me after I told her I enjoyed cross-dressing and our relationship had never developed to the point where it was strong enough to survive and support my transition? It was a huge decision to tell her on what was only our fourth date. There had been nothing physical before then so it wasn't as if either of us were heavily committed. I, for one, was very unsure whether I even wanted a relationship and I guess that was what made it easier to decide to tell her. I couldn't have allowed the relationship to progress to a physical level before telling her, because after my weight loss my breasts were very much more prominent and I had reached a point in life where being honest and open in a relationship was, in fact, the only way I could see myself moving forward.

The fact is, that when I did finally make the decision to transition the time was right. I was with the right partner, received the necessary help from a wonderfully supportive group of health care providers and had the most amazing circle of friends who didn't judge me. They were simply there for me when I needed them.

Epilogue

When I look in the mirror each morning I am amazed and proud of what I have achieved. I no longer see a sad person; I see a person who has finally found herself. Even though the journey still continues, it is in fact a different journey. The progress I've made over the last three years has been incredible. I had always believed that I would take Stephanie to my grave and without Denise I most likely would have done. When I'm out in public I sometimes forget that I was ever Robin, and if I catch a glimpse of myself in a mirror I find it hard to believe the feeling of contentment, peace and happiness I have at that moment. It is truly incredible and I think to myself "You have done it Stephanie Vaughan - you really are that person in the mirror".

Even a visit to the supermarket or a walk up the main street of Busselton makes me smile. People probably look at me and think "What's she smiling about?". When Denise and I go into a shop and the assistant asks "How can I help you ladies?" it just makes my day. I could go on, but I can summarise most of it with a comment made to me by a very good friend after we had been working together at the Nannup house. He turned to me on the drive home and said "You really have the best of both worlds don't you - you can play with boys-toys (meaning the large number of tools that I have) all day, go home, get dressed up in your best frock and be the person you want to be". He was right in so many ways,

I love working in my property maintenance business; I get to meet so many lovely people, do lots of things which involve the use of quite serious tools and get huge satisfaction from doing it. When I'm out in public I am usually over-dressed, especially for Australia as it is such a casual place; but I wouldn't have it any other way as I have waited so long to be able to do so; I really do have the best of both worlds.

As much as I've had my share of hurdles to get over on the medical front and would probably have done things differently had I known then what I know now, I am very thankful for all the help I have received along the way. I know that lots of transgender people never progress to surgery, but for me it wasn't an option and, whilst the end result wasn't what I had totally wished for, I am content and moving forward with my life. For me to actually have the surgery was very important; it was the culmination of many years of longing to be the person I knew I should be. Numerous times over the last couple of years I have said to one or other of the health providers when I have seen them "I realise that the health issues I am experiencing are of my own doing. I elected to have the surgery and no-one forced me to have it". Their replies have been very similar, and one in particular challenged me as to whether I really believed what I had just said. She asked me if I thought I had actually had a choice whether or not to do something about my gender dysphoria. In real terms, I don't think I did have a choice as, by the middle of 2016, I was very ready to throw in the towel and indeed had made plans to do it. If it hadn't been for Denise's nurturing I am pretty sure I would have ended my life before the end of that year. So the answer to that practitioner's question is that, yes, I did have a choice but the other option was not one which offered any hope.

I also know that there have been parts of my life which have been very privileged. Being brought up in a farming environment is a wonderful introduction to life and, even though many of my childhood memories are filled with mixed up emotions, I realise that there were lots of wonderful times as well. I find it sad that children today don't have the same amount of freedom which we had in the sixties and early seventies. There were times when we took enormous risks with farm machinery when in reality we weren't old enough to be operating them - but we survived. I often "talk" with David, one of my oldest childhood friends (electronically or otherwise, as he is still in the UK), with whom I spent a great deal of those happy times, and whenever I see him it's as though it was just yesterday. In many ways he was the bright spot in my teenage years when, inside, my life was so dark at times. I feel an amazing bond with him.

Since the middle of 2012 I can't even begin to tell you how much I have spent on medical expenses but that is not important - I would have used my last cent to obtain the happiness that I now have. There was just no other way forward and I am blessed by all the people who have supported me; all my friends and most of my relatives. As the psychiatrist said to me back in November 2016 "There will be people who have a problem with what you are doing but what you need to understand is that it is exactly that – it's their problem, not yours. If they want you in their life they will support you and those who don't support you certainly don't deserve to have you in their lives". I agree with her and give thanks every day for the people who are in my life. In answer to the question posed by the book's subtitle – When do I get to be me - I am finally me, and life is good.

Acknowledgements

Throughout my journey I have been blessed to have had the love and support of many people; it has indeed been humbling. There have been so many it would take almost another chapter to list them all and I would probably still miss someone. So I've decided to recognise the six pivotal people, without whose support I doubt I would be here today. They have all made such an incredible difference to my life and are listed in the order in which I met each of them (with one exception). Perhaps, not surprisingly, five out of the six are healthcare professionals in one way or another.

Dr Annette Richardson (Holistic Osteopath). I've been seeing Annette since shortly after my brother died in 2011 and can say with my hand on my heart that I have never left her room feeling anything but better than when I went in. My journey started with her suggestion that I see a particular GP about what she suspected was a thyroid issue in 2012. It may have seemed fairly insignificant at the time but it turned out to be anything but! In 2018 it happened again; I was struggling with a number of issues when Annette suggested I see a holistic GP (Annette Cransberg was abroad at this stage) This second one also appears on my list as she too has been incredibly important in my journey. Annette is not only a very talented osteopath, she has been a constant in my life for over nine years; someone I've always been able to talk to about anything and who isn't afraid of 'putting me straight' (in the nicest possible way) if she disapproves of something I have said or done.

Dr Annette Cransberg (General Practitoner) was introduced to me by the above in 2012. Again she was someone I felt an immediate connection with and from my very first appointment I had a feeling that she would get to the bottom of my issues one way or another. She sent me to all the right people to try to find the answers and she just didn't give up on me until the truth was discovered. She was there to guide me through the aftermath of the bombshell which was revealed in December 2015 and was there for me throughout my transition. Like all of the people on this list she has spent much more time with me than she should have done and has become a very dear friend.

Hayley King (Clinical Psychologist). When Annette Cransberg suggested that I should have some professional support to help me through my journey I was less than convinced. However, from my first appointment with Hayley I knew it was great advice and that she was the ideal person. There is a calmness in how she approaches issues and she has given me lots of strategies to work with to get me through the 'doomsday moments' which have arisen. She has brought me back from the brink on numerous occasions and talked sense into me. Above all Hayley has been there for me when I've needed help and has made a huge difference.

Dr Sarah Moore (Holistic General Practitioner). Again it was thanks to Annette Richardson for suggesting that Sarah might be able to offer a different approach to some sizeable issues I was having; I'm so glad I took her advice. Sarah has been truly amazing with me from the start and continues to be a wonderful support. In 2019, when I had completely run out of options to deal with ongoing debilitating pain and swelling for which I was taking opiate painkillers almost every day, she recommended I try meditation. I was very unconvinced, as I just couldn't imagine how meditation could possibly help; but she persuaded me to at least give it a try and with the support of the next lady on the list it has absolutely changed my life.

Sarah Roach (Meditation Teacher). I am a person who makes emotional connections very easily with people who I just know are good for me. I made such a connection on my very first meeting with Sarah. There is a nurturing calmness when I enter her home and I can honestly say that from my first class, I have not missed a day meditating. Meditation has also helped me develop a "different relationship" with the pain I was experiencing in 2019; and since attending Sarah's classes I have not required opiate painkillers. Our weekly class is one of the highlights of my week, serving to "keep me honest" in my mindfulness journey. I am still very much in the learning stage but the benefits are plain to see and I can't thank the two Sarah's enough for their guidance.

The last person in my pivotal six has been and continues to be my rock, my true soulmate and my world. Denise has simply been there for me through all the trials and tribulations before, during and since my transition. She is the most selfless person I have ever met; she has done more for me than anyone should ever have to, and I love her with all my heart. Considering how hard I must have been to live with after the shocking news in December 2015 I'm amazed she didn't throw in the towel long ago but she has stuck with me through thick and thin. There is an ease when we are in each other's company that I have not experienced before; we are a team in everything we do, whether it is cooking a meal or working together at our property in Nannup. She is my everything. Thank you for being you Denise; I couldn't have done any of this without you by my side xxx

Letters to and from my parents

As I left the specialist's office in West Perth in December 2015 the tsunami of emotions which started to hit me was immense. There was just about every reaction you could think of; shock, confusion, disbelief and even hatred. It has taken me many years to deal with these feelings. Indeed, it was 2020 and the first two months of the year saw me in a deeper depression than I'd experienced before. The biggest issue has always been with my parents and how they watched me go through hell at school when they knew the reason for my very mixed up mind and body. They chose to do nothing about it at the time and then lied to me after I saw the specialist in Leeds.

I have spent a small fortune with my psychologist, trying to find some sort of acceptance of my parents' actions and she has been amazing with me. Perhaps, surprisingly, my biggest step forward was after a conversation with a friend one Sunday morning at Nannup. She had some issues surrounding her deceased father, but made great progress by writing a letter to him and, some time later, writing his reply to her.

At the time I thought it was worth a try. I desperately needed something which would help, so I wrote the first letter a few days later. I didn't feel ready to write the reply until a month after that. The mental shift I felt in writing that reply was quite immense. Somehow, the act of writing down what I imagined would have been their reply allowed me to put myself in their shoes and look at things from a different perspective; it has certainly made a huge difference. I don't think I will ever fully forgive my parents for not telling me the truth; your parents are, after all, the two people you should be able to completely trust. But I have reached a level of acceptance I didn't think I would ever achieve. After all, the only person feeling the pain and hurt was me; but it still took a massive effort to get to where I am now.

To this end I decided that the letters were significant enough to include in the book, in the hope that it might encourage someone going through similar issues to do the same and perhaps experience some sort of closure.

Thank you so much for your help Kate xx

LETTER TO MY PARENTS - MARCH 2020

Dear Mum and Dad

It's now almost four years and three months since I learned the truth about my beginnings. The truth which you carefully hid from me even though I went through so much pain and hurt at school, and for many years later. I would love to think you had a logical reason for not telling me the truth but whichever way I look at it I can't find one. Mum, you never really liked me did you? That was why you went back to work and left me with Nanny Joey. She was good to me but then she left me and by that time I had absolutely no bond with you at all. Dad, you were just not strong enough! If either Craig or Natalie had been born intersex and were going through all the shit I did at school, there is no way on earth that I wouldn't have sat them down and told the truth.

What I really don't understand is that you really wanted a daughter Mum. You were half way there with me and in my head, the full way. I knew from around 8 years old that I should have been a girl. Why didn't you fight for me when I was born? Sure, there would have been some difficult times and I would have still needed surgery, but I would have been happy. As it was I had to wait fifty-six years to be the person I wanted to be. I missed out on so much growing up as a boy.

You will never know how much hurt I've been through and am still fighting. Why would you do that to your child? If I'd wanted and had kids it wouldn't have mattered if they had been born intersex, I'd have loved them just the same and been at their side through all the trials and tribulations. You just abandoned me and took the easy way out. I don't get it at all.

Why did you take me to two different specialists then lie to me and tell me I had breasts because I was overweight? The second one obviously told you Dad to tell me the truth but you didn't. Why? I was already thoroughly mixed up so it couldn't have made me any worse. Dad - why did you not stand up for me?

Mum - why, when Fiona and I split in 1997, did you say to me "I think we have unfinished business" and never revisit it. Were you going to tell me then and realised you were not strong enough? How would you have defended your decision not to tell me earlier? Regardless of what the doctors told you, you should have stopped the pain I was going through. Did you emigrate to Australia to get away from me? I bet you expected that would be an end to witnessing the pain I was going through but you couldn't stay away could you? Your favourite son obliged with two grandsons for you so you had to come home. Did you tell Greg about my beginnings before you died? Perhaps you couldn't take it to your grave?

Why, at the eleventh hour on the day of my christening did you change my name from Robert to Robin? Was it just in case things didn't work out and I could go either way as Robin? If you knew there was a chance that they might have done the wrong thing with me why did you let it happen in the first place? I really don't understand it at all.

Mum, can you imagine how I feel about you? I hate you with every bone in my body! Dad, you should have spoken up and fought for what was right, not just given in to Mother all the time.

I very much look forward to your reply, your excuses will certainly be interesting.

In anticipation,

Your daughter, Stephanie

REPLY FROM MY PARENTS - APRIL 2020

Dear Stephanie

Thank you for your letter, there is clearly much pain and anger inside you and we know we contributed to it. Stephanie please try to see it from our perspective. We only did as we were told to do - we weren't given any option when you were born. They just told us that you had been born with a condition and it needed surgery to fix it. We were told in no uncertain terms not to ever discuss it with you. As far as the doctors were concerned, you were now fully male and would most likely never know anything different. We didn't know what to do when you developed the breasts and we agonised whether or not to tell you. We decided not to tell you, even after the specialist in Leeds told us that we should, on the grounds that you were in a pretty delicate state of mind at the time. I know we shouldn't have lied to you.

We had no idea what was actually going on in your head. Could you not have told us that you wanted to be a girl and in fact felt that inside you always were a girl? We might have looked upon it differently. As it was we felt that turning everything upside down would have caused you even more pain.

Despite what you think Stephanie, I did always love you; I just didn't know how to show it when you needed it the most. You have to admit that at times you were a very difficult child. You have to realise that the world was a very different place in the sixties and seventies to what it is now. You would have been treated as a freak and a misfit which would only have made things worse we thought.

We have made mistakes, we admit that, but it's time to move on and enjoy your life as Stephanie. You look amazing and we are proud of the girl you have become. Your strength and courage I'm sure is admired by many and you too should be very proud of what you have achieved. Going to Australia was not to get away from you; we hated leaving all of you but realised that it probably wasn't the right time for any of you. Much as you did twenty-six years later, going to Australia was something we just had to do. We would have always regretted it if we hadn't given it a try and they were ten lovely years. We both believe that leaving you to fend for yourselves was the making of all of you. You, in particular, matured a great deal faster than you ever would have done and let's face it, living at Kelk and working on the farm was never going to get you anywhere.

If only you knew how much heartache you gave us when you first started driving. You were very reckless (probably still are) and gave us many a sleepless night. We appreciate that much of that was to do with your mixed up head and that we probably didn't do all we could have done to sort that out. It was just a very difficult decision and as parents we didn't always get things right.

I wanted to tell you the whole story in 1997 but Dad didn't because he believed that it would cause you too much heartache at a time when you were obviously in turmoil with your marriage to Fiona on the rocks. In the end I didn't tell you and regret that because another opportunity never came, even after Dad died. When you got together with Jayne I thought you were very happy and there was no need to tell you and turn your life upside down again. I did think of telling you before you left for Australia but again you were obviously happy and excited to be starting a new life and I didn't think you would thank me for causing a lot more heartache. As for your name, neither of us wanted Robert to be shortened to Bob, which we hadn't thought about when we decided on the the name. Perhaps also, in the back of our minds, there was an element of uncertainty. The first three months after you were born was a very difficult time for us.

Stephanie, all I can ask is that you try not to hate us and try to see things from our side a little. Don't let the past hurt ruin what you have now. You obviously have so many friends who love you and a team of healthcare professionals who care deeply about your wellbeing. Most of all you have Denise. I so wish I had met her and could thank her for being your support. What she has done for you is more than anyone should have to do and I hope you appreciate her. I know you do. Look after each other and do yourself justice as the girl you should have always been.

Lots of love

Mum and Dad xx

Photographs

Whitehall Farm, Little Kelk - where I grew up

1970 - with my kittens Bovril & Marmite

1974 - busy on the farm

1989 - Katanning, Western Australia

2004 - Southern Ireland

2014 - a friend's wedding

Dec 2016 - Esperance
First outing as Stephanie

Mar 2017 - building wall panel #14 (of 33) - Nannup House

2017
Wild Lily
Dunsborough

May 2017 -
Philadelphia
bound

2017 - ready
for a night out

2 days before surgery
- no sign of nerves!

So proud of our
Nannup build!

It's party time!

Finally me....